MADONNA AND CHILD

Towards a New Politics of Motherhood

by the same author

PUBLIC LIVES

MADONNA AND CHILD

Towards a New Politics of Motherhood

MELISSA BENN

JONATHAN CAPE
LONDON

Published by Jonathan Cape 1998

2 4 6 8 10 9 7 5 3

First published in Great Britain in 1998 by Jonathan Cape,
Random House, 20 Vauxhall Bridge Road, London SW1V 2SA

Random House Australia (Pty) Limited
20 Alfred Street, Milsons Point, Sydney,
New South Wales 2061, Australia

Random House New Zealand Limited
18 Poland Road, Glenfield,
Auckland 10, New Zealand

Random House South Africa (Pty) Limited
Endulini, 5A Jubilee Road, Parktown 2193, South Africa

Random House UK Limited Reg. No. 954009

A CIP catalogue record for this book is available from the British Library

ISBN 0 224 03821 4

Papers used by Random House UK Limited are natural,
recyclable products made from wood grown in sustainable forests.
The manufacturing processes conform to the environmental
regulations of the country of origin

Typeset by MATS, Southend-on-Sea, Essex

Printed and bound in Great Britain by
Mackays of Chatham PLC, Chatham, Kent

For my own precious mother, Caroline Benn

Contents

There's only one way to find out how women *actually* experience motherhood, and that's by listening to what they have to say.

Ann Oakley, from the introduction to
Mother Courage, Letters from Mothers in Poverty at the End of the Century, Penguin 1997

Acknowledgements

Often, during the course of writing this book, I have observed that the whole process is rather like having a baby; it takes ages to emerge and when it does, keeping it all going is just as exhausting. But it also shares some of the 'love affair' aspects of parenthood. I have lived with the ideas of this book for so long that as I prepare to send off the manuscript for the last time, I feel both euphoric and bereft.

Unlike a baby, this book owes its conception to a cast of dozens. First and last, I want to thank the many women, and men, whom I spoke to over the years. I remember them all, their voices, their homes, their plans; after spending one afternoon with a young mother on the outskirts of Bristol, she brought her two children to the train station to wave me off. Railway station farewells are always poignant, but there was something particularly touching about this family of familiar strangers giving me such a kind send-off; at the time it felt like they were wishing me and the book well on our joint journey. A particular thank you to Carol Revell, Eileen Smith, Ann James and all the women in Cardiff; to Jean Selwood of Scoopaid; to Lorraine Glancy, Ruth Morrison, Deborah Curtis, Barbara Ormston of the Mothers' Union, and the Reverend Neville Boundy. Maggie Gibbs deployed her customary energy in putting me in touch with people; thank you to all of them, particularly Simone. Liz Kettle, Paul and Sean made me feel at home in Sheffield, Yusuf Ahmad and Frances Brooke were equally hospitable in Bristol and gave me lots of valuable contacts; Al Gordon helped me find my way around the Scottish side of things. Thanks also to Deborah Easlick of the Rainer Foundation, Joy Crabtree and Rita Heywood at the

CARLI project, Basildon; a special thank you to Jean Hanson for her help and to Linda Crabtree, Hayley Chipchast, Philippa O'Connor, Karen Gerty, Wilma Gordon, Pauline Thomas and Carol Munro.

Two women were crucial to the making of this book. I was lucky to have Philippa Brewster, one of the finest editors in publishing, to work with me from beginning to end. She was always tough when she needed to be and kind when *I* needed her to be! My agent, Faith Evans, was her usual supportive and enthusiastic self, and brilliant at mid-book crisis. Dan Franklin at Cape has been consistently helpful. Annie Lee copy-edited the manuscript with calm efficiency.

I am grateful to the Society of Authors, whose generous grant helped me to keep afloat financially.

Many other people helped me out with information, further contacts and helpful conversation. I would particularly like to thank Liz Speed of the Equal Opportunities Commission; Virginia Valentine of Semiotic Solutions, who generously gave me a morning of her time; Hilary Simpson of Oxfordshire County Council; Helen Garner of the Fawcett Society; Lucy Lloyd of the Daycare Trust, who kindly read part of the manuscript; Irene Pillia of the Working Parents' Association; Beth Lakhani of the Child Poverty Action Group; Ed Mayo of the New Economics Foundation; Bernadette Vallely of the Women's Communication Centre; Rowena Young at Demos; and all at the Maternity Alliance, who were always ready to send information at a moment's notice.

Others helped me with their thoughts and ideas, often over the years. Conversations with Annie Sedley on maternity rights, work, politics and the law have helped me sort out some of the more complex issues concerning mothers and work. Sue Steward and I have ruminated for years about writing, music, Madonna, Burchill, men, sexuality; you name it, it's all in here somewhere. Paul Grant, whom I didn't thank enough at the time, supplied me with some important articles on feminism and motherhood which proved particularly crucial to me at the end of this project; thank you, now. Thanks also to all at the Institute of Race

Relations who put me in touch with the thinking of Barbara Ransby. Meg Abdy of the Henley Centre kept me down to earth. Long conversations in the kitchen with Tony O'Connor during 1995 clarified my ideas on men, children and nurturance. A sharp but good-tempered discussion with my father, Tony Benn, on a journey in spring 1997 made me think again about politicians, family and father time. He also kept me supplied with documents and did the most phenomenal amount of photocopying for me, all with his usual generosity. Dina Rabinovitch is always brimming with opinions about mothers and work, which we have discussed over a long time now. My aunt June Benn is a fount of knowledge about feminism and women's writing of previous generations; she supplied me with plastic bags full, literally, of valuable information, personal and intellectual. My mother, Caroline Benn, sent me a steady stream of newspaper cuttings; her comments on early drafts of the manuscript, and her timely reminder of the importance of society, were invaluable. The unflagging energy of Cynthia Enloe kept me in touch with important developments in the USA.

Thanks also to the *New Statesman*, the *Guardian*, *Community Care* and *She*, where some of these ideas were first aired, in different form.

Denise Winn and our weekly walk has sometimes single-handedly kept me from writer's loneliness and mother's insanity. Other friends – Becky Swift, Edward Pilkington, Tim Owen, Lesley Thomson, Em Farrell and Bob Young – cheered me on from a metaphorical distance. Ruth Richardson and Jeremy Cooper cheered a fair bit too; they also gave me swift and practical help at the very moment I needed it. As always, Barney Bardsley took as detailed an interest in my welfare as my writing. Tony, Caroline, Stephen, Nita, Hilary, Sally, Joshua and Naz, and all my family, have been their usual encouraging selves.

I cannot end without thanking a group of new friends I have met through motherhood. While I am not *quite* sure what they will think of this book – my guess is some of them will agree with some of the arguments some of the time – Katie Fellerman, Chris George, Maggie Gibb, Amanda Martin, Lisa Nicholson, Vibeke

Nope, Francesca Raphael, Hope Samuel, Rachel Verrells, Dawn Waterman and Joan Williams have made new motherhood much more enjoyable for me than I could have hoped.

Thanks also to Claire Ware, who has looked after Hannah and Sarah with complete professionalism and love.

And last, but never least, Paul Gordon, who did so much for me, from that first conversation in the car on the way to Swindon to that last load of washing. He discussed ideas, read drafts, corrected punctuation, pushed noisy girls to the library and back, cooked meals, constructively criticized, congratulated when appropriate, and always, always made me laugh. Our girls, Hannah and Sarah, didn't give much practical help – but I've never had so much fun in my life.

~ I ~

A Personal Beginning

I did not become a mother until I was thirty-seven. Whenever I am reminded of this fact, am faced with the baldness of it, I see my unique self dissolve into a mere statistic. It always surprises me. Medically, I am, of course, a primigravida; a mild curiosity to the handsome young medical students who check my blood pressure; kindly tolerated by the impatient, plump young consultant with a bright patterned tie who happily displays his knowledge of the chances of foetal abnormality on this particular piece of horizontally laid flesh. Culturally, I am part of a new wave too; one of the host of women who now postpone motherhood, in order first to establish a career or find themselves or some such thing.

It didn't feel like that of course. No-one lives their life as if they are a statistic. It simply felt as if there was all the time in the world and suddenly no time at all. Then, there were all the things I wanted to do, articles I wanted to write, books I wanted to read (every year a new set of lists drawn up on pieces of scrap paper: history, politics, fiction, the classics, and always that bloody *Ulysses*), people I wanted to meet, places I wanted to go. In short, a life to live. From my teens onwards – how wearily unoriginal it all seems now! – I had modelled myself on a particular kind of woman, the kind who deliberately refuses marriage and motherhood, the archetypal 'independent woman' who often later writes her story up to more or less conform to this clean picture. I was never that successful at it, as it happens. Being a loving, friendly person by nature, I could never regulate my own feelings or those of others to conform to some abstract principle: the natural chaos

1

of the emotions, the appealing, sometimes appalling, disorder of real connections between real people always seemed obvious to me. But I loved the trying of it. I loved the idea of making something of myself. If I'm being honest there is no four-letter word I love more than 'work'.

I remember an argument I had with a friend when we were both twenty-five. She was disgusted with me for implying that someone else's mother had lived an 'ordinary' life. 'Look at my mother,' she exploded with fury. '"All" she's done is have four children. That's *all*. Too ordinary for *you*.' (I don't know why: I giggle at the memory of my dismay at her anger.) She had to be right but I just couldn't feel it. All I knew was that I had to do what I was doing, which was, I thought then, refusing the more domestic choices of the older women in my family: both my grandmothers, but particularly my paternal grandmother, who was a terrific 'family' person, and even my mother, who had managed to have four children, work and quite a lot of fun. I had to make a different path for myself.

No story exists independent of the time in which it takes place. That angry friend, justly defending the claims of the ordinary, was, in her way, more remarkable, more extra-ordinary, than me. In the fifteen years since our angry exchange, she has pursued a working life and remained childless whereas I am 'saddled' with two babies and a diminishing income if you want to calculate human gain as economic loss. But this was what our generation and successive generations were about: making something of ourselves. (Still are.) There was no question about it; all that fifties feminine nonsense about knocking yourselves out for other people, being there, at the end of the day, the great supporter, especially for men who didn't even seem to notice what was being done for them, was plainly absurd. It was so absurd we didn't even dwell on it much. We had things to do, places to go, people to see.

And then? What then? What happens to those of us more obedient to the laws of self-development than so-called simple biology? What happens to those of us who come to motherhood, late or not, believing we are part of the 'new world' for women?

The first and most fundamental lesson we learn is that the language of 'before' cannot be adapted to, or moulded around, our new circumstances. All that we held solidly dear from the old life melts into air; the ever-renewable sentence that begins with 'I want', 'I plan', 'I intend' now becomes hopelessly entangled with, lost within, the compass of this creature whose tiny hand opens and closes with all the slow definite beauty of a flower.

'Here is the world,' I thought, in those first dreamy months after my first daughter was born, clasping the tiny fierce paw, 'and it does not reside in me after all.'

What a relief it was.

I will wake up, of course, one day. I will begin to look around me. I will read the awesome, exuberant, endearingly awful Camille Paglia, whom I interviewed at eight months pregnant, neither of us referring to this large, neat football tucked underneath my wool jumper (did she even notice, I wonder now?) . . . Camille Paglia, who tells me – and anyone else who will listen – that as soon as a woman becomes a mother, she turns from her grand projects and becomes just another boring human interested in saving the world for God's sake. Like that poor Chrissie Hynde, she says to me, who used to be a half-decent rock chick until she had babies. Then I will read feminist writer Maureen Freely, who tells me that just about every feeling I have is legitimate and it is all feminism's fault that I feel so crazy. War of the worlds indeed.

But the sense of entanglement is what interests me. This is what I have to deal with. I can see that it will never go. It only deepens, finds new valences. The sadness that I once felt as a little girl, setting off for nursery school, waving to my mother's smiling image at the second-floor window, is, now, surprisingly, the same sadness I feel, kissing my little girl goodbye as I go out to teach a class on a dark October night. That same fibrous sense of connection is there when I settle down to sleep. Even at bedtime, I am not alone: that precious private time when once I was left with my own thoughts, swirling deliciously or dangerously around my head. Some part of my conscious and unconscious attention is now always with the little girl, and then her baby sister, sleeping down the hallway.

As if it were a thread, I can almost watch it travel, thin but as strong as steel between my room and theirs. Not exactly thinking about one or the other but, rather, seeing them in my mind's eye, the untidy mound of my two-year-old under a heaped duvet, the skewed position of the baby's head as she leans to one side of the cot; hearing the delicate wisp of her breathing, the near-snorting in comparison of her older, bossier sister. Knowing, hoping they don't need me right this moment – eleven thirty-three – as I try to switch off, into sleep. Guessing but hoping that they won't need me in a moment, an hour, in the grey light of dawn.

A cough wakes me up. My head lifts itself a fraction off the pillow to listen for its continuation or its end. A cry has me standing by the side of the cot before I even realize I am awake, shifting, settling, offering solace. Tense on the balls of my feet. Happy. Exhausted.

This entanglement can be called many things. Maternal anxiety, if you're that way inclined. It can be called love. Exasperation. Joy. Whatever it is it is quite different from the feelings I have had up to now, for family, friends, even a deeply loved partner. It is life-shattering in the best sense. Like all great experiences – serious ill-ness, sudden and complete loss of status – the everyday miracle of birth and the bringing up of a child can make us lose both our arro-gance and innocence. And that is a good thing.

For a while, though, I become rootless, marooned between two worlds, without a way of thinking about myself or quite knowing how to behave. I no longer belong to the old world of me and my plans. How I loved my plans! The myriad daily activities that went with them – saving a letter to read on a bus journey, putting the kettle on as soon as I got home and mooning around the kitchen as I waited for it to boil, staying up to one, two-thirty in the morning for no reason except I liked being awake, alive.

All that was not gone; rather it became an unreachable land. Mine is a petty example but I understand exactly now what people mean when they talk about rights not being abstract, but existing in a context. I can still read books, listen to music, boil a kettle and think while it steams. But, frequently, the amount of planning I must undertake in order to achieve this gives the actions themselves a very different quality. They become almost heavy with significance while my head is light with the near euphoria of doing them. Looking after two children under three is perhaps comparable, in its slowness, its lack of mobility, to carrying a lead weight around each ankle. Or swimming under water.

So that old quickness is gone. When friends ring from offices or I ring and perhaps catch them in the middle of a meeting, the hard-edged, almost suspicious, quality to their voice (which I now hear almost entirely as self-protection) seems so peculiar. I remember using it myself, glorying in it. Quickness. Executive toughness. Control. Covering up. Yet I envy them the noise, the sociability.

I, by contrast, for the moment, live in the land of motherhood. And what is that? I have no idea how to do it or even think about it. It is a symptom of some residual lack of imagination that I tend to think I must do what others did, be what they were, as if every life fits some pre-existing template rather than creating its own original mould. For a short while after my first daughter is born, therefore, I still see other mothers through my pre-maternity (arrogant, innocent) eyes. In the park, in the shops, on the street, I observe a random procession of bleak, slightly tired beings who have given up on many things: the sharp definitions of personal style, the efficiency and satisfactions of a day filled with definite objectives, interest in the real world of wars and Parliament. Meanwhile, I carry my new responsibility without much grace. When I walk one exhausted Saturday morning, buggy wheels stuck with mud, into a local café just for refuge and the distractions of other people's noise, the fury I feel at seeing an old acquaintance sitting at the back of the café takes me aback. I am shaken at the gloss of her well-slept hair, the precision and self-containment of her movements as she drinks some coffee and eats a piece of toast, the apparent order of her quiet conversation with her male companion. Refusing good manners in favour of a quick escape, I simply turn my chariot of chaos round again and back into the street.

Meanwhile, friends endlessly congratulate me on doing well, looking well. They are only mildly puzzled at the mixed messages I send out: that nothing has changed, that everything has changed. I am, unknowingly, angry at their mixed messages: that this new human addition to my life – and their lives – is wonderful, at least for an afternoon, but everything can be the same as it was before. There is a slight question mark around whether I am up to it. Will I be one of those tedious women who now go on and on about their children? I try not to. I try so hard that sometimes I barely mention them and then wonder who is being saved, and from what, and who is being cheated, and of what? Meanwhile, my mum and I gossip for half-hours at a time about the 'girls' and their antics.

Healthy irritation begins to creep in at those who ask me, with a mix of command and assumption, how the 'work' is going, barely concealing their view that that is the thing after all. That lovely word 'work' sounds more complicated now. Or it has different resonances. Increasingly in those exchanges, I seem to leave my body and stand above myself, eavesdropping on the tinny voice (my own) that provides answers on this project or that, the next article planned or commissioned. And I *am* still interested. I am just hearing the word itself differently. I am wondering if getting up at five-forty in the morning and being climbed all over until six-twenty and then watching a Disney video while trying to keep crumbs and juice off the sofa and then clearing up a mess of toys and scrap paper I didn't even see being made, and it is *still* not seven in the morning, how many other people would call that 'work' too. And if it is, how can I, or the girls' father, ever feel as good about that as the other kind? And when we start work 'proper' at nine in the morning, can we (a) stay awake and (b) even refer to any of this previous three hours' labour to anyone but each other? There is the grandest of difference after all between 'having a life' as people have a life in magazines or even books and being seen to live it. That, after all, was the only difference between me and my dirty buggy and the acquaintance in the corner eating toast that rainy Saturday morning. I was revealing the chaos; she was embodying the dream.

I finally understand why that friend was so angry with me all those years ago.

I do not want to lose my new innocence either. When I first walked a buggy round and round the same patch of quiet streets I was happily sorry for myself. I used to indulge myself, just a bit, in 'Whatever happened to my life?' kind of thoughts. Slowly, over time, I began to dwell in the moment. I liked having somewhere to rest my arms while I walked. I began to enjoy the utter invisibility of a Mother with Child in London street. When my second daughter was born, those afternoons of walking alone became intensely pleasurable. They contained all the joy of stillness and the abundance of life, expressed by Dennis Potter when, in the last months of his life, he talked of the beauty of the may tree that stood outside the window of his work room. I knew what he meant in this respect: for the first time in a long time, I stopped wanting anything more than I had been given.

~ 2 ~

Asking the Right Questions: A Sort of Introduction

I offer this brief insight into what might be termed a mild postnatal depression for a number of reasons. The idea for this book came before I had children: I sensed there was a great deal more to be said about the 'new' motherhood than was, as yet, articulated. Women, I believed, had subtly been urged to believe that individual aspiration, or, at the very least, a job, would be their salvation. The values of our time tell us: each of us can 'make it', woman or man, mother or child-free. But just how many of us did – does – this message reach? And how many of us even want to receive it? At the same time, I sensed that women's more private, complex knowledge and experience of motherhood had somehow been driven underground. We all talked about 'mothers'. We all gawped at pictures of famous and important ones. But did we really value reproduction over production?

Several developments led me to confirm this as just the beginning of the argument. Travelling round the country talking to women, I began to realize just how little the values of the market had penetrated the lives of most of them. Many of the mothers I talked to wanted to work or enjoyed the work that they did. It gave them a satisfaction to be out of the home, away from 'the four walls' and limitations of their own and their children's company. They were not, on the whole, working in jobs that brought them personal glory or, more importantly, much money. 'Five pounds an hour, that's a good job.' 'Ten thousand a year,

I'd be happy with that.' The market had not penetrated their thinking in another important way. Almost every woman was involved in some form of spontaneous, voluntary, modest and co-operative arrangement that sprang from the fact of her motherhood but did not limit her within it. Far from it: these were actions that took her out of herself, into the world, whether it was on a coach trip to the seaside or a once-weekly visit to the local school every week to help children with their reading.

For those more successful in the financial or status sense, there was an almost contradictory problem. For them, the twin claims of parenthood and outside achievement were reconcilable at such a high cost that their conversation, with me, with themselves, was a constant back and forth debate about private values and public expectations. All motherhood is tiring and often depressing: social class tends to be one of the significant factors in determining the level of defeat and dismay. But for these women, there was often a particular quality to their exhaustion that came from *conflict*, from attempting to dwell within two worlds that are governed by quite different values. Paradoxically, their very success had often cut them off from the society around them, the co-operative ventures and adventures of women with, apparently, less to lose.

Then I became a mother myself. I began to understand what was really involved in that simple word, 'care'. When I looked around I didn't see that many people – writers, feminists, politicians, journalists – talking about this most fundamental element of experience. So my own motherhood transformed my quest into something both much more personal and yet more ambitious. After all, I could quickly figure out the limitations and possibilities of my own position. I became hungry to know about all the rest.

Meanwhile, popular culture – society's deceptively simple conversation with itself, about itself – was increasingly taken up with the issue, and image, of modern motherhood. When in 1983 the heavily pregnant young Harriet Harman campaigned for Parliament, in the south London constituency of Peckham, it was still unusual to be so 'out' about pregnancy. The sight of this young Labour hopeful, then tagged a fiery left-winger, knocking on doors and delivering leaflets in her conventional maternity smocks, was both a disturbing and becalming image. As the decade wore on, more and more 'top' women began not just to come out about their motherhood but to integrate it into their public personalities. We began to see apparently frank pictures of women writers and publishers and campaigners, squashed up on couches with pretty girls in floral dresses, or bemused at toddlers who shouted down a telephone or banged on their typewriter. The mothers smiled as only parents smile, with pure delight. The new up-front feminism of the period helped shape a new language that allowed these women to talk about the difficulties and challenges of 'combining' work and motherhood.[1]

Hollywood star Demi Moore took the iconography of motherhood into new territory in 1991 with the very public flaunting of her swollen stomach for the cover of *Vanity Fair*. This was narcissism, undoubtedly, but she was also pushing out the boundaries in relation to motherhood, just as surely as Madonna's chained notebook of erotic imagery pushed them out on sex, and k d lang and Cindy Crawford's serious play around lesbian stereotypes, also on the cover of *Vanity Fair*, spoke a new popular language about sexuality. The mother as powerful out-there woman, the powerful out-there woman as mother, became an increasingly ordinary image in western society. So that by the time Madonna – yes, Madonna herself – became pregnant in 1995, while filming the blockbuster *Evita*, and attended both its American and European premières in 1996 within weeks of birth, still breastfeeding but back in shape, we only asked: what took her so long?

The debate about working motherhood was also gathering pace throughout the 1980s, accelerating rather alarmingly from the early 1990s onwards. For the past few years, we have been inundated with features, in both the quality and popular press, television and radio, on every aspect of women, work, fatherhood and family. Unsurprisingly, mothers attracted the most attention and the most criticism, from the mainstream and right-wing press. 'When Mummy walks out.'[2] 'Far too busy to keep a child . . . the battleground of motherhood versus a career.'[3] 'Nannies, neglect and the mothers driven by money.'[4] Women's magazines and the feature pages of the quality press covered the same issues in more sympathetic, if partial, terms. 'Babies – who needs them? . . . now one in five women are saying no to motherhood.'[5] 'When the juggling stops. What happens when you give up a successful career to be mother and wife?'[6] Feature writers scoured their contacts books for leads to older mothers, women who had used In Vitro Fertilization and succeeded, women who had used In Vitro Fertilization and failed, single women who had found a father for their child, best friends who had been divided by motherhood, sisters who had been united by it, women who had been fundamentally altered by it. Articles on fatherhood became the new vogue around the middle to late 90s, as journalists suddenly attempted to analyse the profound shifts that were taking place in the heart of the British home. 'Sorry Mummy, but Daddy knows best,' said the prescient headline.[7] Virtually every 'new father' in the country must have been interviewed, it seemed, at some time or another.

If feature writers were busy on the question of the new motherhood, so were the columnists. It is striking how few of these were, or are, men. Male journalists will take to the word processor with a vengeance when a subject or set of claims arises that threatens their sex, such as the Child Support Agency or the recovered memory movement. They will write tenderly of their new fatherhood. But very, very few write about mothers and home, mothers and children, mothers and work. In a strange and banal reflection of the deep assumptions about 'women's role', female journalists are invariably left to this topic. And they do their job. The new generation of columnist–mothers, a slightly different breed from columnists who happen to be mothers, have, over the years, briskly, tenderly, impatiently, wittily, informed us, over and over again, that *really* women love hanging out the washing or that *really* they need the anxiety and speed of office life; that childcare is the crucial issue and so is women taking power and so is the role of men: that working women are good for their children; that the whole debate is silly anyway because most women are satisfied with the way things are.[8]

These polemics were often sparked off by cases or events, including an increasing number of 'media events'. In September 1993, *Panorama*, the BBC flagship current affairs programme, broadcast its provocatively entitled 'Babies on Benefit'.[9] This programme suggested that one of society's graver problems was the large numbers of young women who were 'choosing' to have babies without men and living off the state. As I discuss in greater detail later in this book, both acts were depicted as cold, calculated choices rather than the more banal consequence of the haphazard mix of youth, sex, love, and both male and female unemployment. In late 1994 there was an extraordinary amount of anxious press coverage of the case of 'high-flying' American lawyer Sharon Prost, who was fighting for custody of her two boys against her partner, the boys' father, Kenneth Greene. Prost, who was employed by a conservative Senator, worked long and unsocial hours. In the eyes of the courts and large sections of the American and British press this made her an unfit parent to retain custody: writers and campaigners more sympathetic to the anomalies, even hypocrisies, of the case, if not Prost herself, tried to point out the double standards in operation, namely that no 'career man' would be so condemned for his devotion to his job. The case was made more complicated by the fact that Greene, the boys' father, was a trade union negotiator who had had spells of unemployment (and depression) but had increasingly taken over the care of the young boys. Prost lost custody and (male) journalists heaped praise on her ex-partner Greene for, in the words of the judge in the case, 'striking a delicate balance between parenthood and career'. As one male journalist commented: 'Put simply he had done more things and spent more time with the children than their mother.'[10]

Academics also found themselves thrown into the media mêlée, and often found themselves misrepresented. In spring 1996, Catherine Hakim, a respected researcher at the London School of Economics who had spent her working life labouring relatively obscurely in academia, caused a minor public storm with her suggestion that two-thirds of women were home-makers, not career-oriented, and that feminism had directed its priorities for legislative change with only the one-third in mind. She said publicly that she did not like the way her arguments were taken up by sections of the press. In early February 1997, female academic Professor Margaret O'Brien of the University of North London spoke in protest to a Sunday newspaper after another *Panorama* programme, 'Missing Mum', used some of her research to suggest the children of full-time working mothers do less well than the children of mothers who work part-time.[11]

The fevered, almost unreal quality to this rolling programme of argument and counter-argument had culminated just a week or so earlier in the strange case of Nicola Horlick. Horlick was a city 'whizz kid' reputedly earning nearly a million pounds a year as a fund manager at the Morgan Grenfell bank. In January 1997 she was suspended from her job after suggestions were made that she had been in talks with a rival bank, ABN Amro. What made Horlick unusual, however, was not her job or her salary or her supposed treachery. It was the simple fact that she was a mother of five. (The children also have a father, who is also a well-remunerated banker.) As soon as the story of her suspension broke, public attention was riveted by this supposed 'Super-woman' who had both risen to the top of her profession and produced so many offspring. For a few days, Horlick's face stared out of the pages of every newspaper, whether it was a sombre city and business section or a garish Sunday tabloid. It was an unreadable image, that pretty, doll-round, dark-eyed face; knowing but somehow blank; a face more interesting in action than repose. Some of the pictures of Horlick during her frenzied week of negotiations with the bank brought a new edge to the 'top public mother' image: journalists and photographers trailed her as she walked in the park, pushing a buggy, with four of her five young children. The most extraordinary of all came in a Sunday tabloid; it chose, for its front page, a close-up of Horlick at home feeding her baby with a bottle of formula, underneath the headline, 'Superwoman speaks of her admiration for Tony Blair.'[12]

Part of the excitement and interest of the Horlick story stemmed from her own dramatic actions, for example her decision to fly herself (and a few journalists) to bank headquarters in Germany to confront her European bosses. But the interest in her was much more. It was as if society, or at least the Greek chorus of cultural commentators that sometimes stand in for the rest of us, needed to define Horlick, put her in her place. Were we looking at something typical of the times or something extraordinary? Were we looking at success or failure? By the weekend after her flight to Germany, the almost universal judgement of the press seemed to be that Horlick was a failure. She had mishandled herself, she was too histrionic. More private verdicts were also condemnatory. The snide and the sane, particularly women, asked each other how much of a parent could she be with a job that demanding? Throughout the affair Horlick herself was desperate to prove her commitment to her children, to her own ordinary life as well as her ruthless professionalism and 'integrity' in the job. Up against two juries – the work world who wanted to dismiss her as a competent professional, the private world that wanted to dismiss her as a mother – she tried to please both, and ended up pleasing neither. Her public anxiety about misrepresentation of her own competence and commitment as a parent fed into endless articles about the impossibility of anyone ever being a 'Superwoman'. At the same time, no-one ever turned the spotlight on 'Mr Horlick', with his own top city job and the same five children, and asked him to account for himself, nor on the countless men like him. As journalist Linda Grant commented, 'It is odd that in business there is no male equivalent of Superwoman. Captains of industry and senior politicians may have big families. No-one ever enquires what magic potion they drink to get them to the top and keep them there, apart from the usual combination of brains, hard work, luck and, often, machiavellian cunning and backstabbing.'[13]

But underneath this public cacophony, typified by the Horlick story, there remain some significant silences about modern motherhood. The increasingly ferocious spotlight on working women and top women has distorted, even erased, a truer and much more interesting picture of modern mothers today. The most obvious point is how narrow a focus the spotlight has; how it illuminates lives not just untypical of, but almost antithetical to the lives of the nation as a whole. Horlick's story, with its excessive salaries and large numbers of progeny, was the epitome of this distortion: her Superwoman tag was a clue to the almost comic – as in cartoon – aspect of her story. It was as if the eighties with all its excesses had come back to haunt us, but this time as farce.

Media representation of, and interest in, working mothers is not always so extreme, but it naturally feels more at ease with a mirror reflection of the women it believes to be its market: the comfortable, pressured, anxious, seriously leisured nanny-hiring classes; those with gardens, fitted kitchens (industrial or neo-Victorian), car or cars, mortgages, teetering, especially in the inner cities, on the brink of choosing a private education. Take the preoccupations of a decent, liberal columnist–mother like Nigella Lawson on *The Times*. Typical issues taken up by her include the guilt that women (wrongly) feel at employing a cleaner, the virtues and benefits of working from home and how to pick the best primary school for your child.

The gap between the lives apparently reflected in the quality press, even the tabloids, and the experience of the women I was visiting became glaringly, sometimes shamingly, obvious. I spent some spring days in Sheffield, where I went to talk to a group of women, mostly bringing up children on their own. None of the carefully crafted questions I had prepared had much resonance with them, which, incidentally, is how I quickly learned to throw out my preconceptions and simply attend to what was before me. So I spent a morning doing just that, listening and talking. On the train home I scribbled the following in a notebook:

The three women live in a vast wilderness of tower blocks and low-rise housing on a ring of hills that surrounds the city and with a beautiful view of it. All the roads are being pulled up, there is chaos because of the road works. A woman standing in what seems to me the middle of nowhere, or nothing but rubble, sticks her hand out. A bus I had not even seen approaching slows down and stops for her. It's as if the place operates to rules of its own. Maureen lives in a neat three-bedroom house. Her parents live diagonally opposite. This group of mothers meets once a week. Maureen and Clare are cousins. Maureen picks Clare's child up as if – but not quite as if – she were her own. They are suspicious and welcoming of me all at once. Why – Molly asks me – do you want to write about us? About women? Is it your hobby? They are friendly, open, carefully attend to even my sillier questions. I'm always amazed at how much human beings do like and need to talk about themselves. Their lives are well organized. But the men are like shadows on a far-away wall. The relationship between them and the men is on the whole amicable but distant. It's them and the children. Them and each other. Two of the three live on income support. What do they want from life? I try to find out. More money, definitely, yes. Some freedom from the kids, yes, in whatever way is possible; a job of some kind. Clare is going to train to be a hairdresser. Molly used to work as a confectioner, making and packing sweets. 'It wasn't bad. I've tried everything, me. I've been a cleaner, worked in a sandwich shop. I don't mind as long as it's enough to get someone to look after her.' Maureen works in a crèche at a local swimming-pool, the one where I went swimming yesterday. She does a few hours but can't do more, unless it is cash in hand, because of restrictions on what you can earn and still draw benefit. Would she like to work more? 'I would. I would. But when you think about it, until she's older, it's got to fit in with taking her to school. So you're limited in what you can do.' She does sewing from a back room sometimes, but she found it hard to do when her daughter first started nursery: 'I was right glad she was going to nursery . . . She was annoying me when I was with her. But I still missed her, I got right depressed when she was gone.' For all of them their biggest problem is that no job pays more than income support, once you've paid childcare. It's not worth looking for a badly paid job. Clare, after paying rent and bills, has £10 left a week. She and her kids are beautifully turned out, but she's 'always borrowing'. The phrase they use most with me is, 'You won't tell the social, will you?' Maureen has a nice house but she never goes out. Loneliness. Boredom. These words crop up often, too. After all my reading about motherhood, about work and 'identity', I see nothing that relates to these lives here. Friedan's exhortation to 'use that degree', Ros Coward's account of competitiveness among stay-at-home mothers, displacing the competitiveness they could not bear, tolerate, in the workplace – it's another language, another territory here. When I get to the station, I buy a copy of *She* magazine and read the first words of Linda Kelsey's editorial, next to a full glossy picture: 'Women who juggle marriage and mother-hood, work and home, often find that not only does their sex life slip to the bottom of the agenda but they lose their sense of sexual identity too. It's hardly surprising given the nature of their frantic lives.' The absolute last words I would use of the three women I just interviewed were 'juggle', 'frantic' or 'agenda' for that matter!

These reflections reminded me of something I had recently read by the ex-Yugoslavian writer Slavenka Drakulic, whose first book, *How We Survived Communism and Even Laughed*, described some of the privations in the old Eastern Europe. In one chapter, she had talked about how it felt, living frequently without basic items and amenities, to pick up a western magazine:

Living under such conditions and holding *Vogue* magazine in your hands is a very particular experience – it's almost like holding a pebble from Mars or a piece of a meteor that accidentally fell into your yard. 'I hate it,' says Agnes, an editor at a scientific journal in Budapest, pointing to *Vogue*. 'It makes me feel so miserable I could almost cry. Just look at this paper – glossy, shiny, like silk. You can't find anything like this around here. Once you've seen it, it immediately sets not only new standards, but a visible boundary.'[14]

For Drakulic and her friends, there is an assumption that 'a western woman only browses through such magazines superficially, even with boredom'. But every western woman? It is an important question: how much the everyday – magazines, papers, videos; the stories we read within them – both unites and divides us and what that means for our images of ourselves, as individuals, as well as collectively; our national conversation about ourselves. That copy of *She* – cover price that day, £1.60 – was technically not beyond the reach of Maureen or Clare or Molly, who had earlier been animatedly talking about the cost of their coach trip fare to the seaside. Yet in another way the magazine was unreachable. If you have ten pounds left at the end of the week, will you even consider buying a magazine that eats up nearly a fifth of that surplus? One of you might buy it and share it around. But would you ever, alone or as a group, buy something whose contents assumed you had at least five times that total to spend on yourself alone each week?

In one important sense, the media have homogenized our experience. We can all read the *Mail*, watch *Brookside* or *EastEnders*, listen to *The Archers*. Vast numbers of us, from all classes and backgrounds, do. We can swap our views, experiences of those programmes, share in the dilemmas of the same characters. If you have ever felt stuck for chat with someone and discover that you 'share' a soap opera, you will know the sense of instant ersatz intimacy this mutual experience can bring you. This language of sameness, then, both brings us together and, at the same time, masks our differences in insidious ways. This is one of the problems this book explores.

This political or social silence, even dishonesty, about certain kinds of motherhood is matched by a more personal one. I touched on this earlier: the difference between real and represented experience, between 'having a life' and living one. I do not think our society/culture possesses a genuine understanding – or, more to the point, a care – for what it means to raise a child, the quality of that experience, the quantity of effort it involves. The much belittled 'housewife' or stay-at-home mother is the contemporary bearer of that neglect. She feels no-one appreciates what she does, who she is. And she is right, on two counts. The mother at home has literally no market value, for the job of bearing and rearing children is not perceived in monetary terms, despite the best recent efforts of insurance companies to 'cost' a housewife's labour should she be taken ill or die, leaving her family unserviced. One of the ironies of women's new status as workers is that the other side of the traditional woman's lot, her domestic life, the thousand physical, emotional tasks of the everyday, has disappeared from public view. We assume it, give a sentimental nod towards it, but we lack real knowledge or care for it. At best, we hug our own private, special experiences of parenthood to ourselves, like proud new parents with a baby just back from the hospital. In one sense, everyone who is a parent, male or female, thinks they know what parenthood is about: it tells us something marvellous not just about ourselves, but about the human condition. But parenting is not just an individual experience: and if it is, we can become locked in it rather than liberated by it. As a society, we should use our private, individual knowledge to tell us something crucial about the social conditions of those who most contribute to this special experience: mothers.

An old friend put it this way to me. She was looking at a group portrait of a primary school class, the rows of children approaching the age of reason; pigtails and gappy smiles, shiny hair and eyes, not a spark of cynicism. 'All those children,' she sighed, 'all the effort that goes into getting them to that place, on time; the faces to be washed a thousand times, the clothes to be cleaned, shoes to be bought and mended, the words and phrases to be taught them, conversations to be had, to show them how to be human. All those tears to mop up. Scraped knees to tend. What a vast amount of labour and it's not exactly hidden, not exactly undervalued, but it isn't really acknowledged or appreciated either, is it?'

If fathers have traditionally lacked knowledge of just how 'vast' this labour is, mothers have not. What has changed is the way that modern mothers seem encased in a new silence: fearful, a little self-contemptuous. We know what we do, but we don't talk about it much, publicly.

Contemporary fiction provides an interesting example. Women writers, young or old, write little of the effort of motherhood directly. It is no longer the vogue. I always imagine the internal, collective conversation might go something like this: 'We know all *that*; about what women do. Now we are more self-contained: there are other things to write about. And anyway, that other is the culture of complaint, even self-victimization. What anyway is there to say any more? It's the same experience, drudgery or bliss; coming round again and again.' Perhaps there is nothing new to say about drudgery or bliss. (I think there is: contexts change.) But let us at least acknowledge the silence.

Let us at least acknowledge how unusual it is for a writer like Helen Simpson, quick-witted epiphanous drawer of short stories, a quintessential modern writer, to break the silence in a *Best of Young British Novelists* collection. There among the surreal tales of abortion, and taxi rides, and teenage sex, and lesbian love across centuries, is a story of painful realism about life with two young children:

> After the holiday, Jonathan would be back at the office with his broad quiet desk and filter coffee while she would have to submit to a fate worse than death, drudging around the flat to Lorna's screams and the baby's regurgitations and her own sore eyes and and body aching to the throb of next door's Heavy Metal. The trouble with prolonged sleep deprivation was that it produced the same coarsening side effects as alcoholism. She was rotten with self pity, swarming with irritability and despair.
>
> When she heard Jonathan's step on the stairs, she realized that he must have goaded Lorna to sleep at last. She looked forward to his face, but when he came into the room and she opened her mouth to speak, all that came out were toads and vipers.
>
> 'I'm smashed up,' she said, 'I'm never alone. The baby guzzles me and Lorna eats me up. I can't ever go out because I've always got to be there for the children, but you flit in and out like a humming bird . . .'[15]

Toads. Vipers. Smashed up. Swarming with . . . despair. The ambivalence of love for man and child ('. . . they fell on each other's necks and mingled maudlin tears. "It's so awful," sniffed Frances, "we may never have another".'). The tone is modern, a little mocking, quick in description, allusive rather than all inclusive but the content is age-old: the reality of motherhood. In this, it reminds me of the writing of Doris Lessing, or Marilyn French. Or Adrienne Rich, in her first quoted diary entry, in *Of Woman Born*:

Entry from my journal, November 1960

My children cause me the most exquisite suffering of which I have any experience. It is the suffering of ambivalence: the murderous alternation between bitter resentment and raw-edged nerves, and blissful gratification and tenderness. Sometimes I seem to myself, in my feelings toward these tiny guiltless beings, a monster of selfishness and intolerance. Their voices wear away at my nerves, their constant needs, above all their need for simplicity and patience, fill me with despair at my own failures, despair too at my fate, which is to serve a function for which I was not fitted. And I am weak sometimes from held-in rage. There are times when I feel only death will free us from one another, when I envy the barren woman who has the luxury of her regrets but lives a life of privacy and freedom.[16]

If feminism opened the Pandora's box on these demands and painful emotions, post-feminism slammed it shut again. Post-feminism is self-contained to the point of amnesia and arrogance. This, I will argue, leaves the modern mother in a strange position: swamped with information and perspectives on who she might be, but robbed of authentic reflections of what she feels.

It is these considerations that inform the purpose and approach of this book. In the beginning, my simple idea had been to find out if life for mothers was better or worse than it had been a generation

or two ago. My basic impulse was that it was better, that modern
women had more choices and that this affected how they decided
upon and experienced motherhood. Certainly, this has become the
commonplace view. Writing in the *New Statesman*, Anthony
Giddens, one of Britain's leading sociologists and Director of the
London School of Economics, observes:

> Look at how the position of women has been transformed.
> New worlds have opened for them which did not exist
> before. Any debate about the family, for example, has to be
> set against this background. The structural basis of society is
> shifting, not disintegrating.[17]

One can find this kind of sentiment repeated, in different forms, in
a hundred articles, books and speeches of the last twenty years.[18]
Certainly, there are examples of much practical improvement in
the lives of mothers today compared to the 1950s for example. We
now have a legal right to maternity leave and protection against
many forms of sex discrimination. We may read occasionally of
women who are sacked for being pregnant, but we, rightly, see
these cases as remnants of a now outdated set of attitudes. Call any
large trade union and an official will tell you of how locally negotiated pay and conditions improve, often significantly, on minimum legal rights. Employers are keen to woo women back to
work. The 'right' of women to childcare is well-established in the
public mind. Even as consumers, parents have an easier time. Stuck
in a traffic jam last year, I found myself staring at an enormous
poster of a small child, advertising a new superstore with crèche
facilities. Swimming-pools, holiday camps and hotels routinely
provide baby-minding services; children are looked after and enter-
tained as part of a total leisure package. Even in the tiniest of ways,
businesses and local government show some awareness of children;
that wonderful smooth dip in a pavement that helps ease the passage of clumsy buggies from the road to the pavement and back
again; those even more wonderful magical doors that whoosh open
for you as you stagger up to the shop entrance. Looking for a loo
in a Manchester art gallery the other day, I unthinkingly followed

the baby-changing symbol down a corridor or two, until a uni-
formed attendant grasped me by the shoulder and pulled me back:
that's the men's toilet, he signalled, nodding simultaneously as if he
too understood my mild disbelief that even men's toilets now separately include nappy-changing facilities. All of these changes tes-
tify to a still limited but definite recognition of the needs of parents,
especially with tiny children. And a recognition, often, that they
have money to spend.

But I could also see that there were new, unforeseen pressures
on women; to be all things to all people: mother, worker, carer
quite possibly of an older relative; pressure to earn enough to live
or perhaps have all or just a few of the wonderful things offered
up to today's consumer. I could also see the flaws in public policy.
Elaborate schemes to help women take career breaks and aid
flexible working did nothing to touch on the fundamental fact
that women are assumed to take the major share of care of
children; they did nothing to promote shared parenting. Fine
statements on the family from politicians of all political parties did
nothing to help women with their caring load. There is a new
post-everything political blindness, too. We talk too much about
'families' and 'parents' these days, rather than remembering who
does what job within these 'families', among these 'parents'.
When the Working Mothers' Association changed its name to the
Working Parents' Association, in 1994, I recognized the imperative of linguistic/political fashion while thinking the decision too
premature. How, I wondered, could a society that talks so often
and obsessively about 'women' at the same time talk so little about
what matters to so many of them?

So I wanted to investigate the gap (or the overlap) between the
two perspectives. I wanted to investigate real lives and the ideas
that surround those lives. I wanted to go out and see for myself.
Listen. Look. Learn. That word 'investigate' is crucial, even if my
own explorations have been of the more personal kind. The
media increasingly favours the columnist over the investigator,
often for simple financial reasons. For a newspaper, it is cheaper
to hire people to sit at terminals and think great thoughts than it
is to send them out into the world. As a result, we are awash with

opinion rather than observation, prescription rather than description.

I have organized the material in this book as follows. The next chapter sets out some of the defining facts and values that have shaped the new motherhood, a kind of 'how we got here' section. Hopefully, this sets the arguments that follow in a definite context. The next part of the book, 'Real Lives', represents the result of my journey around (some of) Britain's mothers. These chapters are shaped around the key questions of work, home, money and men because these are the things we need to ask about, even if there are no obvious answers. In the course of writing this book, I talked to dozens of women and not a few men. I did not aim to be representative, rather to tap what the great cultural commentator Raymond Williams called 'a structure of feeling'. Nevertheless, I did talk to women from differing backgrounds and places: women from their teens to their seventies, mothers at home, full-time career women, part-time clerical workers and nurses, teachers and writers, single mothers, women working in social services and swimming-pools, mothers on benefit; women living in and around Basildon, Bristol, London, Sheffield, Cardiff, Glasgow and Liverpool; black women, white women, women with too much money, members of the struggling middle class, and women with few resources. However, this is not an 'interview' book as such, because I use the material in different ways: sometimes in 'straight quotes', sometimes in longer chunks, sometimes in an impressionistic, almost fictional form At each turn, I have been concerned to get across a truth: I choose the form that best fits description of that truth. The third section of the book, 'Politics', investigates ideas around motherhood; in particular the actions and arguments of mainstream political parties, especially New Labour – the Tories, thankfully, seem less relevant than they have done for years – and the arguments of feminism, historical and modern. How well have these currents of thought, which aim to both represent and change the experience of their particular 'constituencies', succeeded in that task? In my last chapter, 'Towards a New Politics of Motherhood', I look at how we might start to think about women, men and children in new ways. We are at an exciting, difficult crossroads.

But most of all, I would like this book to read like an absorbing story, for I have written it in a spirit of enquiry, trying always to go beyond face value, to get to the bottom of what I see, read, hear. I make no apology for bringing in my own experience, where relevant (which is not that often). Personal experience is a valuable tool, if examined as wisely and as critically as other forms of material. But I do not limit myself to it. That would be merely narcissism, even if covered with the usual explanation that one only ends up writing about oneself anyway.

For fifteen years I have been pretty certain about many of my views on women and feminism. Writing this book changed those ideas. At certain points it threw them into disarray. Sometimes they did not come back to me in coherent form – or not for a while. I would like the reader to enjoy the sifting of the argument, the *trying* of it at least. But perhaps most of all I would like her or him to come away with a picture of a time, now the late 1990s. A picture of some women in this period. The daughter of a committed and conscientious diarist, I have come to realize, over time, the overwhelming significance of simple record.

Great Expectations:
New Ethics, New Icons

> . . . a certain sort of woman . . . came up in the eighties
> . . . a woman who was bloody stroppy, wanted to have
> a laugh, wanted to have loads of money, wanted to have
> her own way . . . For me the eighties is still around
> because what that decade did was promote that type of
> woman.
>
> Julie Burchill, *Guardian*, 23 July 1996

We cannot understand modern motherhood without understanding the new place of work in modern women's lives. But
what do we mean by 'new'? Women, after all, have always
worked. Slaves like Sojourner Truth laboured as very young
children in the plantations and homes of their masters. In her
magnificent first volume of the history of women in late medieval
western Europe, Olwen Hufton illustrates some of the work done
by women in this earlier period, such as dairying, rearing livestock
and primitive farming. From the seventeenth century onwards,
even modest households employed servants to help them with
household tasks. Domestic service remained an option for many
women without money in Britain, Europe and the United States
who, in the nineteenth and early twentieth century, had to
support themselves variously as servants or seamstresses, farmers or
landladies, factory workers or governesses, teachers or traders.[1]

Novels like Charlotte Brontë's *The Professor* and *Villette* give a flavour of the loneliness and hard physical work involved in even the most 'genteel' of these occupations.

We must be clear about what *is* new about our own age. Let us start with two simple but crucial economic and social facts. The first is the mass entry of women into paid work. The figures for the last hundred years still startle. For women with children, just under 30 per cent of those born in the 1910s had a job at some point during the year in which they were thirty. For women born in the 1940s this figure had risen to nearly 50 per cent, and for women who turned thirty in the 1990s it had risen to nearly 70 per cent. (The figures are much higher for adult women without children.) Even in the space of the decade 1985–95, the number of women in employment rose by some 1.3 million compared to an increase of only 0.1 million for men.[2] The vast majority are working in what are demeaningly called 'low skilled, non professional' occupations: 2.7 million women are employed as clerical and secretarial workers. Half of British mothers working on a part-time basis are in the three lowest occupational categories: clerical and secretarial, selling and the personal and protective services.

The second major change in women's economic and social situation has been the rise and rise of the professional woman, the woman determined to learn a skill, practise a trade and compete on equal terms with men. Part of the impetus for women's slow but certain move into the professions came from the kind of work that mainly middle-class women were doing in the nineteenth century, from the voluntary nursing that began Florence Nightingale's career to the charitable and social work of women involved in the politics of housing, prisons, prostitution and so on. Such philanthropy involved literally millions of women. As the American social historian and theorist Christopher Lasch has pointed out, far from being enmeshed in the 'cult of domesticity' Victorian women and their American counterparts played a fruitful and important role, albeit mainly in a voluntary capacity, in the political and cultural life of their times. Such was their significance in the public realm that Henry James wrote in 1907 that 'women had established "peerless possession" of all forms of public life in the true sense . . . which struck him as deeply regrettable'.[3]

The emergent, pioneering 'career woman' undoubtedly drew on her knowledge of, and confidence in, this volunteer tradition as she began to practise her skills for money and a place in professional structures. As Rebecca Abrams records, in her sensitive oral account of the working lives of ten professional British women through the century, 'it is not surprising to find that they had to have a great deal of determination and commitment to their professional lives'.[4] They were still in a significant minority. The expansion of higher education after the Second World War, the rise of new feminist ideas and changes in the structure of employment have all exacerbated this trend. A professional career in law, medicine, politics, the voluntary sector, education, publishing, is no longer unusual for a woman.

But statistics tell us everything and nothing. Numbers and graphs indicate only 'shaping factors'. They do not describe lives or aspirations or satisfactions. A woman in the 'lowest occupational category' may well love her job, long to see her workmates on a Monday morning, do it with definite pride, hope for nothing more – or perhaps dream of a better job with more responsibility. A professional woman may drag herself into work every day, hating the bureaucracy, the boredom, the stifling nature of her routine. Figures on women in the labour force do not tell us anything about *expectations*, rather than achievements, the more subtle ways in which a generation of women *approach* the prospect of their working lives: the arrogance and hope, innocence and tenaciousness of it all. Despite recession and anxiety, the mood of our own era remains a remarkably cheerful one for women. Young women of today have great expectations of themselves; in sharp contrast, young men are surrounded by fears – their own, society's – concerning their predicted failure in education, work and relationships. This buoyancy is apparent in the many young women I know, of all backgrounds and classes. They are ambitious for themselves, but not always in the conventional sense; there is a sense of curiosity about a future that seems more open to them than it did for previous generations. They expect relationships, marriage perhaps, children possibly, but they do not expect their life to be defined by these choices. Compared to women of just twenty years ago, there is a new seriousness about work: the reproduction of the self through activity, not merely biology.

Thus, while most women will still end up having children – and their high hopes may not always be sustained through the unfolding of their particular personal story – they no longer expect to have them in the old way. The widespread availability of contraception is so acceptable, so normal, as to be beyond comment. Even the new technologies for creating, rather than curtailing, life are becoming part of the way we think about the world and our options concerning it. Child-bearing has become a matter of choice rather than destiny, deliberation rather than duty. One in five women, we are constantly told, will not even have a child. She's got other things to do.

Reversal of fortune

The subtle, yet profound, character of this change in destinies is clear when I compare the lives of my (paternal) grandmother, my mother and myself. My paternal grandmother, born Margaret Eadie just outside Glasgow in 1897, was a child of the Victorian era and, like many middle-class women of the period, spent a life in dedicated unpaid social service. She was one of the earliest campaigners for women's admission to the priesthood, a sophisticated theologian, international traveller, a talented lecturer and writer. In 1925 she lobbied the then aged Archbishop of Canterbury, Dr Randall Davidson, seated in 'an imposing episcopal chair', on the question of women priests. She has described this moment thus:

> Do you want to be a priest? I was able to say that the issue was not, at that time, a personal one. I explained, 'I have two little boys, and I want them to be brought up in a world in which the Church gives equal spiritual status to women' . . .

> I cannot recall that [the Archbishop] advanced any argument.
> He just said there never had been women priests and there
> never could be.[5]

To many of us who looked at her life from the outside, these were
the activities that distinguished her, defined who she was. (They
thrilled me.) But from the 'inside' of her life, the way she thought
about herself, there is no doubt that it was her existence as wife
and mother that took paramount importance. Married at twenty-
three to a man twenty years older than herself, she was mother to
four boys, one of whom tragically died just a few hours after birth
when she was in her thirties. Nothing mattered to her more than
her husband and the 'boys'. It used to drive me mad in my teens
and twenties as she and I faced each other across what sometimes
seemed an unbridgeable gulf. Of expectations. Of generations.

I had absolutely no intention of making children – and
particularly not sons – the centre of my life. *I* was going to be as
important as any of *her* male progeny. For her part, she looked at
me with, I believe, puzzlement and well-concealed irritation. I,
after all, had had the much-longed-for university education
which was not open to her as a young woman, although she made
up for it in later life. When the boys were little she had attended
a graduate class in theology, but, as she later wrote,

> with an already busy daily life I did not contemplate sitting for
> any examinations. Nowadays young wives and mothers have
> no difficulty taking all this in their stride, but sixty-five years
> ago such was not considered a possibility.[6]

She looked at me, with my first class degree and the chance of
many a nice man (whom she always treated with a flirtatious
deference that further inflamed me), and what was I doing with
any of it? I wouldn't marry. I declared myself uninterested in
children. I just wanted to write.

My grandmother died a couple of years before I had my first
daughter, Hannah. By then, we had made a kind of peace
between our very different, perhaps incompatible, characters; a

truce, at least, across the gulf of generation and experience. I had come to understand some of her achievements and sorrows and steeliness. She arrived at a wistful admiration of my determination. But even if she had lived to see me become a mother, it would have been too late or not enough. Even now, I do not make my children the centre of my life as she did; for me, motherhood is an act, not an act of faith.

Even as a teenager, I viewed my mother, Caroline, quite differently. She did not believe that children were a woman's destiny: she spoke instead of her great *enjoyment* in us, often quoting the French writer Colette on how pregnancy was like one long holiday. Children were a source of fun rather than a burden. Yet she had still expected to have them and, in a way, she, too, had done her duty by having a family. Typical of Betty Friedan's generation in many senses – an American upper-middle-class woman, born in 1926 – she was one of the first generation of American women to get a higher education. Her own parents were puzzled by, and uninterested in, her academic achievements. Why would this bright articulate attractive young woman need an education when she was probably going to marry young?

Her way of dealing with the possible contradiction of her own expectations of herself and the pressures of her era was clever and, to some extent, concealing. Throughout her life my mother pursued a deliberate but partly unconscious strategy which was to do things society's way (at least on the surface) *and* her own way at one and the same time. There were echoes, here, of the superficial conformity of someone like Sylvia Plath, a near contemporary, who also appeared to play the perfect wife/mother role while making bitter perfect poetry from her pain. My mother, neither bitter, nor driven by inner demons, merely shifted emphasis when the time was auspicious: as we children grew up, she began to work more, to realize more of her life's dreams. So that rather like my grandmother, Margaret (but in a quite different way), we can look at my mother's life and see two very distinct women, two definite paths: the loving mother and the formidable public woman.

The conforming part of my mother did all the 'right' things. She married young, had had four children by her early thirties, although by her own generation's standards, she, like me, thirty years later, was classed a primigravida. She was a 'good' supportive wife. But, in all the moats of time in between, she determinedly pursued her own projects: campaigning, writing, teaching. It was a family moan, and joke, that my mother never sat in the living-room after our nightly tea throughout my childhood and young adulthood. She always went straight upstairs into her bedroom, where she would work on her bed surrounded by papers, or go to her tiny cramped boxroom of an office. To the outsider it looked utterly chaotic, but she could find a piece of paper at a moment's notice.

When I write these potted histories I realize how inevitable it should be that I would have children, precisely because neither 'model' – paternal grandmother and mother – ruled out the possibility of having both, work and family. But it was never my destiny or ambition, nor even my intention, to have a family. I always shiver with pity when I see women searching for a partner – and particularly a husband – or looking to start a family. For a start, like buses, happiness or husbands for that matter never come along if you want them to. Personal satisfaction cannot be sought in quite that way. Pursue your own aims and you are more likely to find a happiness from within that satisfaction. (This, too, was a family ethic.) But am I wrong to see my greater concentration on self and purpose as typical of a shift as a whole? Yes and no. Of course, I see many women, ironically most of them younger than me, who want the whole marriage and motherhood package. It appears, on the surface at least, as if they are returning to conventional forms, but not quite in the old way. For them it is not an 'either/or' way of thinking about their lives – motherhood or career – as it might have been for my grandmother or even my mother, but, rather, a thankful addition to a self-directed life, if all goes well.

The right to work

If you had listened in to a political conversation at the beginning of the eighties there would have been much murmuring about Thatcherism pushing women back into the home. Women were still the 'reserve army of labour' to be utilized when employment prospects were good, abandoned when unemployment soared. There were still angry mutterings over the absurd statement by Tory Shadow Minister Patrick Jenkin in 1977 that 'Quite frankly . . . if the good Lord had intended us to have equal rights to go out to work he wouldn't have created men and women.'

Towards the middle of the eighties, the emphasis shifted to women, work and guilt. As Susan Faludi records in her blockbuster *Backlash*, a book which helped define a moment as much as describe it, an outpouring of dubious research played up the supposedly harmful effects of working mothers on their families. Yet like all assaults, it brought its own answer that moved the argument to a different stage. Books like *Backlash* had made the assault on women a question for popular culture, not just academic or political feminism. Mainstream feminists, then working on the mass circulation magazines like *Cosmopolitan* and *She*, were infuriated at the suggestion that women were being told they could not 'have it all'. They hit back with pieces on the absurdity of the backlash and the manifest necessity and pleasures of work and economic independence.[7] The effect of counter-assaults such as these was to emphasize a deep-rooted change in the culture as profound as anything that has happened to women in the last century.

And the change was this; that at some point in the mid to late eighties, *the burden of proof shifted from the working to the non-working mother.*

Compared to even ten or fifteen years ago, the burden of explanation and justification is now on the woman who does not have a job. I recently met a woman, quite by accident, at somebody else's house: she had a haunted, slightly unhappy look. There could have been many reasons for it – I do not pretend to see into people's souls – but after we had talked, on and off, for a couple of hours, one strand of her unhappiness became obvious to me. She did not have a paid job and perhaps she wished she did: she felt uneasy surrounded by women who did have paid work, particularly professional women. She jumped, almost imperceptibly, when the talk was about money or meetings. She looked away or looked resentful. Like many women 'at home' she seemed to feel not only that her interests were neglected but that, somehow, society had left her behind. Working women have an opposite problem. They are often harassed through lack of time, particularly if they work full-time. They often feel guilty because there are still plenty of people in public life willing to point the finger at working mothers. At the same time, they feel a relatively new entitlement to the life they lead; there is a lack of apology about them.

I look around at some of the mothers I know locally; they range from their early twenties to late thirties. A large number of them are professionally trained or qualified, if now working part-time. Several of them, the younger ones, are studying or completing a training. Those who gave up work, perhaps after a second child, talk about returning to work, even if they have no intention of doing so right away. One has started up a small business, from home. There is an argument, which I shall return to later, that the having of children has seriously undermined their enthusiasm for work but that is not how they talk or, I suspect, even think about themselves. It is not just that their household often needs the money that comes from the work they do, or that they enjoy being in the 'outside' world, both of which are true, but that the *idea* of being a working woman is vital to them. The substance of the sentence 'I am a . . . teacher/copywriter/dance student/ administrative assistant' is as significant to them as the sentence 'I am the mother of John/Kate/Cherelle/Sinead', although, inter- estingly, women often tend not to talk in declarative sentences such as these about either role. They prefer to talk about what they do, rather than what they are, hoping that others will join up the meaning and declare them to 'be' something, almost on their behalf.

Popular culture not only reflects this shift towards the working mother: it has significantly helped create it. In magazines and movies, a woman's modernity is measured by her involvement in the working world, whether at the glamorous or more daily end of the spectrum. A magazine like *Hello!* regularly features new mothers, happily displaying their babies and gorgeous homes and supportive husbands and all-round wonderful lives. The message is mixed and complex. The convention of such soft features is that women usually invoke the importance of their work but then modify it with reference not just to the joys, but to the ultimate meaning of family. Children and husbands (and life-threatening illnesses) bring realization of what is 'really important' in life, an echo of common-sense sentiment but tinged with hypocrisy in the celebrity context. A typical example was a feature on the model Iman, in April 1997. While the main part of the article was devoted to details of a recent trip she had made to Kenya, the country which gave her refuge as a child from the political upheavals of her native Somalia, and to discussion of the workings of her new cosmetics company, the interview drew to a close with questions and answers on her parenthood. 'When you are young, you think spending two hours with your child is enough. With the passing of time, I now know what my priorities are. Having a child is my priority. Everything else comes after that.'[8]

Soap operas on radio and television rarely feature stay-at-home mothers, especially among the younger generation. Female characters have children and jobs, children and ambitions. This is not confined to mothers with glamorous jobs: soap operas with their 'real-time' feel can show the pleasures as well as the tedium of working in a shop or serving in a petrol station. Ironically, they are not so good at showing the reality of motherhood, mainly because child actors tend to be unconvincing and keep looking curiously at the camera: scenes featuring them are cut to a ruthless minimum. But the programmes get it gloriously right sometimes. When Shula Archer, the respectably widowed single mother in *The Archers*, was invited out for a meal by her new boss/soon-to-be lover, large chunks of an episode were devoted to her attempts to find a baby-sitter. Theoretically, there was a whole cast of characters she could ask to help her out: in practice, none of them worked out. Finding baby-sitters who aren't martyrs or charge a fortune is one of the great minor social problems of our age.

Advertising may reflect a truer picture of women in Britain. After all, to sell a product to someone, you must show you both recognize and value who they are. Adverts about women, for women, reflect a highly segmented market, far less homogenized than it was in past decades. In the mid to late evening, one is likely to see the purest image of the independent woman: advertisements that display the virtues of the nifty little car for the equally nifty young woman, just moving away from her 'papa' and hoping to start up her own business, or the dandruff-beating shampoo for the TV star who must stride before a studio camera in a couple of minutes. There is also an entire mini-market devoted to the couple as consumer: two twenty-somethings prepare an evening meal together or sit on a couch dreaming of money or travel or home-owning. But when it comes to fish fingers, gravy, soap powder or nappies, advertisers have their eye firmly on the woman in the kitchen. 'Mum' here is either young, sleek and sexy, or approachably portly, with well-shaped hair and a blouse in bold red. She chides those cheeky kids who want to get their fingers on some goody before she's ready to serve it up, or affectionately castigates a husband late back from work or football. Some advertisements try to have it both ways. An advert for a deodorant, screened in the mid-morning chat show slot, shows a woman doctor working so hard in a busy hospital we must presume the generation of a lot of (invisible) sweat. The anti-perspirant helps her keep cool. But just in case we think she is getting too serious about her job, the story finishes with her affectionately greeting her husband and young son outside the ward, showing that there is an end, after all, to all this work business.

The Rise of the Bourgeois Feminist Triumphalist

It would be foolish not to relish this new seriousness about work, these new great expectations. It would be foolish, too, not to see in it an inheritance directly traceable to a much earlier feminism.

We can see its genesis, for example, in the bossy badgering of Mary Wollstonecraft in the late eighteenth century when she urged women 'to acquire that soberness of mind which the exercise of duties and the pursuit of knowledge alone inspires'.[9] We can see it in the energetic example of nineteenth-century female philanthropy, the Florence Nightingales, the Octavia Hills, the Josephine Butlers, that Christopher Lasch so fondly praises in the American context. We can see it in the example set by a woman like Simone de Beauvoir, who with her ferocious determination to write, her refusal to marry, her polymorphously (slightly) perverse love life and her uncompromising politics did more than almost any white western woman to project a new independent work-oriented identity for the generations that followed her.

But a new twist was added to this story of female seriousness and female power in the post-feminist years (the mid eighties onwards), a twist that was not always for the good. To understand it, we have briefly to return to the new individualism that took root in the early to mid eighties; what was loosely called Thatcherism in Britain and Reaganism in America. The roots of the new individualism were complex, both economic and political; it expressed itself as both a turning away from the assumptions of social democracy and welfare capitalism and the embrace of a new aspirationalism, supposedly for all. Both the grand ideological failure of state socialism in the old Eastern Europe and the continuing economic troubles of social democratic states of the west helped lead the disillusioned and discontented back into the most enduring of capitalist romances: the individual dream. In this country, Thatcherism seemed to offer everyone a home of their own, a route out of poverty into successful economic self-management, but as the burden of taxation and policy shifted in favour of the wealthy, those reliant on the public purse and the public sector became second-class citizens, poor mothers chief among them.

Some women, however, flourished during this period. They somehow came to life during the crazy boom of the mid eighties when money and effort rather than class and education offered a pathway to new power. Former *Elle* editor Sally Brampton, writing in the tenth anniversary issue of the magazine, captured the excesses of that period. She described it as 'a time when everyone wanted to drink vodkatinis and party all night because what else is youth for?'[10] For this generation, it was fast ferocious money-making and 'serious leisure'.

At some point in this partying, money-making, hard-living culture, some psychological rubicon was crossed, some new attitude was forged, that has proved crucial to how women think about themselves even now. The new attitude transformed, sometimes subtly, the values of earlier generations of strong women – those who had, albeit rather earnestly, upheld the virtues of work, purpose, occupation – into a different constellation; these celebrated, instead, the virtue of power, success and the importance of self. Writer Julie Burchill has described this moment, these values, as being about the ' bloody stroppy woman . . . who wanted to have her own way'. But it wasn't just about 'getting your own way'. It was about what you wanted to do once you had got your own way, which was often not very much. It was forcefulness for the sake of self-advancement as much as forcefulness for any larger purpose. As I argue in a later chapter, the politics of feminism changed too. It, too, began to lose many of its connections with an older, socially aware tradition.

Several icons of the eighties were crucial to the shaping of this new female psychology. Previous strong female figures were merely 'famous' or 'role models'. But the growing power of mass communications made women like Margaret Thatcher or Madonna into overpowering images, into film stars without, on the whole, film careers, although Madonna was later to follow that logical route. Supremely, almost parodically feminine, their power was butch, tough, controlling. Lower-middle-class in origin, they took the establishment on and 'won' by becoming richer, more powerful, than the richest and most powerful member of it. As Julie Burchill wrote, in her essay on Madonna:

> The Eighties saw the emergence of what can only be called
> Bourgeois Feminist Triumphalism, exemplified by Margaret

Thatcher in no 10, Martina Navratilova on the clay courts,
Joan Collins on TV and strident starlets like Janet Jackson in
the charts. But undoubtedly the First Lady of BFT is
Madonna.[11]

We are so used to Madonna and her reinventions now, in the late
nineties: the early images have gone stale not only through
familiarity but from what we can now write about them (such as
the change in the woman since she became Madonna and Child).
But rereading press coverage of her first British tour when the star
really took off is to remember the impact of her brashness, her raw
sexuality, and her iron control of her performance and public
image. A double page spread in the *Daily Express*, entitled 'The
brazen Madonna', declared, 'the language of those loins is one of
pure animal power . . . [Madonna] knows exactly what she is
doing. She is dominating the male dancers and the male members
of the audience.' Writer David Wigg enthused, 'Madonna, 29
yesterday, has been a fighter all her life – not just in her
determination to become one of the biggest stars of the eighties
. . . in four years, she has become a phenomenon . . . she is one of
the world's most successful singers.'[12] Playing on the new gap
between generations, and between men and women, that
Madonna supposedly personified, the *Daily Telegraph* found a
grumpy retired surgeon who had, unwillingly, heard the whole of
Madonna's Leeds concert from the balcony of his flat.
'Unutterably dreary,' he declared. The controversy rolled on. In
July 1988 Madonna declared her 'love' for lesbian comedienne
Sandra Bernhard; in March 1989 the raunchy video of her song
'Like a Prayer' shocked respectable and Catholic opinion.
'Women have always had power – they never knew,' she told the
Daily Express in May 1989, and 'I dislike men who suppress their
femininity.'[13]

But sex or even music was never really the point about
Madonna. The point was control, it was publicity and it was *presence*. Her 1991 film *In Bed with Madonna* showed a woman in
charge of everything from her dancers to her daring. Like a series
of tricks with mirrors, we saw how her image of highly sexualized

femininity was achieved through the iron control of a ballet dancer and the fiscal and administrative discipline of the most acute businessman. The message to modern women was not merely 'Run your own life' but 'Be *seen* to run your own life', an alluring if impossible message for mere mortals with lives, not legends, to live. The old split between public and private, home and work was also dissolved. *In Bed with Madonna* showed the star in a shower cap looking early-morning grungy, eating soup from a tureen, her unmade-up self as much a part of who she was as the high-kicking dancer on stage. It was fantasy: we knew it was fantasy. Or did we? Madonna's strength was obvious, obviously laudable, particularly her refusal of the classic pain and self-victimization of earlier women rock or movie stars, the Janis Joplins, the Monroes. But as this appealing discipline and certainty inevitably mixed with narcissistic self-aggrandizement, the humanity that made Madonna interesting in the first place seemed to fade.

Like Madonna, Margaret Thatcher was a famously hard worker. A chemist, then a lawyer, a mother and a politician, Britain's first woman Prime Minister, she was famed for her toughness, her ability to exist on only a few hours' sleep, her uncompromising politics, that so reversed traditional notions of women's greater personal flexibility. But Thatcher's public persona was complex. From the beginning of her premiership, in 1979, she was always running two images simultaneously: super stateswoman and ordinary wife and mother. The latter image – Thatcher pictured with a wire shopping-basket, Thatcher talking about good housekeeping – was more convincing in the early years; before the sculpted bronzed hair and the winged shoulders, we could just about believe she had once been a version of a Grantham/Surrey middle-class housewife, prudently foraging for a good bargain. In contrast, the super-stateswoman persona took time to develop. The 1982 Falklands campaign, a seminal event in her administration, helped a good deal; Thatcher as a modern version of Boadicea, a woman in a chariot, a woman of fire. So did her rapport with foreign statesmen like Reagan and Gorbachev. Who could ever forget the sight of Thatcher in Moscow among the people, after her triumphant visit there in

1987, fur at her throat, shining, on a journey even she declared was above politics? As Hugo Young records: 'When an unfortunate radio reporter asked her if her visit was political, her response was contemptuous. "Broaden your view," she said, "I am on an historic mission representing my country." '[14]

Thatcher exercised a peculiarly strong grip on the feminine and feminist psyche during her long political reign. Female commentators worried, like a dog with a bone, over what Thatcher did and how she did it; unsurprisingly, they did so in a manner quite distinct from male commentators, who were less interested than they in the mechanics of a personality that hid an unusually tough will under the drape of exaggerated femininity.[15] In private, women were equally curious; there was much discussion of Thatcher's toughness, her sheer self-confidence: to where in her personal history could we trace the source of this extraordinary self-belief? It was believed to be in her relationship with her father, the former mayor of Grantham Alfred Roberts, who always encouraged and guided his eldest daughter. Like many a powerful woman, the young Margaret Roberts worshipped her father and modelled her desires for the future on his life, not her mother's: unlike many a powerful woman she had almost nothing to say about that mother.[16] Hugo Young described the relationship thus:

> In Margaret's adult mind, Alfred was as prominent as her
> mother was obscure. Numerous interviews after she became
> famous managed to exclude all references to Beatrice Roberts.
> There was an almost obsessive reluctance to refer to her.
> Whenever a question was asked about Beatrice, the
> interviewee tended to take the conversation straight back to
> Alfred. If she was alluded to at all, it was under the
> patronizing designation of 'rather a Martha'.[17]

But it was the other sort of motherhood – her own, of twins – that marked Margaret Thatcher out as a real pioneer. She had given birth to twins in 1953, a fact that a biographer like Hugo Young rather sweeps over as she herself, no doubt, would have

liked him to do. But women of the period, those with children
or those who might one day like to have them, were more
interested: up to then, after all, the convention for strong women
in politics, like Barbara Castle, had been to remain childless.
Thatcher's motherhood was probably one of the single most
significant contributions to the nebulous idea of 'Having It All', a
phrase, ironically, that was originally coined in reference to single
women. If a mother and devoted wife could be Prime Minister of
Great Britain, surely all the battles had been won? (This may have
been the origin of Suzanne Moore's remark that the election of a
woman Prime Minister made the 'vocabulary of socialist
feminism' meaningless to a generation of younger women.) Of
course, the conditions of Thatcher's motherhood were excep-
tional: she had money, nannies, good luck – she often claimed
that the children only fell ill at weekends – and determination. In
an interview with Miriam Stoppard in 1986, she told of how she
looked down at her newborn twins and was determined not 'to
be overcome by this'. Like a hostile foreign power or the enemy
within, motherhood was a force to be reckoned with, wrestled
with and finally 'overcome'.

Few women liked Margaret Thatcher: *liking* her wasn't the
point, anyway. The point was the new model she created for a
female public life, a model, like Madonna, of the will to power,
of triumph over circumstance, of stepping over and above her sex
rather than identifying with it. For both of them life was work,
work was life; and the point of work was money, power and
unrestrained self-promotion. How much did the Thatcher/
Madonna phenomenon contribute to a feeling among the new,
the young, even all women of the eighties and nineties that they
should be strong and self-reliant, but that they should *never let go*
for a minute, that they should *always be there*, wherever 'there'
happened to be: the dealer's floor, the magazine office, the legal
firm, showing something much much more than willing?
(Willing was for wusses, anyway.) How much did the Thatcher/
Madonna phenomenon contribute to an idea that to be committed to anything other than ruthless self-promotion was
somehow to sell oneself short? How much did the Thatcher/

Madonna phenomenon contribute to the idea that to think about or be one of those million others without money, power and high-octane mobility and, what's more, with no interest in these things, was to stand accused of personal failure and/or piety rather than an enlarged political imagination, a genuine human sympathy? It clearly did. Talking about the eighties, and the feel of that time, socialist feminist writer and historian Sheila Rowbotham has observed:

> The only thing that hurt . . . was the sneering contempt. If you had any thought or ideas of commitment to other people who weren't able to make it as individuals, you were sneered at. I hated that.[18]

A final word on the purest representative of this position: Julie Burchill, the original 'bloody stroppy woman', one of the first women in journalism not just to command a high salary and a high profile but one of the first women to keep on telling us all about it. Madonna and Thatcher, not surprisingly, were Burchill's kind of women, BFTs incarnate. Like them she had come from a non-upper-class background. Like them she conquered the patronage of the upper middle classes by beating them at their own game. Like them, she measured her achievements out in material form: money, a tangible fame and infamy. Burchill's essay, 'Nature, Nurture or Nietzche: excerpts from the Julie Burchill story', still stands as the most naked statement of the new self-seeking sensibility. Of her unhappy childhood in Bristol, Burchill wrote:

> I waited in my room, waited to be Somebody; then and only then would I be Myself. That, I think, is the modern experience – that you don't really exist until you see your name in print. That you are simply *not yourself* till you are famous. That, then, was my youth . . . Too many of my friends' lives are ending in pregnancy at sixteen – working-class women still die in great numbers in childbirth; they just die in a different way, that is all – and I'm too young to die.

She is enticed by the American example: 'I read in my *NME* [*New Musical Express*] about this Americanne Patti Smith who confirms for me Mary McCarthy's line about American women being a third sex.'

As her career progresses, her personal triumphalism grows:

> That resentment which routed me from Bristol – that I was
> too clever by half – is here, too, amongst people who should
> know better. I am a Thatcherite bitch I hear, which is
> middle-class liberal shorthand for a working-class girl who has
> made it . . . Well they can take their frigging First Aid box
> and minister to some other sweet young thing from the
> wrong side of the tracks: I refuse to lose, I refuse to be
> anyone's hard luck story. Coming from where I did, the most
> rebellious thing I could have done was to make it big. And I
> did . . .

When she hears that members of Duran Duran have asked a mutual friend if they actually '*know* her' – well, that's the kick of fame. To have her heroes hear of her, that is life.[19]

No-one cut the cord with traditional femininity, with the conventions of *niceness*, as decisively, as irritably or as openly as Burchill. She was spurred on by, and fed off, other figures of the period who projected a similar will to power, other working-class girls who made it big, like the writer Jeanette Winterson. Burchill's legacy is alive today in the furious narcissism of an artist like Tracey Emin or even the grave ambitions of a Princess Diana. On a more mundane level, hundreds of women over the years have secretly, or not so secretly, nurtured that triumphalist element in their own character; attempts to smother it result in piety; attempts to reveal it manifest themselves in a peculiar feminine self-satisfaction. Few, however, have taken the new ruthlessness and made something of it, something angry and political, something to do with social change, something to do with making the world a better place. Burchill doesn't even try. She nakedly harnesses *her* will to power to her own story and no one else's.

Having It All

One of the predominant ideas of this era was 'Having It All'. The term itself was originated much earlier, by Helen Gurley Brown, the first editor of *Cosmopolitan*, but her book of the same name, being a manual for the new young swinging girl of the sixties and seventies, hardly mentions motherhood. 'Having It All' in an eighties context was more about babies; or at least it was about whether babies were seriously possible for serious women. The Thatcher example suggested they were, but few women thought they had the determination or resources to imitate her. There was another informal line of thinking that prevailed: women should choose babies or a briefcase, the briefcase being one of the arch symbols of the era. Of course, none of this touched the lives of most women: as a proportion of the country's working women, relatively few were entering or working in the 'new media' and money professions – property, accountancy, advertising, journalism – where these sorts of should I/shouldn't I, could I/couldn't I? conversations might take place. On top of this, the eighties was about youth; women in their twenties could afford to see a dream of motherhood deferred, at least for a decade.

In more general terms, 'Having It All' remained true to Gurley Brown's original prescription for an earlier decade. It remained about having a good time and learning some important skills. The supposed message of post-feminism was that equality was now possible, if equality was the ability to do a job as well as any man. The influence of a whole range of 'icons' was crucial here, from Thatcher herself to businesswomen like the ecologically sound large-haired Anita Roddick. It was not even that women had to be masculine, although that was the stereotypical picture of the era. In many ways, the mood was supremely practical; work skills were to be learned, professional kudos to be earned. Growing male unemployment and the opening up of more female jobs from the poor end of the market, in the newly expanding service sector, to professional companies that were, in the new management-speak, becoming more 'feminized' – all implied that this was the decade for women.

A magazine like *Cosmopolitan* in this period accurately reflected elements of the new mood. It has become one of the clichés of journalism that *Cosmopolitan* was, and remains, dedicated to sex, the pursuit of orgasms. This is to fundamentally misread the magazine. One of its primary interests has always been economic independence, even politics albeit in a soft, feel-good kind of way. Throughout the eighties, feature after feature spurred on the magazine's readers to improve themselves. Articles in the magazine covered the art of self-affirmation; how to ward off office bullies, how to ask for a pay rise, how to know if you're bored at work, how to deal with a (female) boss. These were the new realities for a distinct group of modern women: the briskly competitive world of the office junior. For *Cosmopolitan*'s readers were, and remain, primarily aspirational. The magazine is not read by women who have broken through the glass ceiling or even by those who can see it from underneath. It is the popular or down-market equivalent of young women who read densely printed books in cafés at nineteen and take expectation for inspiration; those who in their state of excited anticipation are prepared, at least in theory, for the boredom, failure and complexity of an exciting life but may be genuinely shocked and defeated by the banal troubles when they come. A survey of *Cosmopolitan*'s readers in the early nineties showed that most of its readership earned less than £15,000 a year, far less than the national average wage at that time. Thus, there was a kind of voyeurism rather than realism to those pieces frequently run about women who had made it. This was not how most of the *Cosmopolitan* 'we' – and like all the best magazines, it did create a sense of an 'insider' readership – were *ever* going to look.

Nor was the magazine entirely about the child-free woman and her brilliant career. In the early to mid eighties, still under the influence of an earlier organized political feminism, the magazine ran a strong campaign for more and better childcare for working women. But as the eighties ticked on, the editor of *Cosmopolitan* changed, the campaign faded. The new ebullient editor, Marcelle d'Argy Smith, had a kind of matching ebullient conviction that women could have it all, damn it: under her editorship the magazine glowed red, sometimes literally, with the achievements of all the world's *wonderful* women. Meanwhile, more detailed interest in the fate and finances of mothers, or not, shifted to *She* magazine, where previous *Cosmopolitan* editor Linda Kelsey had moved. Kelsey had a small son: her aim in re-launching *She*, a previously ailing title, had been to reflect what happens to *Cosmo* girl when she grows up, when she becomes a mother. Of that launch Kelsey has written:

> When Erica Jong said that liberation had won women the right to be permanently exhausted, perhaps I should have paid attention. For working mums, Helen Gurley Brown's famous catchphrase 'Having It All' needed a rewrite. Doing It All was more like it. Sales of *She* soared. Meanwhile my son Thomas . . . suffered a number of minor and not so minor illnesses. I worried constantly. About him, about work, about child care, about never having enough time.[20]

But in early 1995, Linda Kelsey herself fell ill with stress-related depression and left her job, provoking an enormous amount of press comment on the failure of the 'Having It All' myth.[21]

Baby boom and backlash

If 'Having It All' was one of the most nebulous phenomena of our time, which we cannot pin down to a place, a person or even a headline, it is much easier to trace popular rebellion against the myth. As Susan Faludi records in *Backlash*, throughout the eighties and nineties, the mainstream press hammered home the message that career women just couldn't make it. In the words of one article, 'reports of superwomen burnout crop up worldwide'. 'Why 90s Women now say no to Careers,' crowed the *Daily Mail* in 1990, suggesting there was a New Feminist who had 'thrown away the shoulder pads and picked up the carry cot'. Every gobbet of information about women's difficulty was seized upon: 'Mother's Misery Amid the Happy Families,' 'Career Women hard hit by childbearing.'[22] Whenever a high-

profile woman gave up paid work to become a full-time mother
and housewife she could be assured of substantial and sympathetic press coverage.[23]

There were more considered attempts to look at the difficulties
that arose from trying to combine professional work with
commitment to family. Ros Coward's *Our Treacherous Hearts*
(1992), which I discuss in Chapter 11, was one of these; but the
title itself was a sign of the times. If the burden of proof had shifted
from the working mother to the non-working mother, the
burden of political proof had gone the other way; not only
feminism but women themselves were now under scrutiny for
their failure to carry out the personal and political project of
feminism. The truth was that the most organized and visible
feminism of even the decade before – the seventies – had scarcely
cast a glance at the career woman: it was Bourgeois Feminist
Triumphalism that brought her difficulties into the public glare.
That earlier politics had been more concerned with working-class
women, the night cleaners, nurses, factory workers, and their
struggles for decent conditions of work and pay. Those struggles
were completely forgotten in the eighties, and the history of
feminism itself rewritten to suggest that it was always about the
babies/briefcase dichotomy and was now failing these top women
or had at least got it wrong. Quality papers like the *Guardian*,
which featured a special interview with Ros Coward on her
analysis of women's weakness, had also shifted their perspective
on feminism away from the so-called worthy preoccupations of
the days of the 'wimmin's page', satirized by Dennis Potter in *The
Singing Detective*. In the early nineties *Guardian Women* reflected
the new in-yer-face popular feminism of Madonna and stars of
the 'third wave' like Naomi Wolf.

But the most mainstream and populist response to 'Having It
All' came in a novel of the same name by television executive
turned writer Maeve Haran. Published by Michael Joseph in
1991, a heavy tome at 550-plus pages, *Having It All* was
supposedly a repudiation of absurd expectations for women while
clearly modelled in many respects on the author herself. The
jacket blurb summed it up:

Power. Money. Success. And a happy family. Liz really
believed she could have it all. So when she's offered one of
the most important jobs in television she jumps at it. But Liz
discovered that there's a price to be paid for her success and
that the whole glittering image is just an illusion. And one day
she's faced with the choice she thought she'd never have to
make. Liz decides she will have it all – but on her own terms.

And how that last sentence is the key to it all! *Having It All* tells
the story of Liz Ward, 'high-flying executive and creative power
house of Metro television', who tries unsuccessfully to combine
life with a wayward husband, work and children into the
unaccommodating twenty-four-hour clock. The plot moves
sharply through a number of crises which highlight this conflict:
impossible pressures at work, power plays, feeling the children are
being short-changed, Liz's husband's infidelity with a seductive
but childless old friend. All this leads her to 'chucking it all' – job,
life, husband – for life alone with her children in the country.
Rural living represents the perfect antithesis of life at Metro
television. But the story is not yet properly resolved: even here,
Liz Ward finds herself building up another business. Only this one
is more 'real': it is about helping place working mothers in local
jobs on terms that suit those mothers. Womanpower becomes a
highly successful enterprise which, like all successful projects,
starts to spin out of control. Once it becomes prey to the
seductive forces of amoral capitalism, Liz is again prey to the kind
of threats that destroyed her marriage and television career. A
powerful businessman wants to take the business over; at the same
time Liz is offered her old job at Metro television back but this
time on her own terms, with greater control of all the things that
really matter, such as policy and budgets. Meanwhile her errant
husband has thrown in his life-wrecking job and is starting again
in the provinces, coming to his own slow realization of what life
is about. The final resolution to this unbelievable story is that
husband and wife come together to run Womanpower. This will
allow them to be both financially successful, socially useful and a
'whole' family.

The book is fascinating, now, as a social document. In almost cartoon fashion, it charts so many elements of the 'new mood', the almost addictive rush of work in the eighties, the rise of the Bourgeois Feminist Triumphalist in the world of television, the threat posed by the young, child-free woman, frequently preying upon older powerful men; dressed in clinging lycra and Doctor Martens she is all silk and toughness. Most importantly of all, it dramatizes the conflicts of women who have had children and remain in the corporate work world: the impossible tensions between home and work but also between partner and partner. If the book has any moral strength it is this: that it recognizes the pull of other human beings, it recognizes the importance of 'real' as opposed to manipulated human relationships as a positive not a negative quality.

What actual solutions does the book offer? The chief idea is that women solve their work problems by successful self-employment. While it is true that more and more women have turned to self-employment in recent years in an attempt to control their working lives, this is more likely to be lowly paid freelance work or even home working than an ever more dynamic small business. *Having It All* also locates the source of all human authenticity within the frame of family. Family and particularly children here act as a metaphor for all human relationships of quality. Obviously the demands of small children are the most insistent, but marriage and children are not the beginning and the end of the story of human needs for connection. Correspondingly, child-free women seem somehow less humanized, as if their lack of offspring has given them a humanity bypass. Thirdly, the female characters in *Having It All* actually ask very little of the men. There is a telling, almost throwaway line at the end of the book when the recalcitrant husband comes home and agrees to run the new business with his wife.

'I'll give up the paper and accept Womanpower. On two conditions.'
Liz felt her heart quicken until it almost hurt her chest.
'And what are those?'

'First that you run down Metro and we run Womanpower together.' He looked down at Jamie, 'With half term and school holidays off of course – if you want.'

That last throwaway phrase of David's says it all: if *you* want. Even in this new equal, caring, sharing paradise, it looks like Liz Ward will be doing the school runs and minding the children in the school holidays. *Plus ça change . . .*

There is a remarkable resemblance between the plot and themes of *Having It All* and the earlier film *Baby Boom* (1987), starring Diane Keaton. Here Keaton plays a high-flying executive in pin-stripes forever rushing from one appointment to another, locked in what is clearly an unsatisfying relationship with another ambitious yuppie. In a plot of extraordinary, almost delicious improbability, Keaton's life is changed not by the ordinary mechanism of choosing to have a child, but by having a child thrust upon her by a long-lost relative. This at least gets rid of the tedium of one sub-plot: career woman agonizes over decision about children.

The impossibility of combining child and deadlines, children and profit, leads Keaton – yes, she, too – to abandon life in the city for rural living. Here she – yes, she, too – begins her own 'organic' business, marketing baby foods. So as childcare is combined with caring capitalism, the heroine meets her true love. Not, as in Haran's case, the old man turned new, but a new man with the right values. And good looks. At least *their* newly constituted nuclear family – mother, father and child with no biological connection (except of the most remote kind) between them – in some way represents the more complex patterns of the real world.

It would be wrong to see in either of these plots a simplistic message, wooing women away from the workplace or even success. One newspaper began its feature on Haran's book with the following mildly incredible introduction: 'Stop the clock. Women can no longer handle a career and motherhood, or so says Maeve Haran . . .'[24] These artefacts have not the nastiness, and not the force for that matter, of a film like *Fatal Attraction*, for

instance, which turned the single working woman into a poison
running through our collective bloodstream. The softer message
of *Having It All* and *Baby Boom* is that a little transformation is
possible, both of men and of the structures of work, and perhaps
that middle-class women will lead the march away from the
excesses of corporate capitalism. But of course such 'answers'
leave the central tenet of *Having It All* unaffected: that ultimately,
individual dilemmas need individual solutions. The traditional
structure is not only to be left untouched, but a new structure is
to be built parallel to it: this is a kind of economic variant on the
nineteenth-century notion of 'separate spheres'. Womanly,
loving capitalism. According to Haran et al, women must escape
or set up their own business, not band together, argue, forge
productive links, make politics.

But the final twist to this muddled tale of *Having It All* lies, as
always, in real life. Maeve Haran may have written a book
repudiating conventional ideas of success and glorifying
motherhood but she did so amid a fanfare of publicity concerning
her six-figure advance. The book itself brought the real Maeve
Haran even greater rewards than the television career she had
rejected for a more home-based life. This irony was not lost on
journalists sent to interview her; post-publication features made
carping reference to her 'media' house in Highgate, her new
highly successful career as a writer. So this, too, was Bourgeois
Feminist Triumphalism, wearing its halo. We still had the power
suit, we still had the babies and the briefcase – or the word
processor. In many ways, the Burchill/Superbitch model was
preferable.

In fact, neither was an answer to the dilemmas of 90 per cent
of Britain's mothers. Few of them were wrestling with the
problem of scraping Farex from their Nicole Farhi suit; few of
them were getting to the country for a holiday, let alone a new
life. The most striking thing about the eighties from the point of
view of working mothers was the silence on those themes not
easily turned into six-figure entertainment. When I was reading
through the press cuttings on motherhood, I did a double take
when I came across the following headline: 'Babies May be

Crippled by Mothers' Poor Diets'.[25] And I never found another one like it: it was like it came from another land, was speaking another language. It is easy to dwell on what is there, before us; it is much harder to analyse a silence, more difficult to draw the contours of what is not there.

To find out what some of those missing stories might be, to hear those tales of love and work, pay and the price of presence, we must now turn to real lives.

REAL LIVES

~ 4 ~

Work: The Politics of Time

Human energy is finite; mental and physical energy must be used discreetly, with knowledge and respect. After all the demands placed upon a parent of young children, how do you expect to have anything left over for more than a superficial sort of involvement in other aspects of life?

Jane Lazarre, *The Mother Knot*, Virago, 1987

Margaret Thatcher may have consigned the story of her mother Beatrice to permanent silence but most women are more thoughtful and generous about the woman they readily acknowledge to be one of the most significant in their lives. Yet what they often reflect upon is the *difference* between the generations. My mother, myself — it hovers above and behind women's talk: what I have that she didn't have; the mistakes she made that I don't want to make; the many lessons I have learned from her.

Sally is in her early thirties, with a two-year-old daughter and another baby on the way. She talks to me a few weeks before the birth, just at the beginning of her second maternity leave. She is heavy, nicely tired. When I ring the doorbell I wake her from an early afternoon nap, she leads me into the kitchen, sits me at a kitchen table, cuts me a piece of cake. She has an air of muted excitement which I recognize from my own experience; in the weeks before birth, it is like one is carrying a wonderful open secret. So she awaits the crisis and euphoria of birth; her first sighting of the mysterious creature she already knows, protects and cherishes.

Sally is a specialist nurse who works for a National Health Service trust in the south of the city where she lives, an hour's drive from her home. Like that of many public sector employers, the maternity leave is generous – considerably improving on statutory minimums – and makes her impending motherhood a pleasure not a worry.

'I became pregnant with my first baby before I planned to be and I was extremely lucky in my manager. When I told them I was going to have a baby there was none of this, "Er . . . that's good." He was brilliant. But when you think about it, the NHS is a culture of young women getting married, having babies, for a first, a second, a third time . . . I always knew I wanted to go back. Partly for my "career". But also because it's very *very* important to me that I maintain my ability to earn money. I saw what happened with my mother. She had an English degree, trained as a secretary but stopped working to have a family. She didn't go back until she and my father went bankrupt. Here was this highly intelligent, cultured woman who always maintained her interest in classical music – she sang in the local choir – and all she could get in her late fifties was a job as a carer's assistant. It was such a shocking waste.'

In contrast, Sally has always kept one eye on her own 'ability to earn money', even though she is married to a man who earns enough to support the family. She is knowing, even canny, about her work choices. She picked a specialism where she knew jobs would always be available; she has improved upon her qualifications over the years; like many nurses under the 'new' market-oriented National Health Service she has a keen perception of how the structures are changing and where the new opportunities, especially for her, will be. As a result, she says she felt 'very positive' about going back to work after her first baby was born.

'I actually enjoy going to work more than before I had my daughter. It's a lot to do with my job, the fact that I'm in control of it. It would be very different if I was a staff nurse on a ward.

But there's no-one else to do my work when I'm not there. Maybe it's because I get bored very easily. Working three days a week means there is time just for me, at work, time for my daughter on the other days and time for the family together at the weekends. When I get it all right, I do feel a sense of achievement. It's all hard work, particularly looking after children. But when it works, there's nothing like it.'

Talking to Sally, it is easy to believe that here is a woman who has got it right. She has kept her financial independence, she has developed and maintained an interesting (and marketable) set of skills, she has the satisfaction that the outside world of work provides, the necessary counterbalance to the claustrophobia of domestic life which, in turn, makes her pleasure in her daughter and her husband and her time at home even sharper. This is her perspective on herself, despite or even because of the 'hard work'. In all the big news stories about the supposed guilt of working mothers, we rarely glimpse the reality of lives like this; lives of busy schedules and a deep satisfaction, in which the many short separations between mother and child can enhance, rather than undermine, the appreciation of, and trust in, one for the other.

Yet there is a more gloomy perspective on working mothers like Sally, one which looks primarily at motherhood as a market loss not a personal gain, the having of children in terms of the loss of finance and status. Bourgeois Feminist Triumphalism has played its part here. According to the values of BFT, the really important women, the only ones worth bothering with, either forswear children altogether or they keep the reality of those children masked by their continuing presence in the market or the public places of our society. In this respect, BFT has uncritically taken over the full-time or nothing mentality from the breadwinning male of old – middle- *and* working-class. In turn, this has consigned the majority of women who continue to work part-time to a form of secondary economic citizenship. Modern women have therefore become divided in a new way; not by the fact of motherhood alone, not by biology, but by the far more crucial question of what time they publicly assign to it.

In her recent stringent analysis of women in contemporary

Britain, Kate Figes opens her chapter on women and work
(entitled, incidentally, 'Punishing motherhood') with the striking
image of economist Heather Joshi in labour, wondering between
contractions just how much women lose economically through
motherhood:

> Her subsequent research revealed that it came to a great deal.
> Against the lifetime earnings of a woman who works full-time
> and doesn't break to have children, she compared those of
> one who goes out to work full-time at seventeen, takes eight
> years out to have two children and then works part-time
> while her children are at school. The earnings of the latter
> were 57 per cent lower . . .[1]

Every time I read this passage I experience the same sense of mild
anxiety and resentment, mull over particular words and phrases:
doesn't break to have children, *against the lifetime earnings* of a
woman who works full-time. Joshi's formulations express a very
simple truth: time is money. If there is one major reason why
women earn less than men, it is their different relationship to
work because of their different relationship to children. Although
women's work lives are getting longer in terms of the overall
number of years in paid work, on the whole, they work less
hours; daily, weekly, yearly. They therefore invest less in their
work life, in training, re-training, re-skilling. Those who work
the lowest hours, and earn the least, are the least likely to receive
even the minimal state benefit for maternity, Statutory Maternity
Pay (SMP); this is available only to women who work a certain
number of hours a week. Currently, two million women are
excluded from SMP.[2] As part-timers, they are less likely to be
promoted. And as the more committed parent, they are less
willing to give time to a job that takes them away from home;
these are the jobs that make money.

Yet Joshi's calculations also show the limitations of making
judgements about humans in solely economic terms. Within the
conventional language of economics, mothers appear less committed, less rational beings; their appearance and reappearance on

the market somewhat whimsical. There is an opposite truth. Women like Sally are making sane, emotionally coherent decisions – for themselves, for their children, for the whole health of their households. One of the major problems for mothers is that society is not 'joining up' its different political vocabularies; politicians, economists, all those quick-feature journalists are not making fundamental connections between the contradictory values of the private and public world. On the one hand, in the world of work, there is a strict, almost unchanged hierarchy of importance that lines up full-time males, and full-time females, at the top, and then progresses down through the time scale to the kind of part-time women like hospital cleaners or 'dinner ladies' who work just a few hours a week. These women, for they are mainly women, earn the least and are seen to mean the least in society. On the other hand, according to the values of hearth and home – the world in which people exist, and children matter, and care is valued – this hierarchy is entirely reversed. There is not only respect but a kind of unspoken social demand that *women* provide the time that will keep kids off the streets, keep them doing their homework, keep them safe and strong and true.

Yet these two sets of values clash. We assign a so-called moral importance to one job but reward those who do it with a correspondingly diminishing importance in the outside world. We talk about a moral crisis of the family and show no understanding that those considered most responsible are, in fact, least responsible. Modern mothers live out the reality of this contradiction, this moral crisis, for us all.

The politics of time

The simple fact is: children take time. They deserve time. Even in the nightmare world of the career caesarean – an increasingly favoured option in the land of the original BFT, the United States – the mother laid out on the operating table is righteously unavailable on her mobile for a few hours. Pregnant women know that for their best health and the health of their baby, they need to 'give in' to sleep and rest, to the lovely dreaminess of gestation, often quite early on in the pregnancy. In the early years, parenthood somewhat resembles the job of junior doctor in a large busy hospital: one is always on exhausted call; the chance to nap, only an occasional luxury. The word most parents use once they become used to this new little person is 'relentless'. It is not the individual job of nappy-changing, face-wiping or feeding that is so difficult, it is the endless repetition of these tasks and, unlike a junior doctor, the fact that there is rarely any time off.

If the first inescapable fact is that children demand time, the second is that, on the whole, women, including all those in paid work, give more of their time to them than men do. Even when a man and a woman are both in full-time work, the average man has seventeen more hours leisure a week than the average woman.[3] The largest growth in women's economic activity over the last twenty years has been in part-time working. Much of this expansion took place in the 1950s and 1960s, but it is a trend that looks set to continue. Currently, 43 per cent of working women work on a part-time basis, compared with only 6 per cent of men. Most important of all, while part-time work tends not to be a positive decision for men, most women when asked if they want to work full-time say they do not. Women's working lives are, to use the jargon, more 'discontinuous': they move in and out of jobs; part-time here, full-time there.

As Patricia Hewitt points out in her book on working time, men's working lives are still, more or less, a sandwich: education and retirement, with full-time employment in between. 'They do more overtime, particularly when they have dependent children. As full-time workers, they work longer hours than full-time women.'[4] This observation was made in 1993; while more men are now forced to take part-time work by necessity, most of them will return to full-time work if, and when, they can. For women, however, 'the typical female pattern is of discontinuous employment with one or more breaks from paid work caused by domestic responsibilities . . . [it is also] made up of a wide variety of *different* employment histories'. For example, some women have what is broadly a 'domestic career', with long breaks from paid work after the birth of each child; another group of women have a 'continuous career' punctuated by very brief periods of maternity leave. Working patterns vary according to ethnic origin, with Afro-Caribbean women more, and Asian women less, likely to work full-time.[5] The trend is towards women's work lives getting longer and men's getting shorter. Thus, 'out of a working lifetime of 42 years (18–60) a "typical" pattern in future might include a total of no more than three years at home full-time with children, a further two years for other domestic responsibilities and two years out of the labour market for non-domestic reasons, leaving 35 years of paid employment. Unlike men, today's young women can expect to add a decade of paid employment to their working lifetimes, compared with women born early in this century.'[6]

Hewitt uses the term 'part-time' to refer to those working not less than thirty hours a week. Many women do far fewer hours than this, but still think of themselves as workers. Afia, Saleema and Kim work at a large urban primary school as School Meals Supervisory Assistants, or what used to be called 'dinner ladies'. 'The children still call us that,' says Kim, 'even though we have nothing directly to do with the food. We clean the trays, wipe the tables, supervise the children while they eat, do playground duty. We take turns at different tasks.' Each of the women took the job because it suited the demands of motherhood. Kim is a single mother with two grown-up children and a ten-year-old daughter. 'This is my daughter's school. She wanted me to do the job here so I came and asked, "Can you give me a job?" They said, "Okay." I used to work full-time as a cashier in a club but the hours were twelve noon to eight in the evening and they didn't suit me. This does.'

'This' for all of them is just seven and a half hours a week, one and a half hours a day. They take home just over £36 a week. 'Some boroughs are better,' says Afia, with benign disinterest, to the other two, 'I know they get about fifty pounds for the same hours.' For Kim, it is the small amount she is allowed to earn before incurring cuts to her benefit. For Afia and Saleema, it is 'their' money, their small contribution to households largely dependent on a male wage. When Saleema, who has four children, uses the word 'pocket money' it recalls an era when all women's money was considered surplus to living requirements. She means it, I think, in the sense of independence; it gives her something all of her own. That independence is more than financial. She took the job, she says, 'because I was a little bored. I wanted company. You make friends, like Afia and I, now when we do our shopping, we meet in the street. We know each other. So this is a very good job and I can still look after my children. In the morning, I clean the home, then I come here. Afterwards, I go home and it's collect the children, do tea, do bed.'

We all laugh, spontaneously, at the jokey weariness in her voice when she says 'do tea, do bed'. It is an understanding of the loving boredom of endless repetition. Would she like to work more? 'No I don't want to. Well, *I* do. I want the social life but, I think, my husband would say, "No way." At first, he didn't like it that I came here at all to work, but now he says, "Okay." But I'm a little bit bored stuck at home. Saturday and Sunday I am never out of the kitchen. So I like the weekdays, because there's a change in the day.'

Afia, the quietest of the three, says, 'I like it that we are all from different cultures and we get to know each other. Like Kim, she's from China ('I'm not, I'm from Thailand. I told you that already.') . . . You see! You learn things. At the end of the shift, we eat together. It's just fifteen minutes, it's quick. But we talk. I like that, our time together.'

Mothers versus the marketplace

Women with children talk about time all the time: feeds, sleep, how many days they are at work, what they manage or don't manage to do at home. Time torments them: time is a treasure. They always want more of one kind, less of another, particularly those in full-time work. Liz is a teacher of special needs in Bristol. She went back to work full-time three months after the birth of her first child.

'It was a perfect job. I needed the money. But there were difficulties. I was still breastfeeding, having to express milk in the loo. I couldn't do it in the staff room. So there I am, sitting in the toilet, alone, pumping away. But everyone knew I had a baby. People acknowledged it. To the dinner ladies, their attitude was just "Shame, what a shame that you have to leave her." The teachers were a bit more supportive of what I was doing. But I was terribly angry and emotional the whole time. If a staff meeting went on five minutes longer than it should, I resented it terribly because I didn't see her during the day. When she was about three months old we went away on a family holiday to show the baby to her relatives. I hadn't realized quite what would be expected of me on the holiday, the social engagements and so on. We came back and I went back to full-time work. Within the month I was suicidal, completely beside myself with exhaustion, banging my head against the wall.'

When Liz had her second baby, she stopped work entirely for the first few months. Liz's experience is a good example of how the logic of an efficient marketplace does not match the apparently more nebulous demands of new motherhood. In today's work climate, most women with jobs will return within months of the birth, even if maternity leave is notionally longer. Since 1979, the proportion of women returning to work within nine months of giving birth increased from 25 per cent to 45 per cent.[7] The Department of Health recommends breastfeeding for a minimum of four months, yet many women have to return to work much earlier. The most obvious reason for this is money. Even in the best maternity leave schemes, women go on to half pay after a set number of weeks. But there is also a growing culture of what I call 'premature returnism', a desire among women, particularly professional women, to show that motherhood has not changed them. As the new mother of a young child and a self-employed writer, I had been back at work, if fitfully, within weeks of the birth, resentfully taking transatlantic calls at some unearthly hour of the night on an article that needed more work on it. This was at a time when all I wanted to do was gaze at my new baby girl and not worry, about money or the outside world, or whether I was still considered a serious person 'out there'. In a newspaper interview, Helen Storey, the fashion designer, reflected on her own actions after the birth of her son, like this: 'I did ridiculous things like going back to work 10 days after I'd had him, lecturing students and feeling my milk coming thru' my T-shirt.'[8]

The folly of this external, and internal, pressure on women was underlined by the guru of natural childbirth, Sheila Kitzinger, at a conference, 'Challenging the Myth of Motherhood', in late 1994. Kitzinger speaks in a quasi-spiritual way about those early months, how women after birth are 'vulnerable and tender', how in the first forty days after birth women are 'passing over the bridge into motherhood'. This period should, she believes, be treated as a 'babymoon', a period when women can enjoy the sheer sensual luxury of new motherhood. Falling in love . . . joining others in love . . . a period when mother and baby should 'tune in'. While this kind of language is not my own, I could recognize the force of Kitzinger's argument when she asserted that 'a "time of special cherishing" is at risk of being lost. Women now have to be cool and clear. They are urged to "get their figure back . . . get back to normal". I am always being rung up about Fergie and Diana and asked if they are "back to normal". This whole myth of women as sleek, glossy . . . getting back to the boardroom is one of the really unfortunate images of post-feminism.'

Sometimes, the wish to be with a child is expressed in the language of the impossibility of *not* being with them. Carol, a social worker working mainly with the elderly, is expecting her second child. 'When my first was ten months, I was supposed to go back to full-time work. I found a really good office. If that hadn't happened, I would have been more anxious. But I still couldn't believe the [change] in me. Five years ago, as a staunch feminist, I would be saying, "Women have the right to work. There should be child care facilities," but when it came to it, it wasn't straightforward when I had to do it. I was offered the job and I thought, *I can't do it* . . . I'm depriving him of all those years he should be with me.' She did go back and she adjusted, but she could never again imagine herself with the ambitions of old.

One of the saddest interviews I did was with a young black

woman called Pauline who worked as a receptionist in a local
health centre. Pauline was not sad, but her story was. She liked
her job 'okay' but her biggest passion in her life was her young
son. 'I was off for a year after he was born, but I didn't want to
go back even then. I wanted to be with my baby. I was enjoying
it. But I knew I had to, financially. I'm only working for the
money and I can't even think about it, my not being with him. It
would give me a nervous breakdown! If I had an absolute choice,
I would be at home.'

We deny these feelings at our peril, but we also simplify, reduce
their meaning, at our peril, too. The real failures of post-
feminism, as Kitzinger called it, is not that it denies women's
natural connection to children – but that it proposes or tolerates
inhumanity; inhumanity to mother, child – and father. Women are
good at saying what they feel: their talk is littered with phrases
that suggest emotional absolutes, defining essences. But they are
also good at understanding ambivalence, complexity, confusion
about those very 'absolute' feelings. They may recognize what the
world does not: that their greater attachment to the home is a
complicated mix of desire, convention, financial reality, and the
role of others in their lives, willing or unwilling, to help them
'balance' home and work. Many women work *less* than they may
want to because of their domestic responsibilities. When in 1996
Oxfordshire County Council decided to offer their Learning
Support Assistants, those who help out teachers in the classroom,
more training and development in order to upgrade their skills,
they found that many of those women working as LSAs were
trained teachers who were now working far below their
capabilities, and earning half as much. Why? Because the hours of
a Learning Support Assistant, without the burden of extra meetings and marking that inevitably fall to a teacher, better fitted their
home responsibilities. These women needed to knock off at three
p.m. and be free to leave.

There are, too, stories of matching sadness to Pauline's, stories
of fathers forced away from daily life with young children,
through the necessity of finding and keeping employment. If we
are not to return, in an over-simple way, to the idea that being

with young children is a woman's natural job, we have to both respect and yet look beyond a woman and her feelings. We have to recognize the truth of what Juliet Mitchell wrote in 1971: 'Emotions cannot be "free" or "true" in isolation; they are dependent today on a social base that imprisons and determines them.'[9]

The logic of the law and social engineering

Society not only accepts; it confirms that a woman's place is to play the largest part in parenthood. In this context, it is interesting to look back at the equality legislation of the 1970s, the campaigns for an end to sex discrimination and unequal pay, from a 1990s perspective. The 1975 Sex Discrimination Act aimed, broadly, to make it unlawful to treat a woman 'less favourably' than a man would be treated in the same circumstances just because she is a woman. The new law covered access not only to education, training and employment, but also to housing, and the provision of goods, facilities and services. Borrowing from American legal precedent, it also distinguished between direct and indirect discrimination, which considerably broadened its scope. While individual cases of direct discrimination might be dealt with successfully, this did not stop an employer or other institution from continuing to act unlawfully. In contrast, successful claims of indirect discrimination often led to substantial and long-lasting changes. One significant example of this was the case of Belinda Price, a single mother of two, who wanted to return to full-time employment at the age of thirty-five. Applying for an executive officer's job in the Civil Service, she found that while she had suitable qualifications, there was an age bar of twenty-eight on applications for the executive officer's grade. In 1976, Price brought a claim of indirect discrimination on the grounds that this amounted to a penalty on mothers, as they were more likely to take time out of the job market than an equivalent man. The Civil Service argued that all women could go out to work in their twenties if they wanted to: it was simply a matter of personal choice. This ingenious and disingenuous claim did not win them the case. The Service then gracefully raised its age bar on applications to the rank of executive officer to forty-five.

The 1970 Equal Pay Act (which did not come into force until 1975) said that a woman should be paid the same as a man if she was doing work that was 'the same or broadly similar' to his. Unfortunately, many employers had used the five-year gap between the passing of the Act and its coming into force to separate firmly male and female work so that it could not be argued that the labour was 'broadly similar'. The Act also introduced a right for women to claim equal pay where objective job evaluation showed that they were broadly equivalent: this attempt to introduce 'equal pay for work of equal value' has foundered on everything from the rock of unfair job evaluation schemes to the vagaries of privatization. In 1996, women's full-time hourly rates of pay compared to men's, while a vast improvement on twenty years ago, still stands at a disappointing 80 per cent.[10] The comparative figure for weekly earnings is an even more dismaying 72 per cent.

However, while both these pieces of law aimed to help women's position and pay in the public world, they did not touch, nor did mainstream debate around them, on women's role in relation to men, home or children. Equal rights meant a woman's right to work, unhampered by old practices and absurd prejudices: a woman's right to get a mortgage, cash a cheque, join a working men's club. Changes in motherhood, family and the private behaviour of men were considered the territory of misbehaving and marginal feminism.

This primary relationship – between women and home, women and babies – was therefore assumed even by progressive legislation. In 1974 the Employment Protection Act gave women a statutory right to paid maternity leave, protection from dismissal during pregnancy and the right to return to work up to twenty-nine weeks after the birth. The EPA has remained the basis of law ever since, although tinkered with for the worse by the Conservative government under Margaret Thatcher, particularly in 1980, when certain statutory rights, including rights to maternity leave, were cut back for any employees who had been working in a job for less than two years.

Generous maternity leave is absolutely essential. It is part of a humane society. But, if not complemented by a recognition of a male partner's role, it only cements women's relationship to the home. Cynthia Cockburn is one of the few feminists to have examined how private assumptions about women are woven into working practices in both white- and blue-collar work. In her detailed study of the employment policies, theory and practice of four major employers, she has written:

> The state routinely provides for maternity benefit and employers for their part are quite free to extend the amount of leave they offer to women at full or part pay and to ease women's return to work by adapting their hours or terms of engagement. Men, of course, do not get pregnant or give birth. They could, however, look after their children in their early months and years. Yet there is no *requirement* in law to offer appropriate facilities to fathers to enable this. Nor do men complain that they are discriminated against on this score.[11]

Father Time

There has been something of a minor revolution in the economy and therefore work culture from the seventies to the nineties, shaped in part by women's increasing employment in expanding sectors of the economy. While, on the one hand, the Conservative governments of 1979–97 progressively dismantled certain key employment rights – including the right to strike – they adopted a slightly more complex approach to 'equal opportunities'. One of the key aspects of the famed feminization of the workforce involved stronger efforts to recruit and retain women staff. In autumn 1991, a visibly uneasy John Major launched the government's 'Opportunity 2000' scheme, which aimed mainly through the mechanism of partnership and persuasion to get more employers to adopt family-friendly policies. Some employers, such as the Civil Service, have long offered more generous maternity leave than the minimum laid down by the legislation.

But from the late 1980s onwards, more and more companies began offering flexible packages to their employees.

So apparently impressive was this shift in corporate culture that feminist campaigner and journalist Scarlett MccGwire was able, in 1992, to publish a solid – 260-pages plus – book of data which looked in detail at over fifty companies that offered some policy of benefit to women, whether it be job-sharing, childcare or merely an anti sexual harassment policy. The title of MccGwire's book, *Best Companies for Women*, is itself instructive. It reminds us that while, theoretically, most of these schemes are open to both parents, in practice it is, on the whole, women who take up the options on offer, whether flexi-time, part-time working, term-time working, job-shares, career breaks or adoptive leave.

According to Jane Herring, Head of Personnel at Boots, which offers an excellent range of flexi-packages to its 69,000-strong workforce, most of whom are women: 'Only a handful of men have approached us in the nearly ten years these schemes have been in operation, compared to four to five hundred women. Of this handful, half have taken up flexi-working in order to pursue a leisure interest or develop other areas of work.' She sighs. 'What can you do about it? We're not into social engineering. It seems that women still take the burden of domestic responsibility.'[12]

But some employers, able to recognize the connection and contradiction between home and work, *are* taking tentative steps into 'social engineering'. In its February 1994 submission to the House of Commons Committee on Mothers and Employment, Oxfordshire County Council, which employs nearly 13,500 women and fewer than 3,500 men, declared:

We have a vested interest in how domestic roles are shared. If an organization employing an equivalent number of men discovered that they all had a second job which was on average taking up 15 hours a week of their time, it would rightly be concerned about the possible effect on performance . . . The organization which employs a high proportion of women also suffers from the prevailing expectation that it will be women who take time off for family emergencies such as

children's illness. Our approach to this has been to give clear
signals, for example through the establishment of paternity
leave, the marketing of flexible working options to both sexes
and the introduction of leave for family emergencies which it
is expected that both men and women will use – that we
recognize that men have family responsibilities and that we
have made provision for them to exercise these. At national
level, the removal of any remaining assumptions about the
different family roles of men and women from the fiscal and
benefit systems would help to redress this imbalance.

I rang Hilary Simpson, the writer of this document, and Principal
Personnel Officer at Oxfordshire County Council, in the early
summer of 1997. I was curious to know how many more men
were choosing to work part-time. She said: 'The numbers are
growing, but slowly. If I was to look back at the last ten years, the
number of men working part-time has increased but we are still
looking at tiny figures. What you find is that while men are
prepared to change their conditions of work – more men will
work from home, for example – they are still working the same
number of hours. We currently have 667 men out of a total
workforce of 16,000 working part-time, but some of those will be
elderly men working as cleaners or lollipop men. I wouldn't say
it was a radical shift. We had one interesting job partnership
which summed it all up for me. A man and a woman were sharing
a transport planning job; their respective reasons for going part-
time were as follows. She was a mother of young children. He
was doing consultancy work with the rest of his time. That was a
kind of paradigm for me.'

The Conservative governments of the early 1990s did not yield
to growing social pressure for a legal right to paternity and parent
leave. The Labour government, elected in 1997, has pledged itself
to the introduction of both, to bring the United Kingdom in line
with other European countries. Policies that enable men to take
more time to be with their families are an important first step in
changing our work culture. But as they stand they are chiefly a
symbol; a stamp by society *on* society that says, men want to

belong in their families, men should belong to their families. They are unlikely to change fundamentally the structure of employment or the different time that men and women give to work over a day, a week or a lifetime. For the problem lies deeper, as we can see when we look at what happens to the ordinary and extraordinary woman who tries to solve the puzzle of her own continuing ambition; a desire which does not, after all, die with the birth of a child.

~ 5 ~

Work:
The Puzzle of Ambition

Things are simple or complex according to how much
attention is paid to them.
Bernard MacLaverty, *Grace Notes*, Jonathan Cape, 1997

This is how it happens, and I am telling the story of a type here,
many women into one:

> She is twenty, twenty-five and she knows it is going to be
> good, different for her, different from her mother. Some of
> her friends go to college and get qualifications or they train
> to be something. Her best friend goes into teaching, but she
> thinks that's a little below her and they drift apart. She is
> admiring of those creatures who go into the city or law, one
> of what she thinks of as the 'high-powered' jobs although she
> is already secretly afraid that she hasn't got what it takes to be
> one of those people. That's what she and her friends call the
> yuppie-type high-fliers: 'those people'. They say it with both
> a sneer and a shiver of admiration. She is not one, not really.
> Slow creeping, she thinks. Eventually, out of desperation,
> she takes casual work in an antiques shop run by a friend of
> a friend. The antiques part of it stops her worrying about it
> being 'shop work'. Then she helps out another friend who is
> doing research for a radio programme on the antiques trade.

She surprises herself, and her friend, with how good she is at all the practical things: cutting tape, using the machines, organizing people, timetables.

She is twenty-eight. Her confidence is boosted by meeting an old friend who becomes a lover and then a husband. They marry, laughing, but she cherishes the secret seriousness of it. He works in television now: she works on one programme, then two, with him. Then she finds her own work, separately, and for a few years they do a slow climb up the job ladder together. Mostly it is fun; gossiping about people they know in common, colliding on the odd project. She finds herself – and it's like a gift, a nice surprise – doing very well in a production job. She is running things, being paid twice what her father earned at the height of his solid working life in insurance. It feels faintly subversive but perfectly possible. She keeps her mind on the job. When they are making a programme it is almost an eighteen-hour day. As boss on this one, she doesn't leave until the job is done. And the job is done well. She begins to see, no, to *feel*, how people think of her: a real professional. She has a reputation. It's only words but she likes the words: fearsome, ruthless, tough. It's as if she's being created again by the use of these words: she parodies the idea of ruthlessness and then catches herself, in a piece of reflecting glass in the office at work, being the person other people have described.

But there's another story going on: the banal biological clock. Her husband says, in the lazy way she loves, 'Oh, let's go for it. Why not?' She is not one of these rigid over-organizing people, but she worries about what will happen to her earning power. The word 'career' is still too grand for what she has done. The months of her pregnancy are the happiest ever. She is finishing a piece of work: the money earned on that will tide her over for a few months. The plan is that she will work on another series starting in the autumn: they are happy for her to put in fewer hours. They want her, her name, her reputation; she can work from home.

Her daughter is born. For the first few months, the world

recedes, even her husband seems a shadowy, insubstantial character in her life. This is complete love. Financial realities mean she must force herself to concentrate on that strange outside place of cars and phones and plans. She makes a couple of anxious phone calls to the people hiring her. They still want her. On a walk to the shops she sings with pleasure at having a foot in both camps. But the job itself is not enjoyable. She hates finding someone to look after her daughter: no-one is even remotely suitable. In the end, she hires a teenager who can be instructed on a virtual hour-by-hour basis – *after the park, give the juice in the green cup, go to the television room, slot in the video that I've placed on the top of the cabinet* . . . her gift for timetables and control feels like lunacy here. Whenever her daughter is sleeping she rushes to her desk in the corner and scribbles; the fax machine spews up imperious and somewhat mysterious demands from 'head office'. It worries her how much she fears meeting any of her old or new colleagues. The old confidence has drained away so quickly. Like a form of exquisite punishment, her previous self stands in judgement on her present self. The job is finished: she has done it well, but this lack of connection with colleagues makes her reluctant to take any more work from them. They don't offer, anyway.

She has other, more pressing problems. By the time her daughter is one and a half, it makes her sad that she may be an 'only'. She now thinks of her own brother and sister as a gift not a nuisance: she becomes convinced everyone needs siblings. A second child is not quite a duty, but it has none of the excitement of the first. Her feelings for the child herself, another little girl, mystify her. The process was less of a mystery, but this child is more inscrutable. There is a new but different intensity. For a while, it seems impossible even to think about work. Getting out of the house to post a letter takes forty minutes' organization and ten minutes to do it. This is the great achievement of the first few months: getting all three of them out the house, getting them back again. Feeding everyone. Laying them down to sleep – or not.

When her husband comes home from work and tells her stories about the office, she feels resentment and fear. She laughs just to show she can join in with the fun. But she doesn't know if it is harder when he talks about people she knows or people she's never heard of.

They love the girls more than anything. This is, without doubt, the most important thing. She can still find no form of childcare that satisfies her, so they decide to stop looking. It is a relief, as if she has decided to be a mole living in her burrow. Her husband suggests she comes to a Christmas party at work: she catches sight of herself at that moment in the glass door of the kitchen, the thought of going 'out there' fills her with horror. 'I'm such a coward,' she says sadly, to a friend, 'but I can't. I can't face all the people who used to know me in my old life and see me now in my mother-life. I don't mind other mothers seeing me ... but that's different.' She leaves the sentence unfinished. She is talking about 'down among the women'.

This is not the end of the story. In a year, maybe five years' time, this woman's situation will change again. In the wayward, ever-expanding, ever-contracting world of the media, in which she happens to work, she may be offered a marvellous new opportunity. A few weeks of worry and she will find herself returning to her old self: tough and professional if no longer quite so ruthless. Or she may find that work never quite takes off again for her: all she is offered is short-term, bitty employment and, without quite knowing why, she can never set foot on the territory of assured success again. One thing is for sure: this woman, typical of thousands of professional women from their late twenties to their late forties, has, for the moment at least, lost her 'brilliant career'.

This tale, of satisfying motherhood but disappointed work expectations, is also another of the untold stories of real-life mothers. Perhaps it is because every professional woman, believing that it is her competence which brought her so many rewards before the birth, secretly believes that it is her incompetence which loses her so much after it. It is certainly a story replete with sad ironies. One of the most forceful arguments of the earlier feminist thinkers, writers like Betty Friedan and Hannah Gavron, was that women should make a professional life or identity for themselves before having children. This generation of women, to whom I'm referring, have done just that, only to find that professional life slips beyond their grasp. They will still work – in fact, they will work harder than almost anyone else – but they will not be working in a way that brings the greatest rewards. Once again, it is nothing to do with bodies or essences, no feminine reluctance to 'embrace success'; no lack of assertiveness or avoidance of conflict. It will, once again, come down to the more pedestrian question of trying to live in two worlds and feeling never fully present in either.

To be a good parent, a loving parent, particularly in the early years, one has to be there. Not always, but often. There at the end of the nursery morning or the school afternoon. There for the casual, nonsensical, all-important chat over messy lunches, plays in the park. There at bedtime. There during illness. There for the school sports days, plays, carol concerts. There during crises. There during homework. To be good at many kinds of professional work, one also has to be there; not always, but pretty often. There for the meeting at the end of the working morning or at afternoons' ends. There for the casual, nonsensical, all-important chat over messy lunches, pints in the pub. There for a drink after work. There during a colleague's illness. There during crises. There during overtime.

This was how one woman described the last months of her life as a working parent, before deciding to give up work to stay at home full-time:

> My job took me to Japan on business. I arranged to fly at night, going straight to work the following day, taking minimal time off in order to lessen the anxiety for my daughter. On my return I still had to go to my London office all week. My daughter developed a temperature and made herself sick. Our GP asked whether there had been any

changes in her domestic routine and diagnosed stress . . .
Finally a combination of my daughter's screaming through the
letterbox, 'Mummy don't go to work, I need you,' and my
disenchantment with the management of the company I
worked for led me to concede that it was pointless to
continue trying to force the disparate parts of my life to work
together: all of them were suffering. Looking back, I realized I
hadn't managed at all. I had become egotistical, permanently
exhausted, incredibly bad-tempered and was compromising
every aspect of my life. At home, I was short-changing my
husband, too tired to talk or make love, sticking endless
Marks and Spencer meals in the oven, rarely entertaining and
wanting to devote what ounces of good humour were left to
our daughter and arrogantly calling it 'quality time' . . .[1]

It is worth paying some attention to the detail of Antonia Kirwan-
Taylor's account. Even in a paragraph she reveals a host of factors
which contributed to her feeling that finally, enough was enough:
'disenchantment with the management of the company', her worry
that she was letting her husband down, even her propensity to cook
quick frozen meals. Here is someone who seems to feel she has the
whole responsibility of the world, or at least her household, upon
her shoulders and who solves it by giving up work.

Anatomy of a temporary disappearance

Fiona is a part-time medical researcher. She did not have her first
baby until she was forty, after what she describes as a 'highly
successful career . . . which left me still feeling unfulfilled'. She
thinks now that she partly put off having a child 'because my
mother had a terrible birth with me. She was haemorrhaging,
nearly died with me. When they opened her up the blood hit the
ceiling in an explosion. Deep down I think it put me off, my own
experience of being born was such a frightening one. I had no
interest in children in my twenties and early thirties. Friends
didn't even give me their children to hold. It left me cold even
though I had a good childhood with strong memories. Then I

met a man and there was this instant incredibly strong feeling, "I want your child." And I got pregnant. I never felt an older mother, was never made to feel it at the hospital either. More and more women are doing it late. I met other women my age. So there I was, age forty, with a young baby. I really don't think I felt it. My sister's children were grown up and gone by now! But I'm not a traditional forty. I was young, strong, fit.

'On my fortieth birthday I felt very positive. A completely new phase of my life. Quite exciting. I planned it so I didn't have to do much work in the first seven months. Just one thing each month. There was still an enormous anxiety about getting it done. Things changed a bit after the birth of my second child, because some regular work stopped suddenly. Until that, I don't think I felt discriminated against. Things were going pretty well. I took seven months off with my second child too but that wasn't as relaxing. I now work part-time, three days a week. There's no way I want to work full-time, even though the boys are at school now. I can't imagine never going to school, not being involved in their lives. To me, that's what I want. I made a decision late in life. I want children. Therefore I can incorporate working and having children. I want to know what's going on at school. Half the time all you get from the kids is "nothing". I want to get a chance to see the teachers, get a sense of what's going on in the classroom. I think I'm always going to want to do more than my partner. When they were babies, I wanted to decide what they were wearing, what they were eating. It's controlling maybe. But you nurture them in your body. I *want* to play the larger part.'

For a brief period Fiona and her husband planned to share the care of the children. 'He was going to work three days, and I would work two. And we would look after the children between us. But my husband is a self-employed contractor and he found it very difficult to fit his work into his days, which meant I was often having to take over at the last minute on one of my working days. That was very difficult. He also found it hard, I think, the limitation on his mobility, the fact that, when you have children to look after, you can't just get up and go out.' In the end, Fiona arranged paid childcare for her working days.

Sally, the nurse I talked of in Chapter 4, was able to feel so good about her three days a week because she felt in control of her work. She also had some confidence in the future, a sense of a structure in which she was held: moving on, or up, might be difficult but she, for one, thought she could do it when the time was right. For Fiona, having children coincided not only with passing the psychologically crucial forty point (crucial for employers, not women) but also with losing an important research contract; this had kept her financially afloat during her first maternity leave; it also kept her feeling professionally connected. Part-time work after the loss of this contract became more insecure and uncertain. Fitting work into hours of childcare and then school made it even harder for her to bid for the interesting work that was arguably her due at this stage in her work life. 'For instance, there are a lot of conferences that I used to be able to go to, just to see what was happening, show my face. I cannot possibly go to any of those now unless I have a purpose there. And it makes a difference. People think I've disappeared.'

In competitive professions, having children can, odd as it sounds, be perceived as a wilful act of disappearance, a conscious decision to exclude oneself from one world in order to dwell in the half-light of another. For women for whom confidence is always a key issue, the act of making oneself reappear and on the right terms can frequently feel impossible. Even those who return and return to a structure can feel effectively shut out. A respected journalist spoke to me for over half an hour about the subtle forms of exclusion she experienced as a part-time worker on a national magazine. She spoke of how, in a world where everything is mediated through the idea of personal talent, which is connected to assumptions about corporate loyalty and individual drive, which are themselves partly unconsciously connected to assumptions about time made available, she watched other people rise and herself stand still. However hard she worked, however good her stories, she was never going to be a 'star'. In her saner moments she knew it was not through lack of talent but because she could not always be there, 'showing your face' as the jargon goes. But how could she ever be absolutely sure? When she was playing in the local park with her children on her days off, didn't she, too, worry that perhaps she wasn't made of whatever it took? And as none of the assumptions underlying her situation were made explicit – and, even worse, as her situation itself was not a 'situation' for anyone else but her – there was nothing to be done about it. She remains in a good job in which she earns and performs well and yet is subject to an unspoken consensus that she is 'going nowhere'. And where is 'going nowhere' written down, agreed upon? Nowhere, that's where. And what laws could ever prevent it, guard against it? None.

Yet I was surprised by how few women appear to feel bitter at the difference between what they once might have hoped to achieve compared to what they had actually achieved. Far from anger, I often felt there was a kind of relief, to be out of a competitive environment that had made them unhappy anyway. For those who chose self-employment, whatever the economic and 'status' penalties, there was a wonderful sense of liberation from a structure that would always judge them wanting while asking too much of them at the same time.

Yet as one designer, who works only some of the week, said to me wistfully: 'I often look at my male contemporaries, the ones I was such good friends with in my twenties, when we all seemed to have the same dreams, be going for the same things. And here I am still doing things but it is as if I'm living in a different, slower world. They have become fathers now and I am a mother and we talk in a pretty similar way about the children, except they can't seem to remember my children's names, while I even remember their children's birthdays and birth weight, for God's sake, but we are worlds apart when it comes to work. I wish there was another formulation but I can only describe it this way: that they all seem now, in their thirties and early forties, to have either prestige or proper jobs, jobs with pensions and prospects and titles. They're starting to "be" things. And I can see that this is their reward for sticking around. That's my new formulation for professional success: you stuck around and the right people noticed it. You have to be good enough, of course. But if you are and you stuck around, well, eventually you get to be something. It's not just a gender thing because the women who have managed to stick around are getting to "be" things too. They're "names" in their own way too. And I look at me and I'm good and I stick around – I'm still working away – but somehow it's not the same. It is tangible, my absence. I'm never around at school holidays for instance. Or after three o'clock on weekdays. Or in the evening. I don't think anyone talks about me that way, but that's part of it. I don't think anyone talks about me, full stop! And those men, the men who are getting somewhere now, they talk differently, they even look different to me, when we meet. They have an aura of power, not world-shaking power, but workaday power. The power of management and good money. They look better in their clothes. I always feel a little ragged. And power attracts power so I see how they will grow with it, grow into it. And I know how that feels, to feel that you're going somewhere, because I felt that in my twenties and thirties and now I feel I'm working incredibly hard just to stand still.'

Women often internalize their conflict as personal failure or, like the Civil Service in its defence against the claims of Belinda Price, they decide that everything they have done and everything that has happened is down to 'choice'. 'I chose children; what do you expect? I can't have everything.' Those women who remain, and remain successful, in the workplace seem increasingly powerful and distant, because they appear to be abiding by its myriad of rules, apparently untouched by this nether world of parallel desires and obligations. Of course, this is not the case either: full-time working mothers resent both the implication that they feel nothing about their separations from their children and the reverse suggestion that they *should* feel something, particularly guilt.

Control is, as always, the key issue here. What women most resent is someone else – *Panorama*, a newspaper, the church – telling them that what they are doing is wrong, for their own children. What was perhaps most remarkable about the *Panorama* programme, 'Missing Mum', screened in early 1997, was not the suggestion that full-time working mothers should feel guilty, but the sense that this was a programme too far. Every working mother I knew was furious; agitated but furious; especially when it emerged that the academic on whose research it was apparently based was herself rejecting some of the programme's conclusions. And although there was the typical spate of articles reflecting, and therefore somehow confirming the findings of the programme, there were some powerful pieces of journalism not only rebutting it, but giving expression to mothers' anger: a backlash against the backlash.[2]

Being there: the costs and benefits of presence

Alison is a tough Scottish lawyer, just turned thirty, with a son of eight and a son of one year. Years before we met, I had heard a story about her that seemed to sum something up about modern women and work. When she was a young mother, working full-time, Alison had come home one night, after picking up her son from the childminder. Entering the flat she had collapsed on to the sofa, as you do; both mother and child had then fallen into such a deep sleep that not even the phone, ringing repeatedly, had roused either of them. The first thing that Alison saw when she woke up was the blunt edge of an axe, belonging to a local fireman, splitting the wood of her front door. When, years later, she tells me the story herself, she remembers the moment with remarkable precision. 'It was a tiny flat, the front door was only a few feet away from where I was sleeping. And I hadn't heard anything. I hadn't heard my boyfriend ringing or banging. I hadn't heard or seen anything till this axe came through the door.'

Her first child was born when Alison was twenty-three and right in the middle of her legal training. When he was three months old, she went back to do the second year of her traineeship as a solicitor. When he was eighteen months old, Alison qualified as an assistant solicitor. Three months later she took up her first job as a public prosecutor.

Leaving her baby in those early months was traumatic: 'I remember I went to see the childminder. I really didn't want to leave the baby. I was still feeding him, totally. I remember just sitting there, crying. But I really *really* liked my job. There were four or five other trainees, my age. It was a great office to work in. I only did criminal work which I really enjoyed. When I was at work I didn't think. I knew he was quite happy at the minders. I could go to work and not pine. But I was really exhausted.' (That was the time of the fireman's axe episode.) 'Looking back, I see it was something I had to do. As a trainee, you don't get well paid. I *had* to finish my traineeship. For myself, too. I had to get a job. I knew I wouldn't go any further in the law unless I did.'

She had her second baby a year ago; this one never sleeps so the old tiredness is back. 'Money is not so important now [she now lives with her second son's father]. 'Now I work full-time because I like my work. I'm *good* at my work.' But there is a story beneath the story. 'Obviously, the Procurator Fiscal's office, being part of the Civil Service, is an equal opportunity employer. In theory I could take a career break, job-share, go part-time. My job would be there for me. But I would kiss any chance of promotion goodbye. There are a lot of working mothers where I am. All those who have been promoted work full-time. I don't know anyone who is now promoted who took a career break. In many ways, part-time is appealing, *but I just wouldn't be treated seriously by management* [my emphasis].'

Alison's choice underlines the true position for ambitious women in the 1990s. You can have your children, as many as you like, but they mustn't interfere with the first claim of professional work. The ambitious woman has to still serve this first master, work, as well as the traditional man has always done. She is likely to know that it is partly a game, something she has to do: she does not do it in a spirit of ignorance or false earnestness as the traditional man might once have done. She knows, literally, exactly what she is doing. She will be asked, frequently, the question: and what about the children? And she has answers, thoughts, strategies. Some are brutal. Interviewed in the *Sunday Times* 'Life in the Day' section, Lambeth Council Chief Executive Heather Rabbatts claimed that she had not put her small son to bed since he was a toddler: that was the price of her ticket. In 1996 *Vogue* ran a piece on top women in the media and how they managed their lives. For those who had children, their timetables were as complex and precise as a military operation. For example, Veronica Wadley of the *Daily Mail*

> gets up at 6.30 a.m. to make sure she spends time with Alexander, five, and Sophie, nine: she does the school run each morning in her Audi convertible and reaches the office by 9 a.m. She gets back to her Hampstead home . . . between 8 and 9 p.m.[3]

Interviewing Tina Brown, editor of America's premier literary magazine the *New Yorker*, writer Ian Katz described a typical day:

> Brown rises at 5.30 a.m. for her daily run. Then she drops her daughter at school before a breakfast meeting, usually around 8.15 a.m. She arrives at the office at 9 a.m. and leaves at 5.45 p.m. to get home in time for supper with her children. Then she works at home until around 12.30 a.m. That leaves only 5 hours sleep. 'There's no other way to do it. I've figured out a way to do without.' At weekends, Brown says, 'There isn't time for anything except the job and the family. That's it. That's my life.'[4]

The interesting thing about both these appallingly self-disciplined timetables is not that they lead to massive neglect of family – the typical picture of the highly successful woman; Veronica Wadley and Tina Brown and all the women like them seem to squeeze in both care for the job and the children, albeit of a fairly over-organized kind. If anyone or anything is being clearly neglected, it is themselves.

But such stories, exaggerated as they are, go some way towards explaining the familiar figures on women's employment. Only 2.1 per cent of women reach the top bracket of income earners, a small rise from 1.8 per cent in 1977. Only 15 per cent of Britain's managers are women. Only 10 per cent of women in senior management have children.[5] Half of all those who qualify as solicitors may now be women, but look at where those women and their male peers are a decade later, and the argument about equality breaks down. According to figures released by the Equal Opportunities Commission in September 1977, women make up only 15 per cent of legal partners, 6 per cent of police sergeants and only 10 per cent of judges. It is no wonder that other women looking at these very public stories of the price of presence – I prefer this word to 'success' – decide to do something else with their time. To have a more ordinary life. A more varied life. Talking to Scarlett MccGwire, one woman in her mid-twenties, working at National Westminster Bank, said:

> I think I could get to the top if I wanted to, but I don't want to go that far. It's something I feel within me. I want an interesting career – doing a variety of things. But to reach the very top you have to be truly devoted. Those people have no time at all outside their work.[6]

Solving the puzzle of ambition

These, then, are some of the real-life limits on a notional equality. It could be argued that they are limits imposed on women by themselves; that the choice is theirs. I do not think it *is* much of a choice. I certainly understand why so many women don't make it. I understand their feeling that it is often playing an inhumane game and, for those with children, life can't be a game because you are playing it with someone else's life. Relatively few women, even now, choose to be full-time workers and parents; even fewer will show the extra 'dedication' that will lead them to the top. Most will take the part-time option if it is open to them; they will choose to be committed carers and take the professional consequences. Interpret these decisions from the conventional view point of success, which measures people in terms of working time, pay and resultant status, and it appears that women are failing, and in rather large numbers.

Sometimes women's refusal of more traditional work patterns can actually be beneficial in work terms; self-employment, control of one's work, the rest from, and pauses in, a relentless schedule can give rise to more creative approaches. Writers are a good example of how control of one's own time is the most precious resource of all: one can continue to exist professionally while largely pleasing oneself in terms of when and how to work.

The vast majority of new small businesses are set up by women, many trying to find a personal solution to the impossible work/motherhood dilemma. Meanwhile, the conventional corporate *image* of presence, a grey man in a grey suit sitting at his desk all day doing what has always been done, is fading. In fact, the most fashionable contemporary picture of the go-ahead executive is a female one. One recent study of fifty women professionals 'showed that women who were characterized by more feminine qualities, such as empathy, friendliness and compassion, did just as well at work and valued themselves as highly'. The researcher, Sara Paterson, a psychologist at the University of Westminster, who declared herself 'thrilled' by the findings, concluded, 'Now women can be seen as powerful women while still acknowledging their femininity.'[7] Quite so. But the point is no longer women's femininity or even their motherhood. It is all about 'being there'.

There are two approaches to this puzzle of women's ambition. The first is to bow to the force of nature: to argue that children change women, and that women do not mind being changed. I have talked to many who would argue that themselves; they accept a lesser commitment to the workplace because, in the world they live in now, they know that they just can't do both and they don't want to feel bad about themselves for not doing both. But acceptance can be a form of fatalism; a making the best of a bad job. I often wonder what these women are going to feel when that period of temporary disappearance – that can last up to a decade or more – comes to an end; I wonder how many of them in their early forties to late fifties are going to feel cheated. Their situation will not be the same as the mother of old, who hit the job market just as the menopause hit her. Many of these younger mothers are already back at work, for two or three days a week, or four mornings or whatever. Will this amount of time be sufficient for them to feel part of their work, their profession, part of the world? Will they feel they have 'kept up' their skills? Or will they, too, feel looked-over, rejected like the mothers of old? Many women have children much later in life: these could be in their mid to late fifties, even their early sixties, when their children are grown up. They will be ready to re-enter the world of work just when the world is ready for them to retire. Will they feel, then, that they have paid dearly rearing the next generation? And will we then see a new form of politics: a greying generation of post-feminists rearing up in fury at the empty promises of the eighties, the illusion of Bourgeois Feminist Triumphalism? We can't yet know. Motherhood is relatively new to this generation.

The other approach to this puzzle requires women to do nothing, *because there is nothing else that they can do*. That is the difficulty and the beauty of it. This approach presupposes that there is nothing wrong either with their wish to care, to spend time with children, nor with their continuing ambition. This approach presupposes not only that they need social supports to combine work and home – private help, childcare, paternity leave, parental leave and so on – but it supposes such a radical change in our ideas of work that it needs only the women to stay still and the world to change around them. This approach presupposes a shift away from the slavish attachment to time and status-building at work, an orientation that the industrial revolution inaugurated and Thatcherism underwrote. Successful men, men with huge responsibility, men who work ten, fifteen hours a day, are as much if not more a part of this modern puzzle of in/equality as the women. Yet these men don't seem to realize they are part of the jigsaw: too often they stand, sympathetic but unknowing, on the sidelines of women's lives – the lives of their wives, partners, sisters, friends – watching their individual choices with envy or pity but not making new choices themselves; feeling unable to or unwilling.

But the story does not stop even here. Like a detective novel in which we discover more of the murdered victim's previous life or the assailant's mixed motive, there are yet more tales to unravel. For under the ship of women and work with all its baffling complexities, assumed possibilities and banal assumptions there lies the iceberg of home truths. There is no 'solution' to the problem of work until we look at what happens to men and women before they even step out of their front door in the morning, after they collapse, free of waged obligations, in front of the television at night; how they spend their Saturday nights and Sunday mornings.

~ 6 ~

Home Truths: Androgyny, the New Father and the Housewife

Democratic nations care but little for what has been, but
they are haunted by visions of what will be.
Alexis de Tocqueville, *Democracy in America*, 1835–40

Of the several images that currently influence our shifting
perception of ourselves, androgyny – the uniting or merger of
previously distinct gender characteristics – is one of the most
powerful. It is there in the pretty girl/tough guy face of
Hollywood star Johnny Depp or the butch beauty of singer and
actress k d lang or the matching haircuts and cool of Hollywood
actors and recently estranged lovers Gwyneth Paltrow and Brad
Pitt. Calvin Klein's advertisement for his perfume CK strung a
line of murmuring stick-limbed flat-chested girl/women and
boy/men together. Watching them, we strain to understand not
just what they are saying but what they are saying about
themselves. And us. Lesbian and feminist photography plays non-
stop with ideas of sex, gender and desire. One of its most famous
current practitioners, Della Grace, astounded and repelled even
fascinated liberals when she transgressed the final female taboo
and grew a beard.

This absorption in the mutable qualities of a once apparently
fixed gender has absorbed writers such as Judith Butler, one of the
most radical of modern feminist thinkers. In her ground-breaking

book *Gender Trouble: Feminism and the Subversion of Identity*, she draws her own distinction between sex and gender. Sex is '. . . the material or corporeal upon which gender operates as an act of cultural inscription'. Gender is a kind of 'act . . . that is open to splitting, self-parody, self-criticism . . . [acts] . . . that, in their very exaggeration, reveal its fundamentally phantasmatic status'. Information technology and cybernetics expert Sadie Plant, the woman 'primed to be the next Germaine Greer', at least according to BBC Radio 4, has spoken of how 'New technology is the engine which will allow women to achieve for the first time in human history their power and potential. [It has made] the distinction between means and ends become very unclear. The new confusion around gender roles is part of that.' And writing in one of their first publications to assert the presence of radically new values among an upcoming generation of British and American men and women, *No Turning Back: Generations and the Genderquake* (1994), the highly influential British think-tank Demos declared that:

> Amongst (younger) women we can see a marked *deepening* of
> the value shifts we described earlier: growing attachment to
> values such as androgyny, balance, risk, excitement and
> hedonism. More than any previous generation they are
> rejecting the whole cluster of traditional values: authority,
> rigid moral codes of right and wrong, the emphasis on
> security (financial and otherwise), older parochial notions of
> community and the puritanism of the past.

The wide currency of these ideas is surely one example of modern democracy's fascination with 'what will be', with what Richard Hoggart, commenting on the de Tocqueville observation quoted at the head of this chapter, calls 'futurism'. These ideas may well outline the way we will live fifty years from now. But as a tool for describing the way we live now? I am not so sure. On the morning I was due to write the first draft of this chapter, I switched on the radio to find Sadie Plant talking about life in 2010 in the Radio 4 series *Beyond the Millenium* – from where I took the above quote. Six and a half months pregnant, I am putting on my eye make-up awkwardly while my two-year-old babbles intrusively in my ear. Plant's mellifluous voice and fascinating predictions float to me in tantalizing fragments . . . 'with economic power comes sexual power . . .', 'the strange transitory period we are living in . . .', 'de-regulation of the sexual economy'. (Missing most of the substantive interview, as I do, I must telephone the labyrinthine BBC and plead for a copy; the producer's very helpful secretary sends it to me in a pristine white box a few days later.)

As the interview progresses, or what bits of it I can hear, I observe my own creeping irritation. Plant says that in the future women will finally be able to become 'actors' in history in a way that they have never been able to do before. I try to figure out what this irritation is about. It is something to do with a conflict between two truths that I take to be self-evident in my own life and society at large: two truths that sit uneasily with each other. Truth One: that women are the engine of radical change, the agents of a largely progressive confusion and disruption of the status quo. Truth Two: that women are the bearers of conservatism in a literal sense. They keep much of what is good in society going. As the writer Toni Morrison said, in a 1985 interview on 'Black Women Writers at Work', 'Men always want to change things and women probably don't. I don't think it has much to do with women's powerlessness. *Change could be death. You don't have to change everything. Some things should be just the way they are*' [my emphasis].

There is certainly something extraordinarily stubborn and resistant in women's daily lives, their ordinary swap-stories-on-the-street existence. Yet we don't really talk about this any more, as a society. We both take it for granted in our present and yet talk of it as part of an era we have left behind. As little as a decade and a half ago, feminism was interested in its origins. Is this greater involvement in life to do with nature? Or biology? Or is it mainly culture? Those kinds of enquiries have quietened – perhaps their job is done; the new territory seems to involve gender as action or, to invoke Judith Butler's innovative formulation, 'gender as performance'.

But I, too, am less interested here in origins than in merely establishing my stubborn observation of this stubborn truth: that women still take on the burden of domestic life and childrearing.

Who cares?

But how do we, as we must, update our descriptions of the domestic?

Here's one small way. Last spring, I went to a Sunday tea party for a group of three-year-olds. Bar one, the fathers were there, each of them involved in the running of the party: this one leading a game of musical bumps; this one catching toddlers and babies at the bottom of the slide; this one hospitably uncorking wine and beer for the other adults; this one clearing away the soggy plates of half-finished crisps and cakes at the party's end. The difference between these young-ish men and my father's generation is palpable and now well-established. These fathers we are told are *present*. They are involved with their children, far less the remote patriarch, more the benign older brother, even if those of them in work look perpetually exhausted by the 'running from morning to night' to which one writer on modern fatherhood has referred.[1]

I am struck also by a surface similarity between the men and women at this tea party. Take one couple. She is in jeans and a fashionably baggy sweatshirt. He is in a stripy shirt and fashionably baggy shorts. Nearly everyone has short hair, the men's marginally more cropped. Everyone, young, fit, healthy, moves easily, without restraint. One woman, in appealingly severe horn-rimmed glasses, sits, lost in thought, with her legs apart, resting her elbows on her knees, chin in hand. Beyond her, through the window, I watch one of the fathers open his arms wide and laugh gleefully at catching his ten-month-old daughter at the slide's end. There is no surface deference here between the sexes. The men possess no obvious public confidence that the 'wives' lack.

We tend to take our picture of modern life from such images. It is the same when we see a man pushing a buggy in the street or struggling with a full complement of children and trolley at the supermarket checkout. Mentally, we make a little tick against the column that notes aspects of the new world. But such impressions, such occasions, tell us only part, and a possible distorted part, of the story. Other sources of information about contemporary life – polls, surveys, as well as more intense or perceptive private observation – suggest a rock of difference still underpinning this superficial merging of styles and capabilities.

For presence, rather than the appearance of it, is the very thing modern fathers are still not giving their children. A recent survey by the National Society for the Prevention of Cruelty to Children, published in spring 1997, questioned 1,000 children aged between eight and fifteen years and found that one in five could not recall sharing an activity with their fathers during the previous week. Children reported doing far fewer activities, whether playing football or helping around the house, with their fathers than their mothers. Eighty per cent of the children would have liked to spend more time with their fathers.

Men still do less around the home, even those who have nothing but time on their hands. Unemployed men, for example, contribute no more significantly to the household than they did when they were working.[2] Young men still come to relationships with expectations of their partners and a lack of capability about themselves. Molly, a single mother in Sheffield, described her lack of patience with the father of her child as follows: 'My boyfriend did live with me for a few weeks but I'm better off independent than living with somebody. We were at each other's nerves constantly so we're better separate. When he lived with me he'd say, "I'll just be off . . ." and he would be back two hours later, and it would put me in a bad mood. And then I'd take it out on her [the baby]. I find it easier on my own. I love kids, I'd rather have a houseful of kids than a man. They need more looking after. He was older than me but he couldn't look after himself. I seemed to be looking after him. It was like two kids. He had no idea how to fend for himself. He didn't even know how to turn on a washing machine. I don't know. We just clashed.'

Even in the many homes where men do a lot more than most, where they are a dab hand at pegging out the washing, hoovering or even dishing up a spaghetti bolognese, there is still not a real equality of sharing. Itemize the tasks to be done, throughout a week, a year or a lifetime, and women are still walking away with the trophy of labour. Poll evidence suggests, moreover, a very interesting mismatch of beliefs and reality. A study carried out by Social and Community Research in the early 1990s asked men and women how tasks *should* be shared and how they were *actually* shared. While almost all the respondents conjured up an ideal world of rough parity in everything from household shopping to repairing household equipment, the figures of most interest are clearly those on actual division of labour. Some activities such as household shopping and the washing up of evening dishes were shared more or less equally. But the core of household work, from making an evening meal to household cleaning, washing, ironing and looking after sick children, was mainly done by women.[3] Studies of more specific communities confirm this finding. An unpublished study on domestic labour in South Asian households in London found older women still keep the household going. Younger couples appear to share more but do so less than they *think* they do.[4]

It is not just a question of brawn but of brain. In most households, women are still likely to be the organizational and emotional intelligence behind the scenes. They may not pick up dirty clothes from the floor every single time, but they spot, before anyone else, that it needs to be done. It's as if unwillingly they play God to the house: hovering above, always knowing what needs to be done next. They may not always be the ones to pack holiday clothes but they are likely to be the ones thinking about what needs to be taken in the days before, figuring out what needs washing and when. They remember birthdays, sign cards for the whole family. This tiny, apparently insignificant practice tells us realms about how couples think of themselves. I know at least two dozen men from whom I, my partner or our children regularly 'receive' cards, whose handwriting I have never seen because their wife/girlfriend always signs their name for them. Women are more likely to make arrangements about the children with other 'parents', for which, read mother. They are more likely to worry about unexplained rashes, uneaten greens, the chance of choking on a roasted peanut and shoes that pinch: emotional intelligence can, of course, easily tip into neurosis. And, as the NSPCC report indicated, mothers are more likely to be the ones children turn to for help and support with non-practical problems.

So while women may now be doing more paid work, and are allowed to glory in the work ethic, neither fact has fundamentally disrupted women's and men's assumption that responsibility for the home and particularly children is women's. Another way of looking at it is this: women remain the first guardians of the vulnerable, the children and the elderly in particular. How, I wonder, has such a high percentage of able-bodied wage-earning men slipped into that net of care?

Small pieces of information fascinate me. A woman of twenty-eight with a two-year-old daughter, now at home full-time, mentions in passing that her husband has never emptied the dishwasher in the course of their married life. He has never taken a cup over to the sink or emptied a laundry basket. 'If he wants a clean cup from the dishwashing machine he just takes the one he needs. It's beginning to annoy me,' she says, with admirable understatement. For a moment, I see clearly how it is going to end, how the young seeds of resentment are already planted; how that metaphorical selfishly grasped single cup will haunt these two into their early and late middle age. Each time the history of the relationship is revised in the light of new experiences and past regrets, they will never escape the question of that cup. There are a hundred stories like this. The Man Who Mistook His Wife for an Iron, the Man Who Still Comes Straight in from Work and Says Where's My Supper? The Man Who Has Never Made a Bed in His Life.

One of the most interesting and detailed discussions I had in the making of this book was with two friends, one who lives in London, the other in Bristol, both of whom see themselves as doing 'equal shares'. Both men belong to that generation, broadly of the seventies, most directly influenced by both the left and organized feminism. Both men believe, passionately, that the men they know and men as a whole have changed far more than I, in our conversation, am giving them credit for. The friend from London said, 'I was in a local park last week, an ordinary park in Edinburgh and there were four kids in the play area at ten in the morning and they were all with their fathers. These weren't access dads. These were daily dads. Don't tell me that's not new.' I could only answer: four dads in a local park do not make a revolution, but he was not claiming a revolution, only a difference. My two friends also perceived something of the martyr in women who always talk of being exhausted, and yet find it hard to rest or take time away from either work or household tasks or the children even when help is offered. Perhaps, I suggested, the word 'help' was the clue here; however 'good' the man, the woman still feels she is ultimately responsible for keeping everything going. A man who helps can be an additional responsibility – an extra worker to get organized – rather than a relief from that responsibility. To which my friends could only shrug their shoulders and ask me, and themselves: so what *do* women want?

There are men who go beyond 'giving help' into 'taking responsibility': those bringing up children alone through death and divorce, or the really considerate, or the man who takes his egalitarian principles seriously enough to break with masculine tokenism in this realm. But to return to de Tocqueville, our fascination with what 'will be', rather than what merely is, means we are almost too interested in these exceptions. For if androgyny is one image of ourselves that absorbs us, shapes our thinking, then the new father is a second.

Always searching for the new idea, the new angle, both the popular and quality press are interested in men who break away from old stereotypes: men who job-share or men who work part-time, the house-husband, the male nanny, the single father. Masculinity in crisis. Masculinity in transition. Men write about their new fatherhood: its joys, pleasures and pains. As the journalist and writer Yvonne Roberts observes:

> The nouveau père is top of the pops. Such is the abundance
> of material on modern fatherhood, including papers,

conferences, reams of newspaper articles, trendy anthologies
and outpourings from self-styled 'unashamed dad evangelists',
one can legitimately ask if we're not all in danger of becoming
dad-dled and confused.[5]

A quality paper publishes a set of passport-size photographs of
men simply holding their children, in their arms, cheek to cheek.
We are touched, we look more than once: but what are we
looking for? What are we looking at? The commonplace or the
rare? Transforming hope into fact, we have almost convinced
ourselves that a personal revolution has taken place, instead of
understanding that the change is very very slow or very partial;
that, in some respects, relations between the genders have stayed
still. Culture misleads us because it deals too often in symbols and
exceptions, not with the painstaking fact-gathering of the
investigative reporter or the authentic detail of the essayist or
realist novelist. A 1997 book on modern fatherhood, excerpts
published with great fanfare in the *Guardian*, made much play of
the near completion of this personal revolution: indeed, it almost
required of us that we take it for granted.[6] Why, asked author
Adrienne Burgess, could we not accept that men had changed?
With skilled sleight of hand, she declared:

> *Though tasks such as cooking or cleaning may not yet be shared
> equally*, the reality is that among families with young children
> both parents are 'running from morning to night' as one man
> interviewed put it. There is broadly speaking parity between
> father's and mother's contribution and *although mothers do twice
> as much family work as fathers*, they do only half as much
> breadwinning [my emphasis].

But this is not so much an argument for the new man, surely, as
a modern assertion of separate spheres, in which men do twice as
much breadwinning as a fair trade-off for doing less domestic
work? In this scenario women's paid work is merely accom-
modated rather than transformative of private lives, and men's
help at home is still just that, help. This isn't about good guys and

bad guys, it is about recognizing when a revolution hasn't taken place. There are many couples who live as Burgess describes and an argument can easily be drawn up for accepting this way of life, but it speaks neither the language of true modernity nor of real equality. It is benign neo-conservatism.

We can see imbalance even in more egalitarian lives. A man who does his share does so visibly. This may be because he has the annoying manner of a martyr or a propagandist: he wants us to see how good, how different he is. It may be because the woman in his life wants us to know how good, how different he is. When Naomi Wolf was interviewed in the *Guardian* in April 1997 about her new book *Promiscuities,* her husband was described, through the interviewer, as 'an egalitarian, nurturing man'. Women often describe their own partner as 'really good' at home or themselves as particularly 'lucky' in having such a helpful partner. Yet such luck may reside in the man doing no more than the occasional bout of washing up.

But our intense vision of men's domestic work is not entirely dictated by the attitude of the man or men in question. It stems, in part, from our blindness to women's labour, a quietness around it, an acceptance, which means it does not register in the same way. A woman washes up. So what? A man washes up: we *say,* so what? The woman who does Nothing – which is usually about twice as much as the man who does Something – is an object of derision, of satire. The man who does Something – which is usually half as much as the woman who does Nothing – courts sanctification from the moment of donning an apron.

Strictly personal

Has society taught itself to forget something it once knew? It was, after all, one of second-wave feminism's greatest insights: that there was a hidden mound of domestic work, rather like a vast pile of unironed clothes, that underpinned our society. Feminist politics produced a new way of seeing: a recognition of the full weight of the private realm and women's role within it. It generated a series of intense public discussions about the nature

and role of 'domestic labour', what it was worth, whether it
should be paid by the state or not, what it contributed to the
economy. Groups like Wages for Housework lit the touchpaper
of aggravated debate with their argument that women at home
should be paid a wage by the state.

In a piece in *Spare Rib* in May 1977, journalist Jill Nicholls
reported on a public meeting in London's Notting Hill, on
Mother's Day, in which both sides of the debate were put.

> 'All of us are housewives and mothers. We do the work of
> mothering other people. We're tired of doing it for free,'
> [argued] Suzie Fleming of Bristol Wages for Housework
> campaign. 'Few of us can get time off even on Mother's Day.
> We appreciate the cards and the flowers but they're just not
> enough. We want a wage for our work,' she went on,
> showing a stack of petitions for a higher family allowance and
> wages for housework which were taken to Mr Healey
> [Labour Chancellor] at the end of the afternoon. The
> speeches that followed referred to the Iceland strike, where
> women withdrew their labour for one day with the slogan,
> 'When women stop, everything stops' and explained the
> campaign's position: all women are housewives – gay and
> straight, black and white, married, single, prostitute – and all
> women's work is essentially housework; as housework is a
> labour of love, so all women's work is low paid and low
> status. If housewives were paid by the state they'd have higher
> status and more bargaining power – they could refuse their
> work.

But as Nicholls – whose own position was clearly against Wages
for Housework, went on – the proposals 'need not challenge
woman's role as wife, housewife and mother, or the way
housework is organized'. She quoted a Finnish nursery worker, at
the meeting with three Swedish women, who 'had a familiar left-
feminist reaction against the idea. "I am amazed that you are
campaigning for women to stay at home. In Sweden where I live,
the right-wing government is trying to get women to accept

money to do that. In the crisis they want the men to have the jobs . . .".'

Wages for Housework was the most public and brittle of those arguing about women's work in the home. But others were making the case, often more quietly. *Spare Rib*'s anthology of its first hundred issues, published in 1982, devotes a section to Housework. It includes a sober, detailed account of the 'history of the Housewife' from the fourteenth century to the (then) present day; a more personal 'Memoir of my mother-in-law' which dwells in loving detail on one working-class woman's care of home and children; and an angry account of a battle to get a partner to do his share of household tasks. Author Wendy Whitfield wrote:

> After the usual nagging, the disguised and undisguised gibes, I decided on an all out fight. All or nothing. I went on strike. I announced that from now on I would do only my shopping, cooking and cleaning. I would not clean up, nor would I keep up my incessant tidying, writing lists, washing and returning milk bottles, putting away the dishes that he left to drain instead of drying them, defrosting the fridge or cleaning the cooker, clearing away the coffee cups or writing to his relatives. In short, I would do no more than a man would do . . . We as women must not be afraid to keep bringing up the subject [of housework] and forcing our partners to reason through their objections. It is up to us to remember that men are conditioned to expect serving, and even if they acknowledge equality in theory, they will relax all too soon into the role society prepares them for . . .

The clarity, force and anger of Whitfield's writing seems faintly ridiculous in our current climate. Why? It is partly, as I argue at greater length in Chapter 11, to do with that naked fury. Women today are so rarely angry. Cool ironic humour has become the chief means of public discourse. But it is not just that. Women have become more interested in the unexplored aspects of their experience; their place at work or in the wider public world; they have left the home behind as a *subject*.

This has had positive effects, in some respects. It has certainly led to a new practicality. Used to rationalizing, organizing and costing their labour in a work setting, many professional women have turned the cool eye of capitalism and commerce back on the sentimental blur of the home. Housework to do? Itemize the tasks and get someone else in to do it. Since the late 1980s there has been a boom in the formal and informal domestic economy. Middle-class women hire other women to do their cleaning, their ironing, their childcare and even their cooking. Thus do low-paid women bridge the gap between the disparity of contribution to housework between well-paid men and women.

Burnout. Backlash. Rather like a couple who have argued for too long about who did what, when and how, radical fervour about the intimate terrain of the home has given way to a more practical but resigned position. Somewhere round the back it has met up with the new conservatism. Young women may, according to organizations like Demos, assume that household tasks should be shared equally, but they don't have a politics or even a tone of voice to use when that assumption breaks down. In modern private lives, most women do not think, as opposed to feel, that domestic work is a problem. Or if they do, they do not see it as something beyond the personal. Moreover, the confusing content and tone of post-feminism tells them they have left both the petty and the conflictual behind them. The unhelpful partner may be worth arguing with, but 'my' personal argument does not connect to anyone else's experience. A failure to wash up is certainly not seen as a political question.

This acceptance of undemocratic domestic arrangements accounts for a stoicism among many relatively young women, a stoicism not dissimilar to that among women of my mother's generation. It is as if they are thinking: this is my lot, or even, I ought to bear my burdens with better grace. Often, they are convincing themselves that they do not have burdens at all: children, a little housework, not enough sleep; what's the problem? It is a stoicism that, politically, conservatives (of all parties) carry with better grace, because it accords more with their world view, that there are separate spheres, different roles and responsibilities for men and women, however updated these roles and responsibilities may need to be. It is a weariness that the wealthy inevitably carry with more grace than the poor because they, after all, can pay for someone else to do much of their domestic work.

Meanwhile, echoes of the 'old' debate linger in empirical rather than passionate form. Groups like Wages for Housework continue, nothing if not indefatigable. One of its most recent publications, *The Global Kitchen*, analyses the domestic division of labour on a world scale. The Liberal Democrats' proposal for a Citizens' Income, an extremely minimum wage for all, whether working or at home, owes something to those seventies arguments.[7] The innovative New Economics Foundation proposes that housework be taken into account as part of the Gross Domestic Product. Even insurance companies will now measure up the weekly cost of domestic labour, as a part of a policy that estimates what it would cost to replace somebody's wife at the current market value.

All change

What of the woman then who devotes her life to the home? Where does she fit into contemporary mores? In many ways, we can characterize the stay-at-home mother of the late nineties simply by her difference from an older model. Read Betty Friedan's 1963 *The Feminine Mystique* and one enters a vanished world where women are enjoined to take feminine pride in 'simple household tasks': the well-made bed, the well-baked pie, the perfectly matching curtains. Women today still make beds, pies, think about carpets and curtains. Many enjoy the tasks but they do them in a different spirit. They do them distractedly, efficiently. Or they do them very very quickly. Or they do them at odd hours. Home and family are no longer part of an empty feminine mission of perfection: the Friedan suburban model. More often, they are merely one more aspect of a swift, metropolitan competence. *Daily Telegraph* journalist Anne

McElvoy recently coined a new term for a new kind of woman; Hyperwoman has a family, a high-powered job and a house to run. A woman with everything but time, she may well end up ordering new curtain material at two in the morning.

There has been a revolution in women's domestic lives over the last hundred years. In *Hidden Lives*, a family memoir, Margaret Forster illuminates the changes through the personal story of three working-class women: her grandmother, her mother and herself. How, she implicitly demands, can we possibly compare her grandmother's punishing life as a domestic servant in turn-of-the-century Carlisle to her own life as a writer and mother sixty years later? For it is not just her own personal success, as a writer, that explains the change but the transformation brought about by everything from labour-saving devices to new sexual mores that makes life for all women of whatever class that much easier.

When in an article for the *Independent* I asked other women to reflect on this legacy of changes in their own family, writer Ruth Richardson described her life as:

> – easier – not better. Just sitting at this table and looking
> around me, I can see a washing machine, fridge, dishwasher,
> running hot water, central heating, a spin dryer . . . There was
> none of that in my parents' house. A coalman used to bring
> the coal up the stairs every week. There were five of us, all
> daughters. My mother was always washing, bleaching, boiling.
> There were buckets in the bath and a great big boiler on the
> stove, like a preserving pan, for boiling nappies. I'm sure it's
> an illusion but I seem to remember it standing there, boiling,
> all the way through my childhood. Clothes were always
> drying in our kitchen. Yet there was always this hangover
> from my grandmother's generation that everything had to be
> spotless. You had to keep up standards.[8]

Household tasks still require organization but one can spend less time on them. One of the most popular of contemporary food writers has published a series of books on 'real' fast food; delicious main courses and sweets that can be made in just half an hour.

Shopping can be done by phone, mail, increasingly through television and new technology. The expanding fast food culture means dinners can be bought and shoved in the oven, ready and 'delicious' the requisite half an hour later. Microwaves heat up everything from cocoa to potatoes.

But the corollary is that a woman who stays at home in the nineties is ironically less likely to do so as a good wife or home maker but almost exclusively as a good *mother*. She will almost certainly begin to do more of the 'homey' things associated with the full-time housewife of old, but her stated *raison d'être* will be the well-being and moral and educational health of the children rather than good wifehood alone. It is an irony, not lost on those who choose to live this way, that in an era when we are supposed to be giving children less of our time, there are some women actively choosing to make children alone their life's work.

New settlements

In many ways the housewife, like the miner or docker, has come to represent the way we were and probably never will be again. Many women who decide to stay at home feel that no-one understands or values them: men, other women, politicians, feminists. They know that they represent the antithesis of modern womanhood in this important fact: they lack independent financial power. They are both embarrassed and blessed by the knowledge that they spring out of an anachronism: a household that can still afford to have only one partner working. Grown women who are publicly dependent on grown men thus contradict contemporary images of women and change in two important ways.

The modern stay-at-home mother can have an extraordinary calmness. I spent a long spring afternoon with a mother of two young children in a suburb of Bristol. A committed Christian, this young woman had been a bank clerk who had willingly, but not enthusiastically, left her job in order to bring up her family. Everything about her life, from her beautifully ordered small house to her poised body language to her cheerful rich voice, spoke of her enjoyment of her life, her lack of conflict about it. Others are more stubborn: they have the orneriness that comes from being outwardly unconfident but internally rock certain. There can be an air of the martyr about them, common to all those who swim against the tide of prevailing public opinion, placing their faith in future justification. For most of them there will have been a period of paid work and then the decision, easy or agonizing, to give it up. They describe, initially at least, a very different, difficult world.

Karen in Leeds, put it this way: 'A friend of mine's just had her second baby and given up her job. She feels like she's unemployed. She says to me, "I've never been unemployed before." Personally, I never thought of it like that. I thought of it like this; "I'm going to have a baby. I'm going to have a *new* job." But my friend is really upset. She *wails* about it.'

Former businesswoman Antonia Kirwan-Taylor described how she gave up her career of twenty-three years to look after her daughter. 'In truth,' she writes, 'nothing could have prepared me for the sense of loss and bereavement.'

All the old satisfactions are gone: a life of mobility, however limited, of decisions that concretely project into the future rather than merely repeat the actions of the present, the comforts of strangers, money, the pleasure of home as a place of refuge and return. Suddenly the place one lives becomes the place one is, all day. I use the word 'is' rather than 'work' deliberately. One of the weaknesses of the Wages for Housework argument was its crude designation of time spent with children as 'work'. It is something both more and less than that. Looking after young children is a strange mix of being and doing; one moment sitting quietly, reading a book with a toddler, the next lifting a heavy weight (same toddler) up several stairs; the next, laughing insanely at a shared joke; the next mopping tears or blood or snot; the next, sticking a finger into an unwilling little mouth and poking around to retrieve a five pence piece, the next trying to fix a meal for a baby and toddler while keeping both happy with smiles and activities. This lack of separation both between tasks and between oneself and another is what can make 'life at home' so tiring.

Many working women are used to presenting themselves for view, to be seen, measured, judged, argued with. The collapse into apparent invisibility can bring with it, at first, a sense of life-threatening nothingness.

Clare, a mother of four, lives in Glasgow. In her twenties, she worked as a clinical researcher in a pharmaceutical department. 'Then I did odd jobs, working as a waitress. My idea, my ideal, was to set up a restaurant until my babies came along. I couldn't imagine myself not having children. But once I discovered I was pregnant for the second time with the twins, I became resigned. That's it. I'll look after the children. I found it very difficult at first, but I think to a certain extent you have to be resigned. You have to sacrifice yourself to your child. Once you do that, it is easier and more enjoyable.'

She describes the classic insecurities of the stay-at-home mother: 'You become a recluse. At home, you know exactly who you are, what you are. But at parties or meeting other people at dinners, I felt very unsure of myself. "What is it you do? Oh you're the one with all the children." I found that if people didn't have children, I was alien to them. But what's worse is when you find yourself asking yourself who *you* are. Yes, there are rude people and you can get angry at their rudeness. But you do find yourself thinking, "All I can talk about is my children. And it's fascinating and I can go on for hours because so many things affect and change them. But . . ."'

When pressed, many women will admit to feeling that the outside world, whether that be the world of work or politics, is another universe, with different clothes, codes and conduct. Meanwhile they exist in a parallel, rather than 'lesser' sphere, populated with small children, other mothers and carers, teachers, doctors and nice ladies in cake and newspaper and shoe shops. One ex-professional said to me, 'I find it easier now to chat to the woman who works in the local newsagent than I do to my oldest friend. When I come in the shop with two kids in a double buggy at least she knows what I'm about.' The degree of estrangement they feel from the 'real world' depends, to a certain extent, on how much they were part of that other universe and for how long, the satisfaction they gained from it, the confidence they have about returning to it – or not.

Women who work only part of the week are constantly negotiating their passage from one world to another. For some, this is what keeps them alive. For others, it is what exhausts and depletes them. But what they inevitably miss is a period of transition, of loss, then acceptance and finally, entry into a new world, which full-time mothers tend to describe as enriching.

Angie is the mother of three young boys. An idealistic state school teacher in her twenties, she underwent a spiritual conversion during her first pregnancy. 'Everything changed. I had to know: where did the baby come from? And why? What do I do with it? How do I raise it? How can I do it right? What is the best thing? I strongly felt I had no idea of what worked and what didn't. After he was born, I did have to go back to work, in part to pay back my maternity leave money. Even then, I was wondering, how would it go? But I just couldn't switch from one world to another. I had always given teaching my all. One hundred per cent. I was leaving my son with a friend who was an excellent carer. He was fine but he was angry at me leaving him. My teaching suffered. My head was somewhere else. I couldn't cope with aggression in the classroom. I'd been at home for a year. In the past, I'd really psyched myself up, got adrenalin going. Fighting, conquering. I had learned how to be in control. When I went back, I was totally disillusioned with what I was teaching, the ideology of it. You can't force children to love each other, you can only punish them if they don't. I felt we had not achieved [in the school] a harmonious atmosphere. In the past I had so much willed it, seen it through rose-coloured spectacles. Now I thought: whoever is going to be in this classroom, building it up, it's not going to be me.'

Angie decided to give up work completely. 'That's my role totally. Absolutely crucial. The children are getting a person in their life who's saying to them, there is nothing more important than them. They are so special, everything else fades. They're never going to get that time again. I'm never going to get that chance again.'

For her, the time she spends with the children is not divisible.

It is a 'life together. It is not appointments. I have an acquaintance who is having trouble with her children. She can't understand it. She says to me, "I make a *point* of us having lunch together." But a child is not a client. He's your best friend. It was chilling when she said that.'

As for her life with her boys, she says, 'I love it. I absolutely love it. I'm astonished to find I'm in my element. I would never have predicted it. I would never have said I was maternal or domestic. It has been a real revelation, a revolution to me. I wasn't remotely interested in small children.' She sees a parallel between her decision to convert to a new religion and her decision to convert to full-time motherhood: 'You have to abandon ideas of status, credibility. I lost a huge amount of credibility when I found my new religion. People thought, "She's cracking up." Once I felt credibility go, I could stop worrying. So the only reason I don't feel defensive is because of my religion. Because of my com-munity. It's this idea that you're not waiting. That this is my life now. But I feel like I am a rare species. If it hadn't been for my religion, I would have felt so lonely. Everyone I knew who was pregnant at the same time as me has gone back [to work].'

Almost every full-time mother I spoke to had a deep belief that she was doing the right thing: the word they used most fre-quently, almost obsessively, was 'settled'. In one obvious way, these mothers were talking about their children. On reflection, I wondered if they were also talking about themselves. 'To settle' has several substantial dictionary definitions. First, to seat; to put in a seat or place of rest. Second, to come to rest after flight or wandering. Third, to descend; sink down; to lower. Fourth, to come or bring to rest after agitation. Fifth, to render or become stable or permanent. Six, to fix (what is uncertain), to decide (a question). Each one of these accords with some aspect of thought or feeling expressed by the mothers I talked to. One woman's calmness at making her decision not even to attempt to inhabit two worlds; another's enjoyment at the sense of physical solidity at being all in one place; a third's unacknowledged misery at her descent into an unseen and undervalued territory, rich in itself but unseen by others outside.

Karen is twenty-nine. She has two young children. She worked as an accounts clerk in a double glazing manufacturers in Leeds before having her babies. She, too, is certain she is 'doing the right thing'. 'In my opinion, the children of mothers who go out to work are not as settled. Friends who've stayed at home and friends who've gone out to work, the children of the ones who've stayed have just seemed better than them. I suppose I mean, not pushed from pillar to post. Settled. Happier. For the mums, it's harder too, being at work.' Of her own children she says, 'Mine are better behaved. I can't really explain it. Maybe it's something to do with . . . children have to stick to one person when it comes to discipline. If children have lots of different carers, they run wild. I'm sure my children have got a better start in life. When I first gave up work it was a big shock. I felt cut off from all adults, from talking. I did miss work. Now I love it. I've made new friends at baby club, a few of my friends are working. One went back part-time but I didn't want to leave the kids. I want to be with them all the time. I've made my choice. I don't even talk about going back now.'

We assume a hostility between the working and the 'non-working' mother. And it is certainly there, particularly when one woman's insecurity about her own choice or envy at another's is projected onto other women or a group of women and expressed as criticism. But we do both kinds of women an injustice if we simply label it 'bitchiness' or 'projection' and leave it at that. For each woman is silently or noisily contributing to a conversation about the meaning of what they do: what is best for 'the children', not just their own; to some extent, all mothers share this concern for all children. Women without children tend to think of the issue of work or home solely in terms of what is best for the *women*. But the women themselves don't. Mothers are both divided and connected by their concern for something quite outside themselves.

Jessica embodies the 'to work or not to work' split within herself. A journalist who decided to stop working and look after her three children, she describes herself as 'the classic product of a mother who stayed at home and to whom I now have nothing to say. But looking now at the kids of mothers who work, mothers who have children with problems at school, problems sleeping, these kids are so unsettled. The mothers ask me, "Why do you think she's like this?" and to me, it's so obvious. They want the kids to have a perfect childhood, these lawyers and politicians and journalists, and they have this whole thing about quality time. Get home at 6 p.m., sit down and hear everything immediately. But the fact is, what kids tell you seeps out in dribs and drabs. Focusing on a child doesn't work like that. And yet,' she adds wistfully, 'the kids, *my* kids, they like you to work. They like to hear about different things out in the world.'

What are we to make of this contradiction?

The aridity of either/or

One answer came in early 1996 with the so called 'Hakim debate'. This centred on the work of an established and respected researcher into sex equality, Catherine Hakim, who published an article entitled 'Five Myths of Women's Employment' in the *British Journal of Sociology*, later elaborated upon in the unapproachably titled *Female Heterogeneity and the Polarisation of Women's Employment*. Hakim's paper was long and complex. One of the 'myths' that she contested was that women's full-time employment has risen over the twentieth century: on the contrary, she argued, it has remained relatively steady since 1850, while part-time work has grown dramatically. More contentiously, Hakim asserted that women are not passively crowded into low-paid and gender-stereotyped work – such as primary school teaching – but that they actively choose the areas because of their concern for children-friendly hours. Underlying her whole thesis was her argument that anything from a half to two-thirds of women are not concerned with career but are instead 'home-centred'. Hakim believed that feminism, in its concern for equal rights, had always picked up the interests of the remaining one-third of women and shaped its agenda for economic and social change with a bias towards them. In a response, some of her feminist critics took issue with both her statistics and her premise.

Broadly, they challenged Hakim's argument that women acted voluntaristically: women's choice, they said, is hedged in by social expectations and pressures. And, in any case, is feminism only concerned with career women? Feminist economist Irene Bruegel argued on Radio 4's 'Moral Maze' that the history of feminism, particularly socialist feminism, is steeped in reflection and agitation on behalf of women carers. What was being distorted most of all in the 'Hakim debate', she feared, was the feminist movement itself.

The conversation between Hakim and her critics, a dense and rather statistical one, was, unfortunately, too good to miss. The resultant row – 'Academic Feminists Scrap about Ordinary Women' – was a newspaper editor's dream and the broadsheets duly gave it ample space. According to a *Daily Telegraph* editorial:

> The most provocative of [Hakim's] observations as far as the
> feminist lobby is concerned will be the most self-evident to
> ordinary people. That is, that there are two distinct kinds of
> working women. 'Careerists' whose commitment to
> professional advancement takes precedence in their lives and
> 'Home Centred' who see themselves as secondary earners. For
> the latter, paid work is an extension of their role in the
> family.[9]

But simplicity, or provocation for that matter, can simultaneously reveal and obscure a truth. I do not want to get into the detail of disputes over the five, or hundred and five, myths about women's employment. But I am interested in thinking about Hakim's central declaration, that women are divided by their concern for home and career, in the light of my conversations with women, working and 'non-working'. At the most obvious descriptive level, it is easy to say, yes, of course, she's right. Here are the 'housewives' and part-timers on one side; over there are the committed Capital C career women. Equally obvious is that when women have children they, on the whole, choose to be with them rather than away from them, and the world makes it easy for them to make that choice. Indeed, they are assigned a dubious, tricky value for so doing. Neighbours and parents declare, perhaps for the first time ever, how very well you look in your new state of motherhood. They declare, with considerable nerve, how much this life obviously suits you. It is as if an invisible hundredweight of nature and convention is waiting to fall on you the minute you bear a child. Years of polite interest in 'work' is replaced by an instant, deep and gratifying attention to this small human in your arms. Mothers become messengers or even ciphers, bearers of the good news of another being.

Yet the decision to spend time with the children you do have, to be with them as much as possible, because you both want to and perhaps feel you should, is that the same as placing children (or home) at the *centre* of your life? What about the many women I know, child-free to the last, simple careerists to an undiscerning outside eye, who cherish their domestic life and are much more 'homey' than most of the mothers I meet? And are those mothers who work more than they wish or can control overtly declaring that their children matter less to them than the job? Many of the mothers I spoke to would argue that pursuing a life of their own, which does not necessarily correlate with work or money, is vitally important to them. They are not 'careerists'. Some of them are, physically at least, 'home-centred'. But they are all independent, interested in the world outside the front door, with a strong sense of who they are, what they have, what they will do one day in the future. They can point to a thread running through their lives from young girlhood through the early twenties through maternity and now stretching into the future when they are thinking of many other things apart from home and children. These things – books, ideas, the companionship of friends and strangers, politics, travel – are just as much the 'centre of their lives'.

There is something desiccated, then, about this division of women into 'career' and 'non-career' types. If we accept this division with regards to women, which incidentally has never been applied to men, then we necessarily limit our thinking about the human condition as a whole. We divide people into those who seek power, money, a place in the world, and those who do not, who then lurk unseen in the shadows, creatures characterized only by their caring and nothing else. It is part of the crippling limitation of the language used so often, chiefly in newspapers and broadcasting, in this current debate on work and motherhood that we all become reduced to one-dimensional stereotypes with fixed and polarized intentions and orientations.

Writers, that ever unreliable category, are an interesting example of the folly of the over-simple division. The nature of their work allows them flexibility. It also allows them reflection *on* complexity. Nadine Gordimer, Alice Hoffman, Toni Morrison: are these women mothers or writers? The question is absurd. Margaret Forster is the author of a number of highly successful books that make her, within her field, very much a 'career' woman, yet she has always stated with astonishing firmness that children and family always came first with her. She has also described at some length the ways in which she managed her children and her work. Novelist A. S. Byatt has also spoken of the bargain she made with herself between the creativity of family and writing. She calculated that if she had four children that would probably mean four fewer books. Yet there remained the books that she could and did write, a sufficient number she would argue now, I'm sure. These women's choices about the management of their time do not indicate more or less com-mitment to paths not taken, for a short or even a long while. They indicate a recognition of hard truths about a world we still live in, that asks women, first and last, how will *you* manage the children? How will *you* fit them in with your life and your work?

The oppressive polarities of the 'Hakim debate' say much about our lack of imagination about lives as actually lived; their richness, complexity, their contradictions and many, many changes. How many women fit easily into an agenda set by the *Daily Telegraph* or the *British Journal of Sociology* for that matter? If there are a few stereotyped 'career women' whose lives and time can be fitted into simply labelled boxes – time given over to an institution, a ladder to climb, titles to hold, then heart attack and regrets at life's end: the classic male way – that may be because lack of imagi-nation among the corporate world allows them no other working path. Men have followed it for years and there is a growing consensus in society that agrees that it is no longer worth much as a model. For women to be 'serious' about themselves, we expect them to follow the pattern and then deride them for their inhumanity if they do. Yet few women do choose this way. Most individuals have much messier lives, with changing meanings, even to themselves. I recently met a nice, clever woman with sad eyes. When we were talking about what we 'did for a living' she said she was 'just a housewife' – it is awful to hear a woman say those words with self-hate. Her regret about her life was not only that her day was mostly punctuated with cooking largely un-appreciated meals, but that she did not, at forty-something, have a career, a particular path to follow. That, I could understand. But then she began to trash her own youth: 'I wasted those early years travelling . . .' she says, then tails off. 'Well, no, I loved the travelling . . . but I see now *I should have been doing something else*, getting ahead [my emphasis].' Her own pleasurable and meaning-ful past has become subordinate to her perceived lack of 'status'.

It is often argued that women's more fragmented, person-centred, flexible approach to work and life is the way of the future, not the past. I hope there is some truth to this, that paradox, not parody of the male way, is the route forward and that men themselves will increasingly follow it. Certainly, many women will shift from home to work and back again, within the space of a few years. They, too, make no sense within the Hakim paradigm.

I have already spoken about Liz, who teaches children with special needs. Originally a plumber, she trained to be a teacher in her late twenties, taught in London until her first baby was born and then moved in with the father of her child. She found the 'perfect job' for her, except it was not perfect: she was exhausted all the time and wanted to be with her child. 'I knew I still did a good job, but when I'd finished, that was it. I just wanted to get home.' When she became pregnant for a second time, she decided she would do it differently. Finances permitting, she would stay at home full-time.

'Once I thought being a full-time housewife was the pits. I

never ever considered staying at home. But the way I think of it now, I'm going through this stage. I'm not going to do this all the time. I may work part-time in the future. All these thoughts have helped with the stresses. And it is just so wonderful, not working. On Sunday night I feel this complete bliss and contentment. Before, we were both working full-time. We used to wrangle endlessly over the housework. Squabble. Now I've taken it over and I don't feel in the remotest bit resentful if he comes in, eats and gets up. It's like I'm playing at it, looking after the house and children.'

So where do we place Liz? Nowhere and Everywhere. A full-time feminist who became a full-time housewife? A committed professional who gave it all up for the lure of babies? The truth is much more complex. Liz remains a tenacious professional, who stopped trying to do everything, please everybody. Home is the 'centre' of her physical life for a while. Does that make her one of Hakim's 'homemakers'? I'm not so sure. For Liz's knowledge of both past and future informs the sentence, 'I'm playing at it, looking after the house and children . . .'. It also informs her perception of the resentment, or lack of it, between her husband and herself, because she knows 'what it is like to work full-time, the horrible pressures of it'. She has been there. She has been the 'career woman'. She will be that again.

Sooner than I think. The last time I saw Liz, now a good friend, she had just begun a new policy job in her area of expertise, children with special needs. It was a job she saw needed doing; so she created the post and lobbied for local council money to fund it. No-one was more surprised than herself when the funds came through. She loves what she is doing. Forty hours a week or more. Career hours, if ever there were. She and her husband also decided to move to a new house. A bigger mortgage, more bills to pay; desire and need combined in equal measure.

~ 7 ~

Down among the Children:
From Self-reliance to Snobbery

Once upon a time when I was still childless, I met a
friend of mine wheeling her baby along the High Street.
I asked, 'How are you?'
With a glassy smile, she trilled, 'We haven't decided
whether to go to the swimming-pool or the toy library
– have we, sweetie?' (This last addressed to the surly
Mussolini type in the buggy.)
Nanny work, I thought. And still think . . .

Kate Saunders, 'This Crying-thing',
Sons and Mothers, Virago, 1996

TALE ONE*

Elizabeth had her baby son John in early April 1994. She was
twenty-five years old: her first baby. No-one at the hospital
commented on the fact there was no father in attendance,
although when her brother came to the hospital the next
day, one of the midwives, mistaking him for the baby's
father, gave him the same 'useless bastard' look she had
caught occasionally on her mother's face. The useless bastard

---

* All three tales are fictionalized, but composite, versions of stories told to me by
various women. For obvious reasons, such intimate detail could not be exactly
recounted.

117

himself didn't come and visit until Elizabeth was back at home: he was entranced, instantly, wanted to hold the boy, cuddle, sing to him, take him away for ever, claim him. He left after three-quarters of an hour.

In the first months of her son's life she couldn't leave him for even an hour. She could never imagine a time when she would. But when the baby was a few months old her mother, who lived in the next road but one, persuaded her out for an evening with friends. 'Go! Go! Go! And don't think or talk about that damn boy once,' she said, playfully pushing her out the door. It was better than she thought it would be. Her friends were laughing at her, but with her. They were laughing at the way she was always looking at her watch, but they were kind and curious about her new life too. When she went back to the house, she didn't feel the absolute relief she expected to feel. Her bodily and emotional fatigue had found its proper, familiar home but she longed to keep walking in the cold air, for the crisp feeling of separation to go on a little bit longer. It was fun, being drunk. So, there was the small twinge of regret at having to go back into those two small rooms, her furniture now no more than props arranged around this tiny life.

Even so, she didn't go out again for a few months. It was easier to spend all her days with the baby, to arrange the days around him, then tell herself she loved the peace at night and needed it so there was no point going out then either. She would have to go back to work soon. Three days a week. Because she couldn't bear to think of it, she couldn't start to make the arrangements. She simply assumed. Assumed that the 'useless bastard', who wasn't working, would take John one day a week, and that her mother, who hadn't worked in a long time, would do the other two. She didn't mind about her mother looking after him, that was like an extension of herself. But she didn't trust the u.b. He came weekly for a visit and he was good at all the loud things, tickling and jigging and throwing her beloved baby up to the ceiling. He made John laugh more than she ever did. He over-excited him sometimes. But he was careful with nappy-changing, too, and face-wiping. Those large limbs could be surprisingly well co-ordinated and tender. She still couldn't imagine trusting him enough to leave her precious child for an eight-hour stretch. She contemplated giving up work as receptionist at a beauty parlour, but even though the money was terrible, she was still ambitious for herself in theory, ambitious for John. She wanted to be something he would be proud of when he was ten or fifteen years old. She wanted to be more than a single mother on benefit.

Her mother was surprisingly reluctant to help out. 'Okay,' she said, slapping her hand on the table. 'For a short while I'll look after him for a couple of days. But not more and not for long. You've got to grasp the nettle.' Was that about the u.b., whom her mother inevitably and cordially loathed, or was it about getting someone else to look after the baby? People at work had used childminders and nurseries. The head beautician actually had a nanny. But Elizabeth's whole being screamed against it. No stranger could know what baby John needed. It was a physical thing with her, an instant recognition of hunger, thirst, the meaning of a particular cry. And when she got it wrong, which she often did, well then, love tided them over till she got it right. She took refuge in the money question. She only earned twelve and a half thousand a year. It might go up to fourteen thousand. That didn't really leave anything over to pay anyone. It left enough for her rent, their food, his toys.

The u.b. agrees, although, at first, he keeps changing his mind about what day he can do. 'I need to know,' she insists, because with her mother doing Tuesday and Thursday, Wednesday would be best for her. She wants him 'sandwiched' between something safe and her mother is safe. 'And it must be here, in his home,' she insists, 'where all his things are. Nowhere else. Here.' He agrees to both the day and the place. He is living temporarily with his mother and he can see it wouldn't work to take the baby there.

On her first week back at work, she feels sick. Every

chance she can at work she is phoning the flat. What are they doing? Has he given John his milk? Are they going to the park? If it looks like it might rain, the rain-hood is in the hall cupboard. By lunch time, when there is no answer three-quarters of an hour after she last rang, she is hysterical, convinced her baby has been abducted: remembering all the old arguments she and the u.b. had during her pregnancy when she dreamed he hated her and wanted to kill the baby. Her boss says, gently, 'Look, do you want to go home early?' But where would she go: what would she see? At five, she books a minicab she can't afford. Impatience will not let her share anyone else's journey on the short bus ride home. Fumbling with her keys as she lets herself into the house, she is relieved that she will know the worst at least. She bursts into tears when she finds the two of them, asleep on the sofa.

Over the next year, she learned to let go. She also learned how to spread the burden around. On one of her non-working afternoons, she and a friend agreed to swap: one week, she would take her friend's little boy and John, the next week she had a free afternoon, which was wonderful. All the bits and pieces of her life could be swept up, sorted out. Cleaning, bills, lists to be drawn up. It never occurred to her to spend it doing something for herself, like taking a walk or going to the cinema. She felt she must use the time to improve her and John's life. Then the arrangement with the u.b. broke down. He got some casual work and he couldn't make Wednesdays any more. He tried to get his own mother to fill in but Elizabeth didn't want that. Instead, she found a childminder, round the corner from work. One day. It cost a precious twelve pounds. It left her less money, but she trusted the smiling woman in her spotless living-room more than her son's father; she trusted a steady professional love more than intermittent infatuation. When one Tuesday evening she saw the tiredness on her mother's face, which she recognized as a form of anger, she wished she could ask the childminder to do another day. 'School soon,' she told herself foolishly. 'School soon', even though it was three years away. It became a personal mantra, conjuring up the time when someone or something else would step in and help her with responsibility she told herself she was always prepared, if not happy, to shoulder alone.

Personal growth

Childcare, formal and informal, has been one of the significant growth areas in the British economy: a personalized service on which the public world depends. This historic shift in the burden of care has been neatly summarized:

> Until recently there was no need for public policy to concern itself too much with parenting. The economic base of childrearing was secure. In pre-industrial societies the family was the site both of production and of consumption: work and home were combined and parenting was one of the myriad of tasks to be done in the domestic economy. During the industrial era work and home became disconnected: men left the home to go out to work, while women ran the domestic economy. Women's unpaid work ensured that children were clothed, fed and socialized. It is only now that women have gone into the workforce in huge numbers, that the economic base of parenting has become an issue. The old economic organization of parenting – essentially dependent on unpaid labour by mothers – has unravelled.[1]

Who provides the new childcare? We know pretty well who does not: the state, national and local. According to the 1995 cross-party Employment Committee's report on 'Mothers in Employment', 'in contrast with the centralized and universal system of childcare in Scandinavia, the UK system is a mixed bag of provision by a variety of different agencies . . . Compared to countries like Belgium, Denmark and France, Britain has one of the lowest number of places – for under threes – in publicly funded childcare.'

In its dying years, the Conservative government of 1992–7

began to recognize the importance of childcare provision. This was partly because they feared younger women Conservative voters might turn away from a party of the family that had no ideas on how to make the *new* family, which inevitably includes a working mother, actually work. Conservative party schemes for helping those on welfare get into work also required nominal recognition of the importance of childcare, but not wishing to appear to echo the priorities of the then opposition, Labour and the Liberal Democrats, the government of 1992–7 put its emphasis, rather eccentrically, on after-school care rather than the early years. In their election campaign material, they made much play of the 60,000 new places created in after-school schemes and clubs between April 1993 and April 1997.

But neither this government of the early 1990s nor the new Labour government, elected in 1997, believed that childcare should be directly funded by direct taxation. Instead, both political parties have stated their belief, if with differing force and emphasis, that it is government's role to encourage others to provide childcare. As I discuss further in Chapter 9, New Labour believe that through the medium of a National Childcare Strategy, it is government's role to persuade everyone from employers to voluntary networks to provide the necessary services. The major resource in its possession – money – is not to be forthcoming.

Similarly local authorities, funded at least in part from central government, put little direct money into childcare. Their priority is to provide places for 'children in need'; many can rarely do more than meet their minimum statutory function. As a result, locally provided childcare has become part of an emergency, rather than routine, response to parenting. The relentless squeeze on local authority budgets over the years of Conservative government has shown in this area. In 1985, 32,900 children had places in local authority day nurseries and with childminders employed by local authorities. By 1995 this had dropped to 28,900.[2]

Enlightened employers, particularly among white-collar workers, have done their share in providing childcare. One of the market leaders in childcare, Midland Bank, set up its first workplace nursery in 1989. It now provides up to 800 nursery places for its employees nationwide; it also provides holiday play schemes. The bank perceives provision of childcare from both a business and equal opportunity perspective; the inevitably high cost offsets the cost of losing trained (largely female) staff. However, a mixture of realism and reluctance has rather halted the bandwagon for workplace nurseries in recent years. Tax relief for workplace nurseries was introduced in the budget of 1990. But as Patricia Morgan points out, in her interesting albeit reactionary book *Who Needs Parents?*, the dramatic expansion did not materialize.[3] Workplace nurseries are actually very expensive to set up. In 1992, Working for Childcare estimated that a twenty-five-place workplace nursery costs £4,920 minimum per child per year to run. And as Angela Phillips, a veteran campaigner on childcare issues, has written, workplace nurseries 'should be approached with caution. We tie children to profit at our peril.' The 'tied cottage effect' of linking childcare to a job means that when one parent loses their job, they lose their childcare place too. Workplace nurseries are not the most practical of schemes: taking a child to work with you and home again, often in the rush hour, is frequently far more stressful, for child and parent, than taking them to a local centre.[4] There are now only 600 workplace nurseries in the UK out of a total of 6,246 private and voluntary sector nurseries in England, Wales and Scotland.[5]

Exclusively private provision of childcare has also risen, with an obvious market among high earners. According to 1996 Department of Health figures, there are over 4,000 private and voluntary sector nurseries in the United Kingdom. The Conservative government's complex and clumsy nursery vouchers scheme, which was due to be implemented in 1997 but was immediately abolished by the incoming Labour government, aimed to benefit these nurseries for profit; in fact, by an ironic and complex twist, they expanded school nursery class places and left some private nurseries worried for their future. In 1996, Britain's first ever twenty-four-hour nursery, a kind of stop-over hotel for children of working parents, opened its doors.

But overall, few parents benefit from these schemes. Employer-provided childcare obviously depends on having a job; private nurseries depend on substantial earnings. More than half of all women – 70 per cent at the last official count – make their own arrangements, the kind of arrangements made by Elizabeth above.[6] In order to work or spend time away from children, they depend on friends, relatives, informal agreements with other mothers, cheap playgroups in their area, babysitting circles: swaps, shares and favours. A large minority of women – 26 per cent of working mothers – use more formal and expensive arrangements like nurseries and childminders.

In common with other social and economic polarities in western countries as a whole, there is within childcare a significant difference between 'work rich' and 'work poor' households. 'Work rich' families are usually characterized by one or more of the following. They tend to have a qualified mother, higher than average wages, an older mother (over thirty), to be in a couple, have a partner in work, one or both partners in full-time work, be in secure work with sick pay and holiday pay, not be dependent on benefits, use formal childcare (nursery, childminder or nanny). 'Work poor' households reverse many of these conditions: the mother is likely to be unqualified, low-waged, younger, single, have insecure work without sick or holiday pay, be on benefits; she is likely to use informal childcare such as a partner, family, friends, or no childcare at all.[7]

But that significant 'work rich' minority have boosted the provision of services to which they have access. The biggest growth area in recent years has been in childminders, nannies and related services like au-pairing. Between 1982 and 1991 the number of registered childminding places in England and Wales doubled. In 1984, 53,000 childminders offered just over 116,000 places. By March 1994, that figure had leapt to 96,000 registered minders providing 357,000 places. More parents now choose childminding over any other option.

Astonishingly, there are now more nannies than car workers in the United Kingdom. Yet the very word has a connotation that is hard to get rid of. We associate it with privilege, uniforms, nurseries in the eaves and listless leisured parents who receive their offspring in the living-room at tea-time. Jonathan Gathorne-Hardy's entertaining book *The Rise and Fall of the British Nanny* (1993) conjures up this largely lost world, with its fill of nasty characters in uniform and much-loved older women who became part of the strange, extended family that was the upper classes in the interwar period. The modern-day nanny is not considered part of the family, in that patrician sense, although she may live within it with an apparent intimacy horrifying to nannies of the old school. She is a worker, essentially, on a short-term contract, with few legal rights and benefits. She is frequently untrained, and may well be a likeable young woman who likes children (or thinks she likes children!), who has just got off the plane from New Zealand and is looking for metropolitan excitement. Nanny (and au-pair) agencies report a sharp rise in 'ordinary' families ringing for their services. Many of these are single working mothers, using all available cash for help in the home.

Watching the professionals

Walk along a completely ordinary city street at five on a summer's evening. You will see two women talking in a doorway; a child is handed between them. The talk is quick, friendly, a little anxious perhaps. It is full of questions, from mother to childminder, about the day missed: the food eaten, the nap not taken, the television programme watched. 'And did you go to the park ...?' The sharpness of the question is worthy of a barrister cross-examining a key witness, except the question will probably be framed within the accepted boundaries of woman-to-woman chat, which assumes the best and fears the worst. Some mothers are brisk: they manufacture their own trust. Some are eternally suspicious.

A few streets away, a gaggle of mothers and babies in prams are waiting for a glass door to open, to pick up their toddlers and small children from a nursery or a playgroup. The question of personal trust has less resonance here: a degree of surveillance is assumed. But there is still a kind of casual but imperative talk about life behind the nursery doors, an attempt to fit the largely guessed-at activities of your own child – everyone knows that children won't tell a parent the details of what they've done during the day – to the outlines of an assumed general experience. The questions of safety and trust are crucial for parents, but they act as metaphors too. The less trust one feels in a particular situation, the greater one's general uncertainty about leaving a child in the care of strangers will be. Parents seeking out nurseries look for clean toilets and airy spaces, educational toys and qualified, friendly staff. All of these factors lead to a sense of safety and containment, both of which are exacerbated by a distance between parent and worker. If there is a tendency among parents to mistrust the personal worker – the sole charge nanny or childminder – there is a parallel inclination almost to sanctify the nursery worker, rather like a hospital nurse.

Paradoxically, parents can feel reassured by both the professionalism *and* the low status of nursery workers. These are well-trained people with a vocation, but, it is assumed, no careerist agenda. This came home to me recently when a mother told me some of the reasons for her suspicion of a man working in her son's nursery. 'Why would a man want to do a job like that, with such low pay and no chance of advancement?' An odd, interesting question, this, that begs the further enquiry: why would a woman want to do it then?

Ann has two daughters and has recently put her eldest into morning nursery. She says: 'Jo, who heads the nursery, is the mother of a young son who attends the nursery. You think: well, that's a good sign. I see her interests as a parent complementing her interests as a professional. The professionalism part is both mysterious and reassuring. I presume, for instance, that she understands things about child development, intellectually, that I know only by instinct. It is reassuring. I trust her to place my child's behaviour within some kind of frame. Even her love will be professional: there will be genuine affection, that comes from knowing my daughter – hearing her confidences, surviving her tantrums – but that love will always exist in a context. It will never be inappropriate or unboundaried.'

Childminders suffer from the opposite problem; dig not so deep and many of us probably do not even think of childminders as professionals at all. As one worker said to me, 'The term itself is unfortunate. Because anyone can "mind" a child in a way. It's probably too late, but we would prefer a term like "professional day care worker".' Or as a National Childminders' Association (NCMA) leaflet both assertively and defensively declares, 'It's a proper job.' Childminders themselves feel passionately about this. They point to the rigorous checks by the local authority, the courses to be taken on everything from first aid to how to deal with allegations of child abuse; the annual inspections. Or they point to the rapid developments in training; the many childminders now taking a National Vocational Qualification (NVQ) in Childcare and Education, or the increasing number of local councils directly placing vulnerable children with childminders to meet their duties towards 'children in need' under the 1989 Children Act.

It is this pride in their professionalism that underlay childminders' anger at the 1994 Sutton smacking case, in which the High Court granted a childminder the right to smack her charges. As one Newcastle minder said, 'It was like we were put in the same category as friends and family. Workers in nurseries, crèches and playgroups are not allowed to smack. Their distance and professionalism is understood. Childminders deserve the same respect.' The NCMA also criticized the Conservative government for not including childminding among the services to be covered by the (now defunct) Education Voucher scheme. As Gill Haynes, chief executive, says, 'Parents know that childminders can often be the best educators that their children can have. And if vouchers are to go ahead, we believe childminders have an important part to play in making the scheme work.'

Unsurprisingly, the entry of men into childminding has led to a quite rapid change in perception of the job. Put a man into a traditionally female job and, like a picture slowly coming into focus, society may suddenly 'see' and value the skills and qualities attached to the work. In the case of childminding, the automatic if unconscious links between 'mothering', 'undervalued' and 'underpaid' may also become clear.

Self-organization

Somewhere between the apparently separate territories of home and community, of employers and employees, of personal and institutional life are the politics of self-organization. The term 'childcare' does not do full justice to the range of these organizations or their meaning to those who set them up and maintain them. They may begin as an individual or group effort to share the burdens and pleasures of looking after small children but they often become much more than that. For some individuals, this effort may dictate the shape of their future as they gain and build on professional skills. For others, it is simply a way to contribute to, and remain part of, the community from where you come and where your children will grow up.

For the poorest women, organizing around children, for children, however informally, fulfils two related needs. It gets you away from the loneliness of home but it also offers an alternative to those public areas of apparent conviviality – the high street, the café, the shopping mall – which only taunt you with what you haven't got: money. Trailing round a shopping mall all afternoon when you've got nothing to spend is not just miserable: it is impossible. Young children, in particular, interpret the signs around them – racks of sweets, displays of cuddly toys, fridges stacked with cans and juices of all variety – as exactly what they are: an invitation to have, to take. They look to a parent, literally, to translate wish into fulfilment; to 'give it to me'. If providing materially for your children is generally considered a sign of parental success – which it is – then those without money logically feel the stigma of parental failure when they cannot provide, however minimally.

Most of the mothers I have talked to over the years have set up some formal – or informal – way of meeting others. One young woman had a house full of friends, all more or less in the same situation as her: teenagers or girls in their early twenties, pregnant or with young babies. The phone rang throughout the afternoon, with calls for the friends, girls and boys, who drifted in and out of the kitchen and living-room. The most common place to meet is in each others' flats or houses or, on sunny days, at the local park. In Sheffield, Maureen, Clare and Molly arranged outings with each others' children, and child-swaps: their self-organization was dictated as much by a need to trust the carer of their child as lack of funds to pay anyone else. Often, what women want most is the chance to be together, as mothers. The children are put in a safe space and left to themselves; the mothers can sit and talk without worrying, as you might do with a non-parent, that your wandering eye is a form of inattention or even rudeness. If these activities and informal groups progress one step further, they begin to make contact with existing local institutions; a new playgroup, crèche or nursery needs money, it needs local council approval, it needs police clearance, it needs workers and it needs children. Informal politics meets established politics; it is not always a happy mix.

Deborah Curtis is an artist and mother of two young children. Two years ago, she and her husband, artist Gavin Turk, decided, with other local parents, to set up a playgroup in the Shoreditch area of London where they live. According to Deborah: 'Part of the way that Gavin and I operate in life is thinking of things in a creative way. It is more useful to get a lot of people together. The idea has always been that when you get a lot of heads together, the input is more exciting. Also, setting up a playgroup was a way to get time off to do other things without distancing yourself from the children. We had been working it informally as a neighbourhood thing. A lot of the parents were local although some came from quite far away. Some were professionals in full-time jobs – one father is a solicitor, another is an architect – but mostly they are self-employed artists, writers, jewellers, people who, at the present time, don't have a lot of money. Shoreditch is a very interesting area because in the south, there are a lot of living/working spaces, close to the city, which encourage these informal, unofficial residences for artists. In the north of the borough, it is different. There are 60,000 people on council estates that are in a pretty bad way. Our playgroup has been a south Shoreditch thing, but my hope is that we can bring together the two communities . . .'

After a time, Deborah, Gavin and the other parents wanted to become more official. They attempted to get the Shoreditch International Crèche off the ground: 'In the beginning, we had just swapped houses, but some of the houses weren't that safe, so then we did a bit of work on my studio and used that and then we employed two people full-time. We wanted to get registered, but the process of registration assumes that you haven't started. The woman in social services said, "But I've never heard of you!" And I said, "Well, we're a new group. We want to register." She said, "You're doing *what*? You know you can be prosecuted for that. You cannot start until you're registered. It can take six months." Another woman from the council came round. She asked, "Do the children have lunch?" I told her that I cook it. I've got a food handler's certificate. She said, "Oh, I'm not so sure about the re-heating." Well, we were talking about pizzas! I could see when she was looking round our premises she was checking all her mental boxes and we just weren't fitting into them. Her eyes were like saucers. She was looking at this second-hand furniture and I could see that what she was seeing in her head was the last private nursery she had gone round. And then there are all these strict rules about the number of children under a certain age which is supposed to limit the number of children in nappies. But you get three-year-olds in nappies and what do you do then?'

For the moment the Shoreditch International Crèche has decided to continue as a playgroup, which it may legally do, although Deborah and the others hope to secure premises in the near future and start up officially as a crèche. Despite her frustrations over her dealings with the council, Deborah says, 'I am still fired up about it. These things are so good for children. It is a pity that these things are so hedged in by rules. The Children's Act in particular is very restricting. It stops the children taking any risks. Basically, it says, until you're three you can't play with anything interesting!'

The story of Kinderflex is a happier one. One of its founders, Pauline Thomas, comes from a large family who have grown up in and around the city. Pauline and a sister live in Birmingham

Newtown; another sister lives in Aston. According to Pauline: 'I've grown up with caring strong women, always working, even if it's just in a cleaning job. The women in my family have always worked. My aunt is a head teacher. My mum has worked with handicapped kids. Another aunt is a midwife, I've a sister who is a teacher. I was in a day nursery working with special needs children and I thought, "I need another job. I could do this better. I could take children earlier, I could set up a place where parents come and talk, where parents can bring ideas to us." In some nurseries, parents don't even talk. I just wanted to do more.'

With her two elder sisters, Brenda and Carol, who have three children between them, Pauline started up a mobile crèche for businesses from home. Then, with a fourth partner, Beheima, the Thomas sisters decided to set up a day nursery. They had to take 'loads of courses' and apply to City Challenge for premises and funds. 'You have to write up a business plan and all that and go through police checks. You do ask yourself, "Is this really what we want to do?" But it was fun, it was something constructive. It was great. Between us we have all the administrative and nursery experience. Brenda has the book-keeping skills, Carol, like me, has worked in a nursery.'

The nursery, based in Newtown, opened its doors in March 1997. The sisters and their partner put £250 each into the nursery, out of money saved from their income support; City Challenge put in £2,000 for equipment. Further toys, books and furniture will be bought from fees as the nursery fills up. There is room for sixteen children on the premises; it is currently half full but Pauline is hoping 'that by August we will have some more kids. Our wages are reasonable. I can live on them for the moment but not for a long time.' All the sisters work at the nursery, Brenda and Carol in the morning, Pauline in the afternoon.

Pauline says: 'I wanted to do this desperately. A lot of parents round here can't find childcare. It is hard. It is very expensive. It is all private nurseries. There are about five day nurseries round here with waiting lists as long as your arm. We take on babies, from four months. And we are a reasonable price here. People who live in the area pay a reasonable fee. We also get funding from the city council. If there is a course going on near the city centre, then we will take six, seven, eight kids for a day or couple of days for a knock-down price. We are a mixed nursery. People say, "Oh this is a black nursery." But I don't know what a black nursery *is*. My community, the community I grew up in, is mixed: black, white, Asian. And we've got a mix of children in the nursery. We really involve parents. We're approachable. They phone us at home any time of the night. We talk about what the kids do, during the day. One of us is always here to open up and close. I've got a mum coming here tomorrow at lunch. She might come and sit down for fifteen minutes or two hours. I've got a dad coming in a moment for a chat with me.'

Some voluntary groups are less institutional or formal; they exist in a more disparate but none the less tangible way. Barbara Kott is President of the National Childbirth Trust, one of the most successful and long-lasting of organizations for new parents. Now fifty, Kott started her own local NCT group in March 1976 when she was expecting her first baby. 'They now have 700 people in the Kingston area,' she says proudly. Nationally, the NCT has 55,000 paid-up members – that is, members who pay an annual subscription. There are 8,000 active volunteers, eight regions, a teaching, research and post-natal branch; twenty-seven posts at head office; a President and a Council of trustees. Begun in March 1956, the NCT is now a rather grand institutional lady. With an articulate, largely middle-class membership, its voice is heard in many national debates; its own internal discussions, such as the argument in early 1997 over whether to accept sponsorship from Sainsbury's, are given significant coverage in the mainstream media.[8]

But one of the greatest strengths of the National Childbirth Trust is its less official side. Local NCT groups are often formed around prenatal classes that teach couples what to expect from the mini-drama of birth; they provide a valuable first point of local contact for women – and men – who return home, in shock, with a tiny bundle of humanity, and think, 'What now?' Like a magazine with its official circulation and then a much larger unofficial readership – all those people who borrow a friend of a friend's copy – Barbara Kott estimates that there could be as many as 200,000 new parents, mainly women, involved in NCT groups at any one time.

In contrast to the active volunteers, the members of these informal NTC groups don't do very much. That's the point of them. As one woman involved in a local group for nearly four years told me: 'In a way, you could say, all we do is meet. Every Tuesday afternoon and twice a week in the holidays. That's it! But to say that underestimates the huge importance of my group to me over the years. It's completely true what people say: the other mothers may not be people you would have chosen as friends but even that is interesting, to get to know, to get to like, people you would never have chosen to be friends with. It's a bit like family. I've got to know these women as well or better than old friends. I've seen them worrying about sleep – their own or their baby's – or when to start feeding solids or whether their toddler is clingy or how their three-year-old plays with other children. I think you see other mothers as they most see themselves, with all the masks of normal life – work life, social life – stripped away. You see them tired and happy and cross, just getting on with it.'

And these relationships last. Many groups keep meeting for years, well beyond school age. Twenty-two years later, Barbara Kott is still in touch with those women she met back in 1976. Has the fact that more women work these days limited the number of those who get involved with the NCT? 'I would have expected that to be true. But when women are having babies, they care passionately about what happens. They will find the time: to meet, to volunteer, to raise money. Especially part-time women. It surprises me, but we are as strong as ever.'

TALE TWO

Gaye came to London from a small village in Leicester in 1995. One of the first things she did was buy a copy of *The*

Lady in the local stationers to look at jobs advertised there, and rang each one from a phone box outside her friend's flat. Her mother had always said she had a good phone manner. Three women offered her an interview, but she didn't turn up for the last two. She was offered the first job on the spot. The house seemed enormous to her and a terrible mess, after her parents' neat ordered bungalow. There were five children, what seemed a dozen bikes, rabbits cavorting around the garden, a baby with a runny nose wailing on the kitchen floor. He was holding a green plastic colander, banging it over and over on the grimy floor. But the money was beyond her wildest dreams. One hundred and ten pounds, and she could eat her meals there. She had a tiny, cosy room at the top of the house; chintz furnishings, a little grubby; a full-length mirror, a rickety wooden cupboard. The curtains were lined with a black material that made it pitch dark when she closed them and made her a little scared. Her first few nights were dreamless; she was so tired, dazed by the complexity of the household.

The father, Richard, was a university lecturer; the mother, Susan, taught French in a local school. They smiled a lot, so she told herself they were nice people. Gaye dealt mainly with the mother, Susan: right from the start she seemed a little impatient, or perhaps it was just rushed, as if she had given instructions to young girls just one time too many. Sentences began with 'What-you-have-to-do-is . . .' or 'The-way-we-do-things-here-is . . .'. Gaye had a hard time remembering even the breakfast schedule. 'Everyone-gets-up-around-seven-although-the-girls-may-be-later-because-they-find-it-hard-to-get-up . . .' The two eldest children were twin girls, aged thirteen; then three boys, aged nine, three and eight months. On Gaye's first morning, the three-year-old came in and jumped on her while she was sleeping. A black room, a head full of sleep and a lot of thumping. She didn't mind it much, but she didn't want every day to start that way. She didn't yet know how to say 'stop' to a three-year-old, especially when he was the child of her employer.

Breakfast itself was a forest of cereals and a cloud of burning toast and spilt juice. Gaye had to give the baby a bottle and warm it to the right temperature while pouring out the older boys' cereal. The girls, thank God, could look after themselves. Then she had to ask everyone if they wanted toast. Susan and Richard seemed to be sleepwalking in the morning. Richard snatched things off surfaces and mainly shouted 'Don't! Don't!' or 'Careful! Careful!' at anyone who came near him. Susan *wheedled:* 'Darling, could you . . . just . . . get me an orange juice/fetch the paper from the mat . . .' or 'Gaye, *could* you just . . . take the laundry on your way upstairs?' and '*Would* you mind . . . putting it in the machine on your way up?' Somehow Richard and Susan made her feel uncomfortable just for being there, as if she was one child too many. The more she helped the more uncomfortable she felt.

Once the bigger children were taken off to school by their father, it was her job to get the three-year-old and the baby into a double buggy and take the three-year-old to nursery; then she had to bring the baby, Arthur, back home, play with him, prepare lunch, go back and pick up the three-year-old, bring them back and give them lunch. Susan said they should both sleep after lunch, but one or other of them never did. If she told Susan that they hadn't slept, she would give Gaye a look, that seemed to say, 'What did *you* do wrong?' Then it was over to yet another school to pick up the nine-year-old boy and take them all to the park. The nine-year-old's family nickname was Middle Boy, or MB for short: Gaye could never use it. She was the only one in the house who called him David. When they heard her the teenage girls would shout, in a united persecutory chorus, '*He's* not David. *He's* Middle Boy.' David was the only one she liked. He insisted on wearing shorts, even when it was a cold spring day. He wore glasses and was sad, a little serious. Most afternoons, when all five were back at home and jumping or crawling around the playroom, David was curled up quietly on the battered kitchen sofa reading a book. While she was preparing the vegetables for dinner he would tell her stories. He was so good at it that she even thought of buying the books that he was reading. Susan came in at about five o'clock. She was always at running speed, she never stopped. And she never said hello, except to the baby. Gaye would be standing at the counter, chopping, and the kitchen door would bang open and Arthur would begin to flap his chubby little arms and the first thing Gaye heard was, 'Hello my little darling, *precious*, Arty . . .' Susan was a woman who liked babies, which was why she kept having them. Once they had grown up she was not so interested in the people they became. There was rarely a 'hello' for David or the girls. And certainly not for Gaye.

After serving and washing up tea Gaye was supposed to get off. That was the deal. She had been working an almost straight twelve hours by then and she was falling asleep on her feet. But Susan had never said whether she was to get off at seven or after supper. She had only said, 'Supper-tends-to-be-about-seven-and-then-you're-finished.' Twice a week, Richard's mother came over for tea; a jolly lady in her seventies whom the children loved. She was pleasant to Gaye but the meal took twice as long as usual because she insisted on every child telling her something about their day and no-one could get up until they'd finished their pudding. It was well past seven-thirty before the oldest ones were up and away and off to do their homework and Gaye didn't finish washing up until after eight.

She found it hard to be 'off' in a house so full of chaos. In the beginning she tried to go into the sitting-room and watch the television, but either the older girls piled in and wanted to talk to her or watch their own programme or someone wandered in needing clothes taking off or pyjamas put on. Worst of all, Richard sometimes came home early and wanted his quiet whisky and newspaper in the chair in the corner. Susan would wander in and out of the room talking to him, glancing at Gaye as if she were a piece of unhoovered dust. Gaye decided to go to her room after supper. There, she heard only thuds and muffled screams. For the first half-hour she lay, blissfully unbothered, revelling in her stillness, usually dropping into a deep sleep.

Then there was a tap. And another tap. Then a slightly impatient bare-knuckled rap.

'Gaye? Gaye? Are you there?' Susan's voice.

There was a problem. Arthur was teething. David had cut his leg. There was nobody to give the three-year-old his bath and it was getting so late, 'he'll be too tired and bad-tempered for nursery tomorrow'. In the first months, Gaye had tried to imitate calm, if not enthusiasm, when these interruptions occurred: 'Fine. Fine. I'll be down.' But by the sixth or seventh such request, in as many weeks, she merely complied, sullenly. 'Yes, all right', spinning out the words 'all right' to make it clear that it was not. Usually, this happened at bathtime. Susan obviously couldn't cope with it and Richard was usually not in.

There was never extra payment for this extra hour, in addition to the extra hour washing up supper. It was still one hundred and ten pounds, flat on the kitchen table, on a Saturday morning. There was never any payment back either for money spent on the children. If she took three of them to the park, for instance, they wanted ice-creams and drinks and she could come back with over five pounds spent. Once she mentioned it to Susan, unable to ask directly for the money. Nothing was offered.

The money remained one hundred and ten. Two gorgeous red fifty-pound notes and the pinky blooded ten. Richard got the money out when he did the Saturday morning shop with the girls and the three-year-old. That was a nice quiet time: Susan, cooing with the baby in the bedroom, Gaye and David sitting in the tidied, sunny playroom playing chess or cards, the sun glinting off his glasses. She felt sorry for him, he was so self-sufficient. He was nine, but he would sometimes come up to her, dressed in the inevitable shorts and a duffel coat and ask if she would help him do up all his toggles. He didn't really need the help.

He just liked her.

'Where are you going?'

'Just a brief walk.'

That was his father speaking: just a brief this, just a brief that.

'Are you allowed?'

'Oh, yes.'

And the door would slam, the only thing loud about the little boy, and he was gone, for half an hour, sometimes an hour. The first time, Gaye panicked. But David always came back. He had to stand on tiptoe to ring the bell to get back in the house. She wanted to know where he had gone but he would never tell her. Having secrets was his revenge against a family who didn't want to know them anyway.

Gaye stayed with the family for six months, March to October. It was winter that did it for her. She knew she couldn't stay through afternoons of rain, and cold so biting they could not go out to the park. There was mutual resentment between her and her 'employer'. She knew they found her sullen, particularly about those evening calls to help with bathtime. She knew they found her inflexible, unwilling to give up Saturday afternoons if one of the children was ill and needed minding while the family went out. 'It's a very special thing, a large family. It requires particular skills,' Susan chided her. They thought she was petty, minding about buying the children ice-creams and lollies, and the children thought she was mean, when she said, drinks only.

Over the months, Gaye had made friends with a few other nannies and mothers in the park. She was careful with the mothers, but she told the other nannies what she was 'going through'. They all said, leave when you can. Look on the notice board of the café. Look in *The Lady* again or some of the free sheets. In the end, she got a new job through word of mouth. She was to 'live in' again; a mother, recently divorced, and her two boys. She told Susan on a Monday. By

Wednesday, a new girl had started and Gaye had to find a place to stay until the following week when she could move into the new job. She never saw David again.

The nanny state

Both literature and popular culture have mined the seam of female 'twinning': the ways in which women, searching for both intimacy and a sense of identity, closely observe and sometimes even mirror each other. This can be in a depiction of pure evil, as in Jennifer Jason Leigh's chilling portrait of a malicious flatmate to Bridget Fonda's easy-going young fashion designer in *Single White Female* or a story as complex and benign as Christa Wolf's masterpiece, *In Search of Christa T*, in which the narrator tells the story of the apparently ordinary life and death of her best friend, whose personal history mirrored that of post-war Germany.

The nanny/mother relationship can, on the surface at least, evoke similar echoes of intimacy and even interchangeability. This is a job without the usual boundaries. There is no uniform, rarely a job description. There is no mission statement or timetable of objectives. Mother and nanny may even be close in age, aspiration, experience. There is little formality: this employee may see her employer more often in a dressing-gown, hair dishevelled, than in her work clothes. She may sit down to breakfast with the family every day, gossip idly over endlessly renewable pots of tea. She may overhear arguments of an intimate nature. She may be party to family secrets, marital problems. She may confide secrets herself. At the end of a working day when she hands over her charges, she and the mother may regularly talk in more detail about the activities and character of the children than the mother does with the father of her children.

As more and more 'ordinary' women hire nannies, cleaners, baby-sitters and even women to iron their clothes, there is a suggestion that female intimacy creates a relationship untouched by the tensions of employer/employee. A 1992 *Guardian* article on the domestic labour boom chose to illustrate the article with a sequence of three shots: two women, standing in an ordinary

living-room, talking, laughing, contemplating. 'Geologist Gill
Weightman and cleaner Jackie Benford.' One stands behind an
ironing-board, the other perches on the side of the sofa; otherwise
they look like friends. The article describes how:

> Jackie Benford works for Gill Weightman near Leicester.
> Both are 34 and have three children; they met outside the
> school. Weightman pays Benford £10.50 for three and a half
> hours. 'I like working for Gill because she's ordinary,' says
> Benford. '*She could be cleaning my house if things were the other
> way round* [my emphasis].'

But things are never the other way round. (Could I be the
Governor of the Bank of England if things were the 'other way
round'?) While many relationships between mother and nanny
are excellent and consistently good-tempered and these invariably
tend to be underpinned by fair treatment, fair wages and
appropriate distance, others are riven by unspoken hostilities,
such as Gaye's experience. Many childcare workers are in the
eighteen to twenty-four age range; there can be a tension
between the generations. The mother weighed down by
responsibilities and the grim fact of ageing feels a stab of jealousy
at the freedom of the young woman, the very fact that she can, at
shift's end, walk away from the family. The younger woman is
still free: she has not yet made the irrevocable decision to have
children. In turn, she can feel envy of the mother's professional
competence or earning power, her place in the world, usually a
middle-class one of airy gardens and ample living space.

There can often be an unacknowledged class element to the
tension. If we had sat and listened to Gaye's employer, Susan, talk
about Gaye we might well have heard complaint, disparagement,
unconscious patronage. Among some mothers, there is an almost
imperceptible sense that the women who look after their children
are 'down there'; sweet but not substantial. Illogically, they may
feel that when a nanny looks after their children, it is, to use Kate
Saunders' disparaging phrase, 'nanny work', whereas when they
look after their own children they are as likely to call it 'quality

time'. Some of the patronage undoubtedly results from that peculiarly unattractive quality in the British character that unconsciously classifies people according to ethnicity, class, education and income. A few women talk to, and about, their nannies with that 'edge' to their voice that some men use with their secretaries or some arrogant rich people use with waiters and waitresses. At its absolute worst, it is cruelty. At its best, it is an unimaginative patronage that cannot see the lives of others having equal weight to one's own. In both cases, it amounts to a profound lack of respect.

This lack of respect is doubly ironic. First, it often comes from women who demand respect in the 'outer world' of work and public affairs, who believe they have intrinsic value, social and financial, as working women. Second, most parents assume their parental love; they declare, however unthinkingly, that their children are the most important thing in the world to them. It should follow from this that those who look after their children are doing the most important job in the world. The more modest a parent, the more likely they are to act as if that were the case: to be concerned for the carer's well-being and conditions of work. The more unthinking a parent, the more likely they are to think a badly paid carer is getting all they deserve or a well-paid carer is 'very well off indeed'. (Note the tone of voice.) 'It costs me an arm and a leg' is one of the less attractive phrases used by parents about nannies. And yet, following through the notion that looking after children is the most valuable job in the world, nanny work should be paid somewhere between a solicitor's and a stockbroker's rate of pay.

TALE THREE

Every Friday, Paula, a part-time medical researcher, goes to her building society and takes out a hundred and fifty pounds. She stuffs it in the deepest pocket of her trousers because she is nervous about being mugged coming away from a cashpoint. The money pays a childminder for two mornings and a nanny for two days a week. The childminder, Yvonne, is registered with the local authority. But Catherine, the nanny, is not. Neither Paula nor Catherine declare the income for tax.

Most weeks, Paula is paying Catherine more than she has earned. Her husband tops up the rest on a monthly basis. As well as the basic pay, Paula keeps a scrupulous watch on everything Catherine pays out in fares, drinks, sweets, trips and outings. If the boys go somewhere interesting, like a museum, this 'additional money' can amount to ten or fifteen pounds a week. Very occasionally, Paula lets Catherine treat the boys and pay for outings or food herself. But only if Catherine insists.

'If we go out in the week as well, just once the two of us, that could be another thirty or forty pounds. That makes it two hundred pounds a week just to have our children looked after for a part of the time. Neither of us have relatives living nearby, only my brother, who loves them and visits frequently, but has never offered to baby-sit. Friends have not either. The ones with children are too busy. The ones without don't seem to think of it or want to do it. It's like everything is done on a cash basis nowadays. All the people we know are just too busy.

'Sometimes I wonder if I'm mad to work. It's not an economic thing, obviously. I mean it's not for profit. After paying Catherine I have virtually nothing left for myself. Clothes, books, CDs, all that is a thing of the past. I wait for birthdays or Christmas and just try to look as smart as I can in the meantime. I enjoy the work very much. But it's also the idea of myself as separate from the children. I'm paying for the continuation of my sense of me, existing out there in the world, the separateness I used to take for granted, the separateness I never had to pay anyone for. I keep thinking that by the time the boys get to school, I'll be glad I shelled out all that money just to keep going.

'At the same time, I feel bad that Catherine, in particular, is getting so little money. We pay her better than most of her peers, but it's still only six pounds an hour. A hundred and fifty seems a lot in a lump sum, but as an hourly rate it works out a lot less than I would expect to get for most jobs. It's like this double standard is in operation. The work she does which is supposed to be the most important work in the world gets the lowest pay. And there's mine, that can command a much higher market value. It's mad, I think. But we all accept it, parents and workers. Some parents don't even have the imagination to question it. But someone like me is just too bloody scared. If we paid her a living wage, I wouldn't be able to work. Simple as that.'

Money talks, and the women who count

The fundamental contradiction of childcare in Britain today is this: for those who can afford it, childcare can be a family's major expense, eating up a larger share of the annual income than food, rent or mortgage. Yet they are paying wages for one of the lowest-paid occupations in the country. In a 1997 assessment of a Coventry family where both parents work full-time with two children, aged two-and-a-half and seven, the Daycare Trust found the family paid £5,915 per year for a combination of private nursery places, out of school clubs and play schemes, compared to £3,868.28 per year spent on food for the family.[9]

Childcare workers are frequently on breadline wages. Childminders earn anything from an appalling £1 an hour up to a barely adequate (but rare) £4. Rarely do these fees take into account the hidden costs of childminding: annual insurance and daily wear and tear on just about everything from clothes to domestic appliances and furniture plus the cost of food, toiletries, cleaning materials and that most expensive of commodities, toys. One childminder, who looks after two one-year-olds, one of them her own, told me that toys, resources of an educational nature and the cost of washing or replacing covers and cushions costs her as much as £1 out of her £2 an hour fee. An au-pair can expect up to £40 a week plus board; an 'au-pair plus', who works longer hours, up to £80. Nannies can earn anything from £80 to £260 a week, depending on hours worked and whether they live in or out. Compare this average hourly rate to other jobs: a sales assistant at £4.20 an hour, a secretary at £6.10, a primary or nursery school teacher at £13.

The childcare gap indicates how society has polarized in two distinct ways; first, between those who can afford any kind of formal childcare and those who cannot, between the Elizabeths of Tale One and the Susans and Paulas of Tales Two and Three. The really 'work rich' can buy time to work more, which then earns them more money to buy more time away from their children, and so on. It can be a spurious freedom, because it is freedom from the core concerns of one's life: no-one has children in order to leave them in someone else's care twenty-four hours a day. Those who do are none the happier for it.

But the other polarization, between those who pay for formal childcare and those who provide it, is equally telling. In all its aspects, from attitudes to finance, it tells us more about how some women 'count' more than others. It tells us something about the new, strange ways that class and class-as-income differences exist in modern Britain: how the counterpart to the successful woman is often the woman who services her. Our knowledge of the first is far greater than our knowledge of the second.

This was the often unspoken set of values underlying the resignation of Zoë Baird, President Clinton's nominee for the post of Attorney General in 1992. Before taking up office officially in January, Clinton selected Baird to be America's first ever female Attorney General. In late January of 1993, he had to withdraw the nomination after it emerged that Baird had knowingly broken the law by hiring two 'illegal aliens' as household help – the so-called 'Nannygate' scandal. On the face of it, this was a story about a top working woman whose career was sabotaged by her difficulty in reconciling home and work commitments: many professionals employ nannies, cleaners, drivers without officially registering their status or paying tax. According to one press report:

Ms Baird, 40, a corporate lawyer who last year earned $500,000 [£325,000], and husband, Paul Gewirtz, a Yale law professor, hired a Peruvian woman to look after their infant son, and also her husband as a driver. Each was paid $12,000 plus board. But neither had permits to work in the United States. Ms Baird did not pay social security taxes on the couple's wages, a lapse for which she has paid a civil fine . . . to the immigration service of one of the departments which would come under her authority as attorney general . . . *Ms Baird told senators of her desperate search for childcare and of having the Peruvians because no-one else suitable could be found. The modern dilemma of juggling career and motherhood is making some senators reluctant to judge Ms Baird too harshly* [my emphasis] . . .[10]

Baird's bungle gave us a rare insight into how some very rich, very competent women have come to organize their lives – the price of it, the cost of it; whom they rely on, and whom they don't. But it was interesting for other reasons. While we learned, in some considerable detail, about Baird's life and salary, we did not even learn the names of the 'illegal immigrants', a man and wife, whom she had hired. They remained types, defined simply by their nationality (Peruvian) or their labour (Baird had hired them to drive and baby-sit). But this man and woman showed us something very important about current assumptions about working parenthood and particularly working motherhood. It was rather like watching a play and suddenly the spotlight swings to the 'wrong' part of the stage, deep back. And there are a group of people, talking. We realize immediately that they are central to the action, in some way that they should not be: that their presence and demeanour illuminate a set of relations crucial to the play proper being enacted out front. The smart among us see: this may not be part of the script but it is certainly at the heart of the story.

If our contemporary politics is to be complete and have real meaning we must not only know who these people at the back of the stage are. We must know their story as well as we know Zoë Baird's and the women like her. We must not only know its objective conditions – everything from conditions of work to pay and housing – but we must enter it as subjectively as Baird asks us to enter hers. We must practise its nuances, imagine its resentments and joys. And politically we must continue to ask: why do some working mothers count more than others? In current political and media discussion, the working mother tends to be someone like Baird at the top, moving down the professional scale to a woman like Paula in Tale Three: struggling, part-time but still a professional. Yet many women who look after children are also working mothers. Perhaps the Peruvian woman that Baird hired was a mother. Who looked after her child while she baby-sat Zoë Baird's? Whom did she pay and how much? What were *her* arrangements?

I sometimes sit and make a mental list of the mothers, working or not, whom we know about and those whom we don't, those who count and those who don't. Working mothers who *don't* count include childminders, factory workers and secretaries. Mothers, in general, who don't count include women in prison, unemployed mothers and, of course, the biggest hate figures of them all: the single mother on benefit. From whatever part of the political spectrum you come, no account of modern motherhood is complete without reference to her. What, then, is her story?

~ 8 ~

Babies on Benefit: Alternative Cardiff Conversations

> The first and most general expression of the contented
> majority is its affirmation that those who compose it are
> receiving their just desserts. What the individual
> member aspires to have and enjoy is the product of his
> or her personal virtue, intelligence and effort. Good
> fortune being earned or the reward of merit, there is no
> equitable justification for any action that impairs it – that
> subtracts from what is enjoyed or what might be
> enjoyed. The normal response to such action is
> indignation or . . . anger at anything infringing on what
> is so clearly deserved.
>
> J. K. Galbraith, *The Culture of Contentment*,
> Penguin, 1992

Over the last ten years, one kind of mother has come to be seen
as central to society's trouble. In the United States, she has long
had the grand and racialized title of 'welfare queen'.[1] In Britain,
the debate and disgust has coalesced around the figure of the
single mother. For the new right and traditional liberals,
increasingly authoritarian from the mid eighties onwards, it was
the single mother who was at the root of all that was wrong in
society; crime, lack of gainful employment, especially for young
men, the growing benefits bill, rising divorce rates. What actually

terrified people was their fear of a growing lawless minority; men who mugged pensioners for their weekly money or boys in balaclavas, joy-riding on the roads of housing estates long abandoned by hope. But in the new attempt to draw everything back to moral – rather than economic – causes, the metaphorical mothers were held as responsible, if not more so, than the actual sons.

Such an attitude has deep emotional roots. There are surprisingly many adults who hold their mothers responsible for what has gone wrong with their lives. Even the well-cared-for are, at some level, disappointed and resentful; successful men of forty will deliver long, bitter perorations about a love not given, a care not shown to them, all those years ago. They may not know their anger; it may instead be projected onto a woman or child. Alternatively, they may demonstrate a surprising unkindness to a now frail older parent, all the while betraying a still strong connection to their first love.

But the panic over single mothers has a social history, too. We understand the social character of prejudice only too well when the story takes place a generation ago (or a country away). Here, now, we can *feel* the injustice meted out to young girls who 'fell' and had to be ferried away from the community to give shameful birth out of town, in secret and alone. Back then, too many of us might have silently accepted the moral language that allowed such misery. We can too easily forget the terrible shame that attended the 'unmarried mother' as recently as the 1960s. That spectre of immorality may have faded – and we should be glad for it – but it has arisen thirty years later in new form; this time imbued with more, not less, class fear and hatred.

For the single mother most despised over the last few years has not, on the whole, been the financially viable woman in her late twenties or thirties who chooses to have a child on her own, or the one who finds herself separated or divorced but quite able, economically speaking, to cope. Within this category, lesbian mothers have been the most persecuted, once more accused of unnatural practices, this time, in divorcing procreation from heterosexuality or arguing for custody of children born from previous marriages.[2] But the growth and new strength of single mothers was beginning to have a noticeable impact on society. A black single mother in Bristol, who had her first child in 1970, and her second ten years later, told me that she had found it 'much easier to be a mother and alone in the 1980s. There was a lot more said about us, a lot more places for us to go.' The real pariah of this era is the woman without man or independent means who 'falls', this time on the state. As the 1980s progressed, morality became tied in with Thatcherite economics. 'Dependency' on welfare, lack of dependency on a man, became the real crime.

Yet it was, interestingly, in the period after Margaret Thatcher left office (1990) that the real crusade against single mothers took off. Thatcher herself had prosecuted a prolonged ideological war against the welfare state but she had, on the whole, restricted her named enemies to socialism and Argentina. Her replacement as Prime Minister, John Major, appeared a more sympathetic figure: he had a single-parent sister, Pat, who told the *Daily Express* she always found her brother willing to listen to her. It was the more militant forces of the party, who were gathering and jostling for position in a possible post-Major party, who took up the particular war against lone mothers. John Redwood, then Minister for Wales, and a marginal figure in the Conservative government, emerged as what the pundits like to call a 'credible' figure when he challenged John Major for the leadership of the Conservative Party in 1994. One of the key planks of his campaign was his stated disapproval of the breakdown of the family, and in particular the flight of fathers from those families.

Visiting the St Mellon's estate in Cardiff, in 1993, John Redwood described the phenomenon of families without fathers as 'one of the biggest social problems of our day'. It was this visit, this statement, which marked out more than any other, in the public eye at least, a Redwood version of conservatism. In September of that year Michael Portillo, another leading right-winger, further fuelled the debate. *The Times* reported Mr Portillo as expressing the view that 'Teenage girls could be lured into a life of poverty-stricken dependency by over-generous benefit – pointing out payments to lone mothers were the fastest growing item in the £80 billion social security budget.' 'How,' Mr Portillo asked, 'can we help people to avoid becoming poor?'

The touchpaper was lit. The British media do not love so much as need a debate. In this era of a hundred outlets and fierce competition their commercially powered voracity is such that a single scrap is enough to cook up a feast. Following up on Redwood's comments, a team from the BBC's increasingly populist *Panorama* visited the St Mellon's estate. However, while the ostensible aim of both John Redwood and *Panorama* was to illuminate the problem of absent fathers, *Panorama* trained its guns on those who were there and constant: mothers and young mothers in particular. One of the harshest of many harsh criticisms of the programme was that it conveyed the impression that the actions and motivations of a relatively small number of teenage mothers, nationally speaking, somehow represented the problems of single mothers as a whole. In fact, most of Britain's single mothers are older and have been in partnerships, often for years, that end for many complex reasons.

But *Panorama* found their teenage mothers, and the cameras were trained on the apparently calm faces of young, irrational and selfish choice. The young women were presented not as lacking in choices about their lives, but as calculating, almost castrating, creatures; in turn, the babies on their childish knees seemed not symbols of care, concern and love but a further aspect of their coldness. If anything, the programme presented the absent fathers as both more sympathetic than the mothers and yet pathetically bewildered that the women didn't need them. There was little concentration on what they, like the young women they had once made love to, did not possess, like a job or real hope of fulfilling a greater aim in life. The young men's failure to be good parents was presented not as a social, but as an entirely individual problem. Not only was it beyond their control, it was as a result of the *women's* misplaced strength. The chance to explore the more complex reasons for teenage pregnancy was lost. As Angela Y. Davis has written of this phenomenon, in relation to the question of black teenage pregnancy in America:

There are reasons why young Black women become pregnant and/or desire pregnancy . . . few young women who choose pregnancy are offered an alternative range of opportunities for self-expression and development . . . Is it really so hard to grasp why so many young women would choose motherhood? Isn't this path toward adulthood still thrust upon them by the old but persisting ideological constructions of femaleness? Doesn't motherhood still equal adult womanhood in the popular imagination? . . . I would venture to say that many young women make conscious decisions to bear children in order to convince themselves that they are alive and creative human beings. As a consequence of this choice, they are also characterized as immoral for not marrying the fathers of their children.[3]

Politically, the programme ran with an almost entirely right-wing agenda. 'Babies on Benefit' examined American attempts to 'cap' the state payments of women with more than one child on welfare. The potential or actual tragedy of mothers and children not having enough to eat or anywhere to stay was not fully explored; rather, the state was presented as the hapless victim of individually selfish procreation. In Britain, the programme went to the Conservative flagship borough of Wandsworth, where a well-heeled chair of social services confronted a group of young single mothers about their irresponsible behaviour in having children without fathers or an independent income. The confrontation was a little forced and more than a little absurd, although the young women gave as good as they got. 'If you're going to wait until you've got enough money to have a child,' said one, 'you're never going to have a child.' 'I need help to get out to work,' said another, bristling at the suggestion that life on the 'social' was a happily chosen or easy option.

'Babies on Benefit' is a good example of the way the media can intervene in, shape and distort an issue. But in this case, it backfired. Campaign groups were not just furious about the distortions of the programme, particularly about the idea that a significant number of single parents are teenagers; they made sure

that they set the record straight *publicly*. The memory of the insult
lingers on, however. I, for instance, still remember the reporter:
her voice, its exact intonations. Whenever I see her, now on quite
different 'duties', I feel a shiver of professional dislike. Mention
'Babies on Benefit' to most single parents and they will grimace
with fury, exasperation or sadness.

Nearly three years after that defining moment in 1993, I returned
to Cardiff, to visit an estate just a few miles from St Mellon's, to
talk in detail to three single parents. It had not been a good three
years. 'Babies on Benefit' did not staunch the flow of criticism of
single parents: it kept it boiling over. Both the main parties had
accepted that one of the problems of our society was the rising
benefits bill. Peter Lilley, the cherubic fiscal Conservative, had
made a number of speeches as Social Security Minister in 1993
and 1994, including his famous *Mikado* spoof 'I have a little list'
speech about girls who jump the queue to get housing for
themselves. Tory party conference speeches are always a chance
for exaggerated, sometimes camp, performance but they do not
always result in petty or substantial enforcement. In this case, they
did. In the winter budget of 1995/6, additional payments on child
benefit to lone parents were scrapped. New claimants from April
1998 will receive only standard child benefit, a measure that New
Labour has sadly decided to uphold.

These financial changes were little remarked upon in the
mainstream press. To the comfortably off the cuts appeared to
involve minuscule amounts, a few pounds a week. Yet most
women on benefit are managing on what the well off spend on
food alone. A single mother with two children under eleven
receives approximately £98 a week (at April 1997 rates). Like the
government, and the then Labour opposition, the core of Middle
England could not see that, as in a nightmare, a little money taken
away from a small amount has a correspondingly larger impact on
those so deprived.

It was warm and sunny on the day I visited Cardiff. In the wavy
heat, the estate looked like something between a peaceful
American suburb and a model village. The bus deposited me, a

lumbering eight and a half months pregnant, off at the side of a wide boulevard: the streets had the feel of a rational plan; plenty of grass, space. They were almost empty, this weekday lunchtime. The estate is to the north of Cardiff. Like most of Cardiff's housing estates, it is largely made up of houses, with a few blocks of low-rise flats. These days they are a mix of council and privately owned.

Jackie lives in a chaotic, cheerful house, overstuffed with pictures, knick-knacks, dusty bottles of half-drunk brandy, figurines; *things*. A mongrel dog, half rottweiler, gently paws the baby kitten Jackie rescued from the local post office a few days before. A baby blue budgie screeches in its cage, as insistent as a parrot. The living-room is stuffed with old, soft-covered deep chairs and a sofa. Prints and paintings of tigers line the wall.

Jackie has two boys, aged thirteen and fifteen, whom she has brought up on her own since her husband walked out nearly ten years ago: two tall, handsome, self-contained, curious, fed-up teenage boys. The younger wants, one day, to train as a crèche worker. At one point he interrupts our conversation to tell us, insistently, that there are lots of good dads, that men can look after children, and this after hearing a roomful of women bemoaning men's lack of care for families. When I leave, he is sitting at the bottom of the stairs, looking wistful.

Jackie was married at twenty. She had her first son a year later, 'both events, far too young'. Her husband was in a peripatetic job, 'He's a megabucks in the Far East now,' she says without rancour: '1987 wasn't a good year. My father had died earlier that year, in the July. My husband said to me, we must move back home to be near your mum. We'd just moved when he walked out in the December. He had chosen the house and everything. I would never have chosen a place like this, the garden's too big. I hate gardening. He left me with huge debts, not just the mortgage but gas, electricity, the lot. I'm still paying them off. After he went it was horrendous. We had, still have, a complete change of lifestyle. It was that year interest rates zoomed up, I got an Attachment of Earnings order against him, £375 a month and thank God the CSA (Child Support Agency) didn't fiddle with it.

I was working as well, part-time in a local supermarket when he first left. But I was worse off on that and family credit, than I was on income support. And the childcare was costing me too much. I stopped when the shop closed down, anyway. But I enjoy working. I'm a people person. I just found it really difficult, working and being worse off, rushing round and getting the kids and then having no money. So when the shop closed down, I lived on the maintenance topped up by income support. It was a complete change of circumstances. We'd had a good wage and I'd worked because I wanted to work but also at the end because I couldn't stand being in the house all day because of the affairs he'd had. I believed then that if you were married, you should stay married. The me now doesn't but the me then did. We could go out a couple of times a week. We ate well. There was always good food in the cupboard and there was always a choice. We invariably bought beer and wine. Decent clothes. If the kids needed a pair of shoes, they got them. My youngest now has just got a new pair of trainers. He had a hole in the last pair for three years.'

Does their father stay in touch?

'The kids haven't seen him for two years. He wrote to them to tell them he had had a baby by his new marriage, nine months previously. That was two years ago.'

While we are talking, Stella arrives. A small woman, she is a whirlwind of energy. Her blonde hair is smartly cut, she wears a pressed white blouse, neat blue skirt, pearl button earrings. She knows Jackie's story, picks up a point in the middle of a sentence, as if this is a very familiar conversation to her. For a while, Jackie and Stella bat the questions back and forth: why do the men go? What went wrong in our case? Is there something in us that picks the bad ones?

One of the assumptions of the participants in the morality debate that took off from the late 1980s onwards is that single parents have somehow chosen their situation. There is an assumption that they have 'let' their marriages fail, that they didn't work hard enough at them. It's as if lone parenting is the result of an over-assertiveness on the part of women and a misplaced feminist belief in autonomy. They lay the blame on a new kind of politics that has broken down people's ability to endure, women's ability to endure.[4] Yet there was hardly a woman I talked to who did not express a longing for the once-upon-a-time certainty of the old relationship, if not the particular man of old. There was hardly a woman who didn't wish for a new relationship to work as well. What struck me about Jackie and Stella was their deep sense of hurt, their unresolved anger against their faithless ex-husbands, but there was absolutely no rejection of men as a whole.

Stella met her husband 'when I was working behind a bar. He was lovely. A relative of his introduced us. I should kill her really, shouldn't I? I thought he was a nice enough man; quiet, shy. We got together. We had a lovely child. And then things changed. He started working for his brother who ran his own business. All the business was arranged through his brother. There was this one client, I knew my husband knew her and liked her. She started ringing the house three, four times a week. I got on the phone and said to her one time, "You listen to me. This is my husband's home number. You want to talk to him about business, you ring his brother." I know he even told her not to ring. But things started changing. His mother got very ill. I fell pregnant again. In the meantime I knew he'd seen her. You know you can tell when things aren't fine. You just know. It's your marriage. There was friction. When the baby was born, I was down. I was down during the pregnancy and then down after it. I was very, very depressed. Harry, our second child, must have been about eight weeks old when I got this job cleaning. It was partly because my husband said some of our problems were money problems. So I got this job cleaning; five until eight in the morning. I had to be home in time for him to leave for work. But he hated me, for bringing in the money. He hated me for trying. The more I did the more he resented it.'

Convinced that her husband was having an affair, but unable to get him to admit it, Stella eventually filed for separation and then divorce while he was still living in the house. Her husband later confessed to her that the affair had been going on for years, as she'd thought, but he would not leave. 'I literally had to inch him out the house bit by bit.' The pain and anger of that time are with her still, six years later.

'Whatever I did was wrong. He would turn his back on me. I said to him, "You've got to understand. I'm a person. I've got to be loved too." You couldn't have asked for a better father for the children; loving and caring. And we never rowed in front of the children because I'd had all that in my childhood and I didn't want it for mine. But everything about me was wrong. He hated that I could do things men could do. I could change a plug. I could earn money if I had to. I could even get under the bonnet of a car and fix a spark plug. I could do what men do, you see, and he hated that in me. He said that was the problem with us. I was too *emancipated*. That was his word for me.'

He finally left. Stella had to go on income support. 'He even filled the form in for me,' she says drily. Shortly after, her husband became unemployed and couldn't give her anything. Even the Child Support Agency agreed. Stella's housing costs are paid and her part-time wages are topped up with family credit. She says, 'I work part-time, ten till two at the local hospital. I love my work. I hated being on social security. I like to be out and doing. That's me, the kind of woman I am.'

Stella's job pays her just over a hundred a week, plus she gets £245 family credit a month and £25.90 a week in child benefit and (what was then) single parent benefit. She said: '£460 goes in bills and mortgage, gas, electric and my one extravagance, the catalogue club. But the catalogue is for necessities, really, winter shoes, curtains when you're desperate. We spend £25 a week on food. One week, we do a big shop for tins, you know, cheap soups and whatever. We all tell each other whoever has an offer on. The other week we buy washing powder, washing-up liquid, bleach, shampoo. Toilet rolls; we use them sparingly in our house. One packet of biscuits a week, crisps for their school bag, juice, squash, cheese and ham for their sandwiches, my daughter won't eat anything else. Don't buy coffee and we make our tea bags last.'

When did she last go out? 'Let me see. It was my birthday. May.'

'This May . . . ?'

'No, last May. May 1995 . . .'

Jackie breaks in, 'That's not true. You came to that committee thingy . . .'

'No I didn't.'

Jackie agrees: no, she didn't.

'I don't mind all that . . . going out.' Stella waves it away. 'I made a decision about what I was going to do for my children. Their security comes first. Anyway, we're going on our first holiday, me and the kids. Two weeks, a package. We've been saving for I don't know how long. My daughter gave up her bike money to put towards it. When my contract on my job was renewed, we booked it.'

Her face is a picture of triumph. If you looked at that face, without words or explanation to accompany it, you would think, this woman has won ten thousand on the scratch cards or met the lover of her dreams. The delight is so intense, so particular.

How do they get away with it, I wonder later? How do government ministers and well-paid columnists and conservative 'thinkers' get away with attacking these women who talk, without self-pity, even with a laugh, at the ways they make twenty-five pounds a week buy enough food for a house of one adult and two growing children? And why aren't the women themselves throwing stones through windows or overturning cars in the street when told to tighten their belts or pull their moral bootstraps up? Stupid question: history shows that women have never thrown that many stones or burned cars in the street. Energy: that's part of the answer. Most of their energy goes into calculating the numbers that rule their lives, and loving their children. They are proud with me, the very pregnant stranger, but they tell me that they tell each other a lot, if not everything. They are alone, spending most nights in, and they are often lonely. But they are not lonely in one important sense: they have each other. They know all the other women are on their own too. It's a communion through the evening, through the night, of sorts.

And for the hundredth time I think how true that social being determines consciousness. You don't understand the dimensions of a life you are not required to live. Empathy, imagination, the best political and personal will in the world, won't vault you over that chasm in experience. It won't take *me* there. I can only try to match it to roughly similar experiences: the way that since having children and working, there's been these eternal, infernal sums in my head: weekly, monthly, yearly sums. Will it balance out by the end of this month or the next? Will that bit of money come in, in time to pay for that item that I need, that bill? I take small but definite pleasure in my own saving. I enjoy the excitement of generating a surplus; it sends me into a local shop to finger the silky soft material of new shirts or a skirt on the rack that I can now afford. But, as one of the comfortable if precariously employed middle class, I am thinking sums on a different scale.

Jackie and Stella, however, are doing their own imagining. Later in the afternoon, they talk about one woman in their group: 'You go to her house. And there is absolutely nothing. There is *nothing*. No knick-knacks, nothing on the walls and shelves. All the things that make a home.' For a moment, they sound desperately sad. So they are better off than someone else: we all are. In their case, this awareness of relativism makes for absolute generosity and anger. In the month before we met, Conservative Social Security Minister Peter Lilley had made a speech about how people aren't poor any more because they've got television and videos. 'I need my television,' says Jackie, 'and my video. They are not luxuries. They are necessities.' It sounds odd, at first. For a second, my ear retunes to middle England and hears the expected reactions: necessity, what nonsense! And then I am listening again to what is being said to me about these lives, here and now. Jackie is right, in general and about herself. As community and the old convivialities that went with it diminish, television represents the technological version of necessary companionship. The number of times I have switched it on, when at home alone, both before and after the babies were born, just to hear human voices, to believe myself not alone with the creaks and echoes of an empty house and my own thoughts. Television and radio and the telephone are the cheapest forms of confirming that you are not alone. (In Sheffield, Jean Selwood, a worker at Scoopaid, an organization for single parents, told me she thought that the government should pay one-parent families' phone bills because it saved so many other kinds of trouble, depression and self-destruction. She was not entirely joking.) A trip out at night involves all sorts of fares and forfeits. Even a pizza with a friend is going to cost you over twenty pounds if you include babysitting and a beer. Twenty pounds is an impossible sum for Jackie and Stella. But they can, at least, watch people eating pizzas on television and feel part of that cosy, busy world. If government ministers had any sense they'd be doing more than paying these women's phone bills. They would be giving away televisions to those on benefits. Let them watch Channel 5!

This question of other people describing, despoiling, legislating for other people's lives haunts me in the days after my visit to Cardiff. On the train home I think about Members of Parliament who have recently voted themselves a pay rise of 26 per cent. When taken as a question of parity, it seems utterly fair. Why should an MP be paid less than a head teacher of a largish comprehensive? I am the daughter, granddaughter and great-granddaughter of Members of Parliament, the sister of a local councillor; all of them conscientious and hard-working. I know what they deserve. No, my problem lies somewhere else: where exactly? It is partly in the fact that even representative democracy has an unattractive element of *de haut en bas* within it. Perhaps that can't be helped, particularly on the Tory side. But it goes deeper. I am permanently uneasy about modern definitions of res-ponsibility and value. We may quarrel with and snipe at MPs, journalists, school heads, hospital managers, but we also grant them a value based on their public profile and financial impor-tance. Listen to the barely audible wheeze of admiration when someone's salary or position is mentioned or we are told the number of people they have 'under them'. Even in the mid to late 1990s the spirit of the eighties is, as Julie Burchill perceived, still around us. (She just happened to think it a good thing; I am not so sure.) In contrast, a raft of other jobs based on the idea of public service such as nurses and teachers are both disregarded and financially unrewarded. As the idea of public service has waned,

fewer and fewer people respect those who work towards the
social, the public good. I read somewhere the other day that the
highest percentage of graduates want to go into the media: what
a terrible thought. At the bottom of the pyramid of value are the
many women who draw money from the state to do their utterly
disreputable (sic) job of bringing up two or three children to be
decent, loving, committed citizens. In our current hierarchy of
values, these women are so far down the bottom of the pile they
almost do not register. It makes me angry and ashamed of our
public values that we have got so many things about people and
work and priorities so wrong.

The day after I get back from Cardiff, I hear Frank Field,
Labour MP, being questioned about his plans for social security
on an unbelievably pompous BBC Radio 4 programme called
'The National Interest'. Sally Witcher, the plain-speaking head of
the Child Poverty Action Group, says simply and effectively,
'Everyone agrees that no-one can live on social security. Yet
nowhere in your plans do you talk about uprating benefits.' Frank
Field, now a Minister of State at the Department of Social
Security, comes back, quick as a flash, utterly calm: 'That's
because the problem is that people *are* on benefits. We want to get
them off them, not increase their level.' How the language has
changed! How easily can even the well-intentioned, high on their
own expertise, sound disconnected! The vocabulary of the
market has seeped into everything, falsely opposed at every turn
to the language of the state, when the real dichotomy is surely
between a willingness to challenge or underwrite inequality? At
another point in this silly programme, a professor of social
sciences accuses Frank Field and George Walden, another MP, of
not being radical enough. At last, I think, slamming down the
knife I've been chopping vegetables with; now, we will hear the
real argument. Nudged along by chair Jonathan Dimbleby, this
professor elaborates, 'In market terms, I mean . . . not radical
enough about the market.'

That's how much the language has changed.

The Cardiff women are outside the language, outside the
argument and outside the market. And yet the irony is, Jackie and

Stella understand how the market works better than most. When a third friend, Margaret, comes to join us in the late afternoon, the talk turns to jobs. The jobs they want to get. The women with older children are desperate for work. They do odd bits on the side, to supplement their benefit, a fact on which the 'Babies on Benefit' programme made much pious, dramatic play. But to these women, it is merely common sense. They don't know anyone who doesn't do it. 'God, even the man at the social security said to me, "How do any of you live on this?" Well, we don't, that's the answer.'

Margaret is a very very tall woman, mid-forties, with a fine-boned, drawn face. She has two young sons, aged eight and eleven. She had the children in her mid thirties with the father's approval but not his involvement because she wanted to be a mother. He is a good father and a good friend, she says, but she shoulders the care. She has been trying for jobs for months. She has a degree, has done social work and some editing in film. But all that was 'back then – the seventies' when she was young and carefree. 'When I came out of university, I had a choice of three jobs. I took the one with the lowest pay because I thought it was the most interesting! Hah! I would never do that now, can you believe it?' They all shake their heads in degrees of amazement; amused at the hopeful, believing people they once were. That was also BC. Before Children.

Margaret says: 'In areas like television, you know, it's who you know. You don't *apply* for jobs. And the work is twelve hours a day, fifty hours a week. It's a young man's macho industry. Working practices discriminate against women with children. It's such a well-known fact you could yawn about it. The last time I did that kind of work the kids were at school till six and then the woman from the club took them home and put them to bed and their father would have them sometimes. But I don't want to work like that. I'd rather pick them up at nine p.m. I'd rather *be* with them.'

What she wants now is a nice regular job. 'I'm trying to move into teaching. Anything that pays at least ten thousand. I've got five different areas I've been trying for. Computer jobs, because I did this training. Anything to do with women's initiatives, to get women into work, because I used to work in that area. Television, editing or scriptwriting; co-ordination or management. Anything that pays ten thousand. That's what I've set myself.'

Jackie chips in, 'I used to say to myself, "I'll take nothing below thirteen thousand," but it's amazing how low you'll go. Ten thousand is my bottom rate now. I've done everything myself. I've worked in factories, done silver service waitressing, party plan selling stuff. But it was different then. Not exactly pin money but extra money.'

These women understand the market. They know exactly how the job situation has changed. Everything is fixed-term contracts. The work is there for women but it is part-time and low-paid, designed for those who have a partner, either with a full-time job or himself bringing in part-time low wages: between them, they make up a wage. But for Jackie, Stella and Margaret there is no 'between them'. The hard-nosed decisions they are making about money and possible careers are men's decisions, without men's traditional freedoms or advantages. They are the sole bread-winners now. Or they want to be. It makes a lot of difference, not having a wife behind them, helping them with the children while they concentrate on getting the work. Everything they do, they do with the weight of caring on them, twenty-four hours a day.

'When I used to work in editing,' says Margaret, 'and we were going to have to work late, I'd be on the phone making all these complicated arrangements with carers and friends and arranging swaps and what have you, and the men would make one neat phone call to the woman at home. And they were taken care of.' She stops and then says, 'And it only gets more complicated as the children get older.'

These women also understand politics, although they talk of it in the slightly jargon-ridden, nervous way that most people do, on the one hand, thinking there is so much they ought to know but don't, and, on the other, giving a mildly exaggerated respect to the sovereign territory of their own feelings. Single mothers have been 'scapegoated'. They are rightly sure of that. Politicians are all out for their own gain. Jackie says, 'I saw Shirley Williams once and I thought she talked a lot of sense. She wanted to unify tax and benefits. The way she talked about it, people like us wouldn't be penalized if we worked a bit.'

They themselves met through a local single parents' group. They meet once a week, go on group holidays – 'life-savers'. They arrange courses for women. The group itself is a 'lifeline'. Jackie says: 'None of this lot would believe it, but I wouldn't say boo to a goose before, in my local group.' Their faces as she speaks show that they don't believe it. 'Then they had the AGM, needed a secretary. I got put forward. I got elected. Then I started going on my courses.'

Margaret joined at first because she was making a film about single parents. She was one herself but she didn't quite think of herself like that: 'I was vexed. This stereotype that all single parents are young, scroungers, living off the council. That "Babies on Benefit" film, I was furious about it. I was going to make a film about it. I got totally obsessed. And I came along to the local group and they said, "Why don't you join?" So I did. But there are times I despair. There are women coming along, we can't help. New women coming along, on the edge, materially and psychologically. One woman, do you remember her?' She turns to the others. 'Five kids under five. Really poor. She was a bit mentally unstable I think.'

Subdued again, they talk a little bit about that woman and her kids. Jackie says, about the group, 'It's someone you can ring up if you need to. I've had phone calls in the middle of the night, women on the verge of suicide. My closest friends now, they're all single parents.'

Throughout the long afternoon the women have made deliberate distinction between survival and life. In a way, they're saying, we do both. We survive and it's bloody hard. There is a tiredness to all of them, the inevitable tiredness of those that hunt and gather: two historic roles merged into one, giving out all the time and making ends meet. Margaret says that when she works, on ideas for scripts or just filling in job applications, she does it from ten at night until two in the morning. 'And you get up when?' I can't help asking. 'Seven as usual,' she grins, 'which is why I look like this.' But there is much more to them all than just enduring, because of their generosity of spirit and mutual understanding. I am certainly the outsider but they are kind, very kind to me. They are full of secret and not so secret jokes; there are lots of smiles in the summer dark of the cramped Cardiff living-room. Somewhere, somehow, they believe in a better future. Somewhere, there's a place for them.

POLITICS

~ 9 ~

Party Impressions

I wouldn't say he is intimate with our washing machine,
but he does know where it is.
Cherie Booth, talking about her husband Tony Blair,
to *Prima* readers, October 1996

It is some measure of the gap that still exists between the laws of
men and the experience of women that to write about party
politics and motherhood feels about the same as attempting an
audible conversation across a wide ravine. Indeed, several times
during the research for, and writing of, this book I have been
politely asked: what has politics got to *do* with motherhood? ('Is
it something to do with that woman who was thrown out of the
council chamber for breastfeeding?') In the immediate period
after the General Election of 1997 which saw the return of a
Labour government for the first time in nearly two decades, I
thought back to many of the women I had talked to, particularly
those who had been, effectively, exiled from political society by
the *zeitgeist* and policies of those years. On the night of 2 May
1997, at three, four, five in the morning, when an exhausted
gaggle of us were still watching the results of the Labour landslide
roll in, I wondered if any of them were up and watching and
whether they thought this change would bring them any good.
Like so many, I wondered about the answer to a question that had
seemed largely irrelevant for years: what good can governments
actually do?

It quickly became apparent that the new Labour government represented a cultural rather than political revolution. Like President Clinton in America, the Labour leader Tony Blair is one of the first of the baby boomers – a man born after the Second World War, rather than a man who fought in it – to take high political office. Much play has been made of this political generation's 'sixties' experience; the brush with drugs, the shoulder-length hair, the flirtation with rock and roll. Interestingly, little has been declared of these liberal men's encounters with, or interest in, feminism, one of the great social movements of their time. Instead, their professionally competent, high-earning, glamorously young wives have been offered to us as a sort of substitute: here is my position on female strength and independence! Voter, I *married* her! Like President Clinton, the cultural importance of Tony Blair lies as much in his wife, and young attractive family, as it does in him.

The 1997 election also brought an influx of young Labour women into Parliament; some of these were the deliberate product of women-only shortlists, others were the more accidental but cheerful face of a landslide. It was not just the number but the heterogeneity of these 120 'Blair's Babes' which made them such a heartening spectacle. Thin, tall, round, short, smart in an efficient, square-shouldered sort of way, the new MPs looked more or less like women around the nation; so much so, they caused a problem for *Vogue* magazine. In an interview of delicious comedy with the *Guardian*, in the aftermath of the election, *Vogue* editor Alexandra Shulman declared:

> It's fantastic having all these women MPs. I was really
> interested though. I was fascinated to see that every one of
> those women was wearing a jacket. And our mantra is that
> you don't have to wear jackets any more, that sweaters and
> cardigans will do. I'm interested in *Vogue* being part of
> that . . . [But] Trying to find an entry-point to the world of
> politics, *Vogue* staff vainly searched the massed ranks of new
> women MPs for one, just one, who looked even slightly
> glamorous.[1]

Many of these new MPs are working mothers with young children. One new entrant who attracted a lot of attention was the economist and journalist, Ruth Kelly, eight months pregnant with her first child at the time of the election. Newspapers and magazines described the domestic arrangements of these new women in loving detail; in one or two cases, the new MPs' husbands were giving up work to look after young children and run the home while their wives toiled late at Westminster. So, we read of husbands who filled the fridge, stocked up on loo rolls, kept up the children's homework and got home early to cook suppers.[2] Here, at long last, was the massed political arrival of the bastard child of feminism and Thatcherism, left-leaning women who were, at last, able to put themselves first. Here was a political class that might actually know something about motherhood. 'We women will change the Commons culture,' one woman MP told the *Express* a week after the election. 'There's a shooting gallery in the House of Commons but no crèche. Things have got to change now.'[3]

Yet the *New Statesman* magazine, a much more sophisticated animal, sounded a quite different political note when it wrote about the new entrants. Deputy editor Jane Taylor warned:

> Any loose talk about how co-operative, caring and consensual women are is guaranteed to provoke rapid and vituperative rebuttal from some aggressive and stroppy sister. With good reason: bright, serious women understand very well that to concede gender difference or assume gender solidarities too often means denying personal ambition and ceding the high, dry intellectual ground to men . . .[4]

The new feminism of New Labour might not be so simple, after all.

Keeping Mum: anatomy of an election campaign

As I write, the Labour government is relatively young; buoyant and supremely confident after its impressive election win. It has already indicated that it recognizes the existence of Britain's mothers – or at least the needs of parents – and the fact that they require practical help. However, it is worth briefly returning to the election campaign of spring 1997 when New Labour set out its stall, to use the political jargon, to the British people. Nervous, and authoritarian in its nervousness, the party gave no indication that it planned a cultural revolution on any grand scale. If anything it mimicked the tired, tough-guy style of its Tory opponents. One cool evening during the extended phoney war, I found myself outside the Tory Party headquarters in Smith Square, Westminster. Giant colour posters of John Major adorned the building; official cars slumbered in the specially reserved parking spaces. A famous BBC commentator walked quickly past us: eyes glassy, still wearing his television make-up, he looked unreal. Young men glued to mobile phones strutted up and down side streets or gossiped in the pub around the corner. I had temporarily forgotten the theatricality, the impersonality of politics: its hard, public face which so characterized this campaign. And I thought, then, it is no wonder that so few women – or modest men – make it to the very top of British politics and stay there. Too many of them still lack the cock-strutting enjoyment of public performance, the vain wish to be projected a thousand times larger than they are.

My uneasiness was confirmed by a report issued a week before the 1 May election by the Fawcett Society, the stalwart of liberal feminist campaign groups, based on observation of several weeks of lacklustre campaigning. Among its devastatingly simple findings was the fact that female politicians from every major party were being sidelined by the leadership of their respective parties. Several women journalists, themselves marginalized by their editors according to the Fawcett report, had already remarked on the macho feel to the theatre of campaigning. It wasn't just the new/old problem of hacks on the campaign buses calling up pornographic images on the Internet. At the big set-piece press conferences, top politicians jousted with their counterparts in broadcast and print journalism.[5] With news programmes beginning to feature footage of their own star journalists on bulletins, the matching star-power of politics and the media was becoming visually apparent. Sheer intimidation was one reason given for the small number of women journalists to even ask a question, a fact drily noted by Shirley Williams of the Liberal Democrats.

Another report by the Women's Communication Centre, also published during the campaign, argued that women's issues were being sidelined by all three political parties. The WCC, quite logically, defined 'women's issues' as 'measures that would particularly benefit women', including action on childcare, domestic violence, part-time workers' rights, low pay and equal pay and support for carers. It was not that the parties had failed carefully to consider them but that these played little part in the real campaign, out in the streets or in the television studios. In the words of the WCC, such issues 'do not feature strongly in the mainstream policy agendas, even though they may figure prominently in the parties' separate strategy documents'.[6] Rather like a man who tells his mistress he loves her but lives his public life in the limelight with his wife, the parties faced both ways when it came to women. They were crucial and invisible at the same time.

The WCC also found that politicians tackled 'people' issues in a 'male' way. When work was mentioned, politicians tended to concentrate on unemployment while the WCC found that women's concerns focus 'on equal pay, access to pensions, child care, a minimum wage, genuinely flexible hours, parental leave, part-time workers' rights and equal opportunities'. The policy most directly relevant to motherhood in the campaign was Labour's proposed Welfare to Work scheme, which aimed to help both the young unemployed and single parents into paid work. But, using the sex-neutral language of contemporary politics, the link between single parents, most of whom are women, and motherhood was never directly made by the politicians themselves. In any case, the Welfare to Work scheme was represented more as a measure that would prove Labour's economic caution to middle England than as a policy that would rectify an economic injustice to some of Britain's poorest women.

For some commentators, this failure to speak meaningfully to women was symbolized by the meaningful silence of the most reported-upon woman in the whole campaign: Cherie Booth. If Jane Ashdown and Norma Major are the kind of mothers we all wish our own had been – homey, smiley, cake-baking and garden-pottering – Cherie Booth is the kind of mother many of us think we ourselves might be: professionally competent, smartly turned out and yet still a warm human being. Even her initial awkwardness in front of the cameras, which was no more than an endearing lack of restraint in demonstrating her feelings, was appealing.

Cherie Booth remained silent throughout the campaign. I heard her speak no more than half a sentence. Mostly, she performed the standard political wife routine, loyally stuck to her husband's side as he made the same speech on the stump over and over again. As one young woman journalist who followed her on the trail observed:

> Cherie Booth is a spectacularly successful barrister. Her academic record is immaculate: her outside interests, child abuse and battered wives, eminently laudable. She was one of the youngest women ever to take silk, and has found time to fit in three young children. She ought, by rights, to represent a glittering electoral asset. If Tony Blair wins the election, we will have in Downing Street a political wife who confounds every convention. And yet, it seems that New Labour is determined to downgrade her into a mute Norma Major.[7]

How should we interpret this neutrality which continues into government? After all, Cherie Booth holds no elective office: nor does she desire one in the future. (The past is another matter.) Being married to an important person does not make you an important figure *in the same way* as that spouse. Denis Thatcher knew that only too well, but Hillary Clinton's greatest mistake may have been her failure, in a democratic system, to make this crucial distinction. However, in the real world of a crucial election campaign, Cherie Booth was not a neutral figure, nor was she deployed as one. While the anxious pre-election Blair talked tough to the guys on the big issues, Booth played the low-key women's card, usually the more human card. If she was seen doing anything independently of her husband, it was likely to be having a confidential chat with some sick children.

Cherie Booth's ordinariness had already been famously displayed in her decision, the autumn before the election, to guest-edit an issue of *Prima*, the mass-circulation women's weekly which is more *Woman's Own* than *Cosmopolitan*. Journalists, predictably, sneered at the endeavour – and Booth did make the odd, arch observations: 'As a keen knitter myself, I love the mother and daughter jumper which Kathryn and I will wear again and again.' But overall, her guest-editorship of the magazine was well judged. In her own signed column she chose to highlight three subjects: good childcare, domestic violence and the unsung work of carers. In a round table interview, at the Ritz Hotel, with eight *Prima* readers, she said, 'I feel strongly about the need to help mothers. As a working father, Tony knows about these things.'[8] Yet the terms 'childcare' or 'working mothers' or 'carers' did not figure significantly in the campaign. Tony Blair did not say, 'I feel strongly about the need to help mothers. As a working father I know about these things.' I daresay he did on the stump in Bolton or on a visit to a nursery in Brighton, but these were never key themes in the big set-piece interviews, with David Dimbleby or Jeremy Paxman, the places that everyone knows really count.

The welfare of women

Labour's confidence in its own interpretation of social problems and proposals for their solution has grown since the spectacular 1997 election win. Nevertheless, its key priorities were forged in the long years in the wilderness and particularly by the Tories' distorted obsessions with the family, the benefits bill and a reduction of the role of the state. Directly reflecting these concerns, New Labour fixed its sights on the one kind of mother that it could do something about: the single mother in receipt of state benefits. Solving the single parent 'problem' was one of the key notes of the election campaign. Both parties made major statements about their respective schemes – Labour's Welfare to Work, which also included plans for the young jobless, and the Tories' Parent Plus scheme – within days of each other. Both used disingenuous language. Tony Blair described Labour's scheme almost entirely in terms of extending individual opportunity. He made Welfare to Work sound like a nice Sunday afternoon tea party. Single parents, he said, were to be 'invited' to a job centre, 'encouraged' to look for work, and 'informed' of what childcare was available locally. There was no question, he emphasized, in private, of anyone being forced out to work.

The Conservative Parent Plus scheme also talked of 'helping' lone parents back into work. Social Security Minister Peter Lilley said, 'Most lone parents want to work but this group need particular help to break out of the benefit trap.' Lilley's next sentence was even more telling: 'It is important that children grow up seeing parents as breadwinners and not the state as sole provider.' (Uncouple that sentence and take the first half to a middle-England household where the mother has never had a paid job and see what *she* says.) There is some similarity here to the motives behind the establishment of the Child Support Agency in 1991. This was presented by Margaret Thatcher as a moral, almost enabling, gesture by government, an attempt to face fathers with their paternal responsibility, but it was also widely understood as an attempt to recoup millions of pounds for the Treasury.

Welfare to Work has continued to be one of the big ideas shaping Labour's first thousand days. Blair chose Welfare to Work as his subject on one of his first big set-piece speeches after the election, when he visited a 'deprived' south London housing estate. Soon after the election, Chancellor Gordon Brown declared, 'I'm interested in developing a welfare state built around the work ethic.' He wanted, he said, to remove disincentives to work for jobless households and single parents. He also indicated that he would not be reversing the Conservative government's cuts in lone parent premium and one parent benefit.

The new government was keen to stress the positive side of its programme; Brown pledged that government training measures would increase the chances of single parents finding work. Certainly, if Welfare to Work means what it says, if it really promises a passage from unwilling unemployment to a decent job, it should be welcomed. Campaign groups for single parents have given it a cautious greeting on these grounds. Most of the single parents, particularly of older children, want jobs; but like everyone else in the world, they want jobs that suit them, as individuals. In their dreams, they wanted really good jobs. ('Jobs over £10,000 a year', remember?) But despite government promises to invest in the creation of a limited number of new jobs, a serious question mark hangs over the quality of most of the work that will realistically be available.

Many single parents are also worried about compulsion. How coercive will Welfare to Work be, even for hard-pressed single parents? What happens when the first woman, or hundred women, say they will not accept a job washing up, paying £2.80 an hour, at a local restaurant? Tony Blair may have said during the election campaign that no-one will be forced to work but, more recently, he has said that life on benefit is not acceptable to the new Labour government. What does 'acceptable' mean in the real powerful world of government policy? The appointment of 'thinking the unthinkable' Frank Field to Minister of State at the Department of Social Security heralds a possibly harder line. Field's appointment, said one experienced senior commentator, was 'one of the most significant' acts of the new administration.[9] Field is known as a zealous critic of benefit fraud. He believes the entire welfare system must be geared to getting people into work. Early reports on the relationship between Field and his senior Minister, Harriet Harman, Minister for both Social Security and Women, suggested 'tensions . . . especially on the issue of compulsion for those on benefit, and single parents . . .'. As one newspaper reported:

In a frank speech to a conference arranged by the New Zealand government in March [Frank Field] argued that all single mothers with children aged over four should look for work or undertake training. If they refused, they should be denied benefit . . . Trailing another major shift in thinking, he argued that the biggest welfare bills did not stem from the jobless but from the number of single parents. 'Between four and five times more children grow up in single parent homes on welfare than children in unemployed households,' he argued. 'Britain's single parent population is not only larger, it is younger and includes a higher proportion of never married mothers.'[10]

Punishing the poor

There are growing and worrying parallels here with Clinton's America. As in the UK, the mother on welfare has been the territory on which the Democrats have sought to cut away ground from the old right. Under attack from militant right-wing Republicanism, President Clinton introduced severe curbs on welfare in the 1996 Welfare Act. Under this law, the head of every family on welfare has to work within two years or the family loses benefits. States can provide payments to unmarried teenage parents only if a mother under eighteen stays at school and lives with an adult. A welfare recipient who refuses to co-operate in identifying the father of her child can lose at least 25 per cent of her benefits.

Clinton backed the Act with obvious reluctance. He vetoed an earlier draft but then signed the law, after some renegotiations. Among the Democrats dismayed by his decision was representative John Lewis of Georgia, who, just before the Senate approved it, addressed the chamber in 'anguished tones': 'Where is the compassion?' he asked. 'Where is the sense of decency? Where is the heart of this Congress? This bill is mean. It is base. It is downright lowdown. What does it profit a great nation to conquer the world, only to lose its soul?'[11]

According to Barbara Ransby, a respected commentator on politics, writing in late 1996, 'The [Act] . . . signals an unprecedented assault on the well-being and survival of millions of poor Americans. [It] eradicates the notion that citizens are entitled to basic subsistence resources, despite the fact that they live in one of the richest countries in the world . . .' Ransby goes on:

> The crux of the problem with the so-called welfare reform programme is the underlying assumption that the problem lies with the culture, behaviour and morality of the poor, rather than with poverty itself . . . [it] ignores the absence of real jobs for unskilled and under-educated workers and instead blames unemployed people for not being resourceful enough to find non-existent jobs. The alleged moral agenda of the current welfare reform crusade – to reduce out of wedlock births and instil a greater work ethic in the poor – applies higher moral standards to poor people than those adhered to by many of our public officials instead.[12]

The United States legislation is far more draconian than anything so far put forward in Britain. New Labour has learned many lessons from Clinton, including what not to do: this act of savagery may be one of them. But Ransby's analysis is still relevant: the unemployed cannot find jobs that do not exist. Nor is poverty an act of individual will or a question of individual fault.

New Labour: new work ethic

When Tony Blair launched his Welfare to Work proposal to a party of business people in Amsterdam, he stated that his aim was to give lone parents a 'proper and decent stake in society'. If one decodes lone parents to read mothers bringing up their children on their own, which most lone parents are, this is a rather odd statement. Are parents bringing up their children alone not already performing a 'proper and decent' role in society? And is *requiring* of them that they take on an additional task – paid work – implying that they do not have tasks enough? One would search far and wide to find a speech by any government minister, Labour or Tory, that suggests married women without a job are not performing a proper and decent role: on the contrary, they are doing 'one of the most important jobs in the world'; isn't that the usual formulation? Yet such women are supported by both a male wage and male presence, however limited; their domestic lives are far easier than those of their single-parent counterparts.

Welfare to Work is not only about money; it is not only about the work ethic; it is about the ethic of paid work. Seriously committed to the importance of work as economic activity, New Labour seems to have developed a rather authoritarian and misplaced belief that paid work *alone* is the route to a satisfactory life and a pure soul. What's more, New Labour's famed modernity now compels them to include women in this formulation, whether through sanctioning an individual's choice or coercing an unwilling group into the market.

Compare the following two statements; old and new, 1983 and 1996:

Statement 1: 'Labour's objective is to achieve equality between women and men. Over half the population is women, yet in our society, paid employment is seen as important while domestic skills – involving caring for children – do not enjoy proper status. Women should have a genuine choice between staying at home to look after the family and going to work.'[13]

Statement 2: 'By supporting women who want to continue in their careers, we will ensure that British business has access to a full range of skills and experience . . . Giving women the support to return to work is crucial to the economic success of this country.'[14]

It is a subtle change, but a profound one. There is little public acknowledgement from New Labour of the extent to which women still work in the home, regardless of an outside job, nor of the value of what they do there. Let's not romanticize the Labour party of old: it showed limited awareness of the needs of both women at work and women at home. But in the early 1980s, when the impact of socialist feminism upon it was probably at its height, feminist pressure at least provoked the party to start thinking about women, even if such thinking was mainly translated into an extension of Labour's considerable shopping list of spending plans. Divesting itself of these commitments of old, not only has New Labour concentrated its focus primarily on the working woman; it has chiefly identified itself with the ambitious or, to use New Labour terminology, the aspirational woman in society. Equality is no longer so much a question of social justice as of economic opportunity, economic power. Within this scheme, New Labour is able to prove to business that women's careers are good for capitalism.

The Tory party has traditionally defended the interests of the woman in the home, particularly the affluent woman. As Beatrix Campbell writes in her interesting account of women and the Tory party: 'What works for women in the Conservative's family ideology is the sense that women are important to society because they are important to the family: they take care of it, after all, and the family is important to society.' But, Campbell adds, 'The rhetoric of familial ideology is rarely about the content of the relationship with children and the work of motherhood, and still less about many if not most women's experience of solitude and abandonment.'[15]

Some sections of small c conservatism have remained faithful to the idea that home-making and child-rearing have an intrinsic value and no intrinsic conflict. In a scathing article about New Labour's 'humbug' on family values, the influential conservative philosopher Roger Scruton argued that while Tony Blair was a 'family man, happily married with children at good middle-class schools', he was hostage to a feminism within his own party. This politics, Scruton claimed, 'destroys the feelings on which family life depends. It portrays the domestic sphere as one of weakness and timidity, requires men to play an equal part in running the home and rearing children, and is suspicious of motherhood as an obstacle to a fulfilling career.'[16]

And, in her attack on the value of pre-school childcare, Patricia Morgan of the right-wing Institute of Economic Affairs attacked the increasing tendency of all parties to welcome the working mother as an unequivocally good thing; 'The ruling consensus dictates that Britain is, and must be, a society where it is economically necessary for both parents always to work. The assumption that everybody is now self-supporting makes any allowance for domestic responsibilities an "anomaly" in the words of one Tory Chancellor.'[17]

But such views are, as Morgan herself implied, lone calls in the wilderness. By the early 1990s the Tory party was acutely aware of the changing nature even of its own supporters and particularly of the increasing number of young women interested in work and careers; the party pitch to women on the primacy of paid work was similar to Labour's. To the Tories, too, the modern woman was a *working woman*. As the Women's Communication Centre found, none of the three major parties had anything substantial to say on the existence, let alone the value, of women's unpaid caring load. In this context, John Major's last-minute offer in the election campaign of 1997 of a tax allowance transfer from spouse to spouse – worth just £17.50 a week or £900 a year – if one partner gave up work to stay at home to look after the children looked just what it was: last-minute, and purely tactical. As writer Blake Morrison observed: 'Even those women already staying at home to look after children or ailing relations, who will be happy for the little bit extra, may object to the exploitation of the family by the current campaigning.'[18]

Family favourites

How, then, does this new love affair with women's economic power square with the political parties' other great romance, the family? Where Thatcher used the family mainly as a weapon against the state and John Major used 'Back to Basics' as a bungled tool of moral propaganda, Tony Blair has brought genuine vigour to his defence of the modernized but still strong family. Even as shadow Home Secretary, he was making speeches about the importance of the institution. 'Blair supports role of the family' was the headline carried by the *Guardian* as early as 1993.

Reporter Patrick Wintour wrote: 'Mr Blair admitted that the left had in the past sometimes been perceived as regarding the issue of family values as irrelevant, or even in extreme cases, politically incorrect.' Some commentators, such as *Observer* columnist Melanie Phillips, reacted enthusiastically to this fresh young face expressing an older common sense. But, to the public at large, Blair's persuasiveness on the family question stemmed as much from simple example as complex argument. Roger Scruton may have praised him as happily married with children at 'good middle-class schools', but he omitted the important fact of Cherie. The Blair/Booths personify the *modern* version of the family; 'old values in a new setting', to use the Labour jargon. Here, after all, are two highly successful working parents and three stable, apparently happy children.

On the surface, the Blair/Booth family picture suggests an attractive gender parity. We know that Cherie Booth earns £200,000 a year or has the capacity to do so. As Prime Minister, Tony Blair now earns a reasonable wage himself. Both are presented as caring, involved parents. It used to be said that Blair could change a nappy while discussing the Public Sector Borrowing Requirement. But look a little closer and this apparent sameness breaks down. In what was billed as 'his frankest interview ever' with the *Daily Mail*'s Lynda Lee Potter, Blair talked about his own family background, the tragedy of his mother's early death, his relationship with Cherie and the pressures of the job:

> One minute you're an averagely rising political star. The next minute you've got people camped outside your home wondering what you had for breakfast. *Cherie's got her practice and she's got the family to manage.* In some ways it's harder for her and the children than it is for me [my emphasis].[19]

This was not a slip-up, just the simple statement of an assumption shared by millions: we both work, but my wife manages the family. Here is a private acknowledgement, at least, of the work involved in such management; the work of stripping beds and ordering curtain material or hiring staff to strip beds and order curtain material, the myriad tasks that make up the creation of a happy, well-ordered house. 'My husband,' Cherie Booth told *Prima* readers, 'has been known to cook a meal – if I am late in . . . I wouldn't say he is intimate with our washing machine but he knows where it is.'[20] The appeal of the Blair/Booth family is that they look new but they run their lives along conventionally agreed-upon principles. The most time-honoured of these is the belief that the strong family still relies upon the greater contribution, physical if not moral, of the mother.

The Blair/Booths, as a private couple, are not particularly important. It is what they symbolize that matters. For a discussion about the new family to be truly 'new' we need a political conversation that first acknowledges, rather than assumes, these realities. We need to strip away the generalities about 'family' and 'parents' to which both Labour and Tory subscribe. 'Parents', they say, must restrain children who indulge in truanting or juvenile crime. 'Families', they say, must be responsible for their own members. 'Families', they say, must look after each other in old age.

In the real world, mothers and fathers do different things and they are expected to do different things.

In one of the most perceptive articles written on the subject of family and community, Anna Coote, then of the Institute for Public Policy Research, argued that one of the factors that handicapped Blair (and all politicians) in their pursuit of 'community' was that they do not tend to live in one. Instead, they live in a 'tiny exotic political community'. Anyone who has visited the House of Commons, as one example of a tiny political islet, can see that it is, in its way, very much a community with all the squabbles and pleasures of any neighbourhood or workplace: it is simply without the chief humanizing element of any ordinary neighbourhood – children. Those who continually talk about the importance of community tend always to talk about what is not being done, said Coote, instead of paying attention to the positive factors within families and local life. Ordinary communities, she went on, are made up of children and adults, mostly sustained by women:

They scarcely need to be reminded of *their* 'duty'. They have a powerful sense of obligation to their children, their elderly relatives, their friends and neighbours. Most of them *have* problems but they are not *themselves* problems . . . Take 'parents', for example. Blair says parents should be taken to court for allowing their children to truant. But the duties of parenting are not equally shared between mothers and fathers. Men are mainly absent from the lives of children, unable or unwilling to take charge of them in that intimate, intricate way that women do.[21]

The absence of concrete truths from political discussion makes even the most thoughtful work on modern problems unhelpful. In one of the more reflective pieces of writing on the conflicts between work and private life, written in 1995, Michael Young and A. H. Halsey, one of the architects of the 1945 welfare state, argue that the care of our children is now the big theme of society. The issue, however, has been abandoned by the Conservatives for whom family used to be the main concern, but no longer. Young and Halsey point to a number of factors that are 'hurting our society and our children', including the growing gap between the highest and the lowest earners and the gap between work rich and work poor. In work-rich families, they note, working parents have become slaves of the clock:

> The people who succeed in holding their own best in a modern economy are those who make themselves the slaves of the clock. They need an acute sense of time and how to ration it out, even when they are with their children. Creatures of the clock can be abstracted, always aware of what they are missing, of what they are not doing, even while they are doing what they have to. The children can be restricted to contact only with part of a person, the whole person being not quite there. The adults can be so taken up with what they are going to do next that they have no time for the moment in which children live.[22]

They then go on to observe that 'the balance between the moral

and material economies has been upset. In the material economy
. . . people are valued for the contribution they make to
production (and their income) . . . in the moral economy. . . they
are valued for who they are.'

What we need, they argue, is a form of moral 'conservatism'
that, literally, conserves the moral values of our society, including
tenderness, discipline and the giving of proper time to other
people.

Young and Halsey are absolutely right. Yet like most liberal
participants in the family debate, they take up a position of
unconvincing neutrality on the mother/father question. They are
unwilling to criticize working women, yet one senses they regret
the fact of working women because it is this change, above all,
that has upset the old relation between the two economies,
material and moral. They also do not recognize the large amount
of work that women still do put into the moral economy. Few
women are such slaves of the industrial clock that they do not
have time for their children; the vast majority of them work part-
time. And while the once leisured middle-class woman may now
have less time for traditional forms of unpaid community or
charity work, women of all classes are still at the centre of
networks and initiatives that keep neighbourhoods going. These
are not just the childcare-related activities I describe in Chapter 7
but other organizations in civil society, from tenants' groups to
anti-drug campaigns, food co-ops to credit unions, church groups
to community safety schemes.

At the same time, Young and Halsey are unable to go further;
there is scant analysis of men's inability, failure, unwillingness – call
it what you like – to maintain the moral economy; nor an *active*
call for men's greater involvement in the private world. Amitai
Etzioni, the communitarian thinker who has greatly influenced
the New Labour project, has said firmly, 'I think men and women,
mothers and fathers, should have exactly the same rights and
exactly the same duties.'[23] Yet he has little to say about the fact
that, at present, mothers and fathers have quite different duties.
One sees this sex-blindness in many contemporary discussions,
even when the politics of gender is apparently under review.[24]

Childcare! Childcare! Childcare!

During the election campaign of 1997, I had an interesting dream. Tony Blair came out of No. 10 Downing Street and walked to the bank of microphones they set up outside No. 10 for important announcements. 'I have today decided,' he declared to the assembled photographers and reporters, 'that from now on childcare will be the passion of my administration.' Behind him, supporters of his radical new policy clapped their hands and smiled. With him was the new Minister for Women – unfortunately a little breathless, as she had just rushed from a meeting in connection with her other job as Minister for Social Security – and the Minister for Education and Employment. Among the campaigners present were members of the Umbrella on Childcare, and representatives from on-the-ground initiatives as diverse as the Shoreditch International Crèche and Lucy Hovells, a local party activist in Sedgefield, Tony Blair's own constituency, where she has been fund-raising, networking and pursuing her own training to extend childcare facilities in the area.[25] As he completed his announcement of extensive measures to provide high-quality, low-cost childcare in every region of the country, Prime Minister Blair lifted his hand into a clenched fist and echoed the call of the election campaign with this revised mantra: 'Childcare! Childcare! Childcare!'

Then I woke up.

Three months later, in July 1997, I turned on the television to watch Gordon Brown's first budget, live. Was I dreaming again when I heard him say: 'A generation of parents have waited for their government to introduce a National Childcare Strategy. From this budget forwards, childcare will no longer be seen as an afterthought or a fringe element of social policies, but from now, as it should be, an integral part of our economic policy.'

Things looked even more promising when, a couple of weeks later, I read the following press release from the Department of Social Security: 'Childcare should be as much part of our economic infrastructure as transport or communication – childcare is as important as the roads which take women to work.'[26]

We are back to the issue of confidence, again. Once securely in office the new government has been able, fairly quickly, to give real voice to an important part of the nation's needs. For the moment, it need not fear the Tories' baiting in the House of Commons; it is they, with their diminished rump of women MPs, who look out of touch with society. In its first three months, the new government has introduced some small, but significant, measures which indicate its seriousness about providing a new infrastructure for women at work. The small improvements proposed so far include an increase in the amount of money a working parent can spend on childcare before Family Credit is deducted (known as the 'childcare disregard'), and making this disregard available for children up to the age of twelve. Childcare is to be one of the priorities of the Single Regeneration Budget – that is, money received from Europe. During his budget speech Chancellor Brown also declared his intention to create several thousand jobs in the 'childcare industry' over the next few years.

These are the promising beginnings to the fabled if vague National Childcare Strategy which Labour has long promised. There are still many things left to do. Groups working in the child-care field, such as the Daycare Trust, point to schemes in other countries, such as the 'Jet' scheme in Australia, which provides a set number of days of free childcare for parents looking for work.[27] They also want to see employers encouraged to offer employees childcare allowances to spend as they wish. Workplace nurseries are no longer the sole answer to working parents' needs, and many employers have already developed more individual, flexible solutions that government should encourage and underwrite. The Umbrella for Childcare group has also devised plans for local agencies that bring together local employers, Training Education Councils, local authorities and parents to devise a childcare strategy for each area. They propose that funding come partly from European sources – an idea already taken up by government through its supposed use of the Single Regeneration Budget – and partly from national and local government. New Labour should also promote New Values; why, for instance, can individuals and businesses claim tax relief on company cars and other expensive toys and no working parent in the land can claim back a penny for the money they shell out for childcare? Can New Labour find the confidence and political will to significantly redistribute wealth in favour of parents – in favour of *mothers'* needs, and particularly poorer mothers' needs – over the longer term?

Challenging the successful male

The old code for a politician's ultimate career failure was his stated desire to 'spend more time with his family'. The largely correct inference was not only that politics allowed no time for the family, but that a successful public life required the sacrifice of a private group. Paternal images, if not practice, have changed substantially. President Clinton has, apparently, been advised on his paternal image by feminist writer Naomi Wolf. Tony Blair, more than any other politician, appears as a contemporary father. *She* magazine recently labelled him as 'ultra modern'.[28] We imagine Blair to be deeply and continuously involved in his children's lives: school work, leisure activities, friends and community life. In reality, this cannot be so, especially since he became Prime Minister. Blair admitted as much himself when he said, in a speech in spring 1997, that his children complain of never seeing him. It is partly, of course, the rigours of his current position, but the lives of many women politicians, some quite senior, show just how they do manage to do the job efficiently and make real time for family.[29] Tony Blair is not just a busy politician. He is a typical example of the overworked successful man whom society both highly values and yet bemoans, in another context, when academics, journalists and politicians themselves attack the 'long hours' culture.

The government has set itself against this culture. It has announced its aim to sign Britain up to the European social chapter, which will notionally cut the working week back to forty-eight hours. Yet paid employment and highly committed paid employment is still very much at the heart of how a man thinks of himself. Being away from the home from seven in the morning until ten at night is still a sign of success for many men, and a few women. These men may very well want to make more time for their children; they may be keen to make the most of the time they do spend with them; there is no apparent kudos in not being with them. But they are unwilling or, more likely, unable to break that fundamental and often addictive tie to a world that demands more than a decent day's work from them. I recently spoke to a male friend who had just had a new daughter. It was five-fifty in the evening and I teased him about still being at the office. 'You're kidding,' he said in a weary voice. 'Half past nine is more like it.'

There is still an unwritten rule that a man's time is his to do what he wishes with it. His responsibility to his family, his duty is fulfilled if he gives money, guidance, kindness. His success is still defined by the extent of his availability, often without limit, to an employer, a business, a specific project, a personal dream, artistic or political. Any new public conversation would have to explore how much of this behaviour is a form of parental irresponsibility. At the very least it is irresponsible to a partner; a wife; the person in the background. Even if that partner has no personal ambition – and who does not have personal ambition, as in a wish to do something other than be with children from time to time? – they can still feel abandoned by the fevered partner who works at the office till all hours. Many women today have more tangible ambitions, in relation to work or 'self-development'; they, too, are blocked by a partner's refusal or inability to yield up his sole place on the road of career fulfilment and success. One mother of three, now in her sixties, who has spent her life with the typical successful male, talked to me recently about how she and her husband might have negotiated their home and work life differently. She said: 'When I look back, I see that it could have been done differently if he had accepted doing things at a slower pace while the children were young and they needed him and I needed him. And you know, it would have done him good. It would have given him more perspective. Instead, he got addicted to his work and the way of life that went with it and it all spun out of control. His lack of control of the time he gave over to work actually damaged, not enhanced, his success.'

Government policy has traditionally been directed at the 'unsuccessful' male: the unemployed man or, more recently, the man who abandons his family responsibilities. The Child Support Agency was inaugurated in 1991 for the purpose of making men pay up for families they had left. Some feminists welcomed the largely unpopular Act for this reason: its symbolic call to accountability. In public debate, too, we hear a great deal about the man who is failing – be it in relation to work, welfare, education or even his falling sperm count. Now it is time to tackle the successful man, to call him to account.

Politicians give no indication that they think such men – themselves – are a problem. They may individually, but not politically – bar mild hints in policy documents when they talk of the need for 'men and women to share domestic and work responsibilities'. This government is pledged to cut working hours and introduce a limited amount of unpaid parental leave, rectifying a disgraceful failure of John Major's government. But it will take more than laws to break the habits of a lifetime. The introduction of flexible family policies, as we have seen, has largely 'benefited' women, not men. Only a handful of men take advantage of these schemes, even where the employer is encouraging. In its 1997 election manifesto, Labour merely echoed the old assumptions when it talked about flexible family policies allowing 'women . . . to juggle home and family life'.

We should start by example, and where better place to start than the politicians, the Ministers of the Crown, the first men of a generation to be directly influenced by feminism? Where better place to begin actively to promote flexible working? So far the most publicized part-time appointment to the government has been the special adviser to the Minister for Women, Anna Coote. Why does the Prime Minister not appoint more, or all, Cabinet ministers and junior government posts and special advisers on a part-time basis? Why does the Prime Minister not stipulate that all civil servants should be sent home on a Thursday afternoon? Why does the Prime Minister himself not begin, modestly you understand, by working a four-day week and banning all red boxes from his sight on the weekend? Why not indeed?

~ 10 ~

Feminism I:
The Not So Secret History

It is 1971, and Mirek says that the struggle of man against
power is the struggle of memory against forgetting.

Milan Kundera,
The Book of Laughter and Forgetting, Penguin 1981

If the story of feminism is the story of ideas about women, then
mothers and motherhood should, surely, be one of its natural subjects? After all, no woman is born without one: most women still
become one. Yet one recent charge against feminism has been that
it is not, and never has been, interested in motherhood. In her
polemical *What about Us? An Open Letter to the Mothers Feminism
Forgot* (1995), journalist Maureen Freely sketched the outlines of
her argument. Of modern feminism, she asserted: 'When I was at
university, the women's movement was dominated by women
fifteen years older than I was who were desperate to escape from
motherhood. Now it is dominated by women fifteen years
younger than I who hardly seem to realize that it exists.'[1]

We can all recognize the feeling that, in the same way as a social
event, the really important *political* party was always happening
somewhere else. Or, like Woody Allen's character in *Stardust
Memories* (1980), we remain trapped on the grey and white bus,
looking over at the colourful revellers in the neighbouring
vehicle. But is the charge true? Freely takes issue with both the

young branch of feminists – for which read the Americans, such as Naomi Wolf, Camille Paglia et al – and the 'great writers' of feminist tradition as well. She suggests that many of these, in particular Mary Wollstonecraft, Simone de Beauvoir and Betty Friedan, had an instinctive revulsion against the maternal experience. This disdain or, in many cases, self-hatred, seeped into a body of writing that was supposedly pro-woman. As a result, feminism has become a kind of hypocritical poseur; the engaging friend who talks about you behind your back.

Freely's book was a deliberately witty polemic, not a detailed political analysis. Her argument, however, catches a popular mood of the moment, a mood which suggests not only that much of the feminism of the past is irrelevant but that its history might even be malign. It poses a tension between ordinary women living ordinary lives and grand feminists with no connection to those lives; it projects feminism as a politics of the already powerful rather than the self-righteous voice of the once powerless. Thus, Freely can take the existential formulation, used to such devastating effect by Simone de Beauvoir in *The Second Sex*, and turn it against feminism. 'It is through well-meaning silence that Mothers became the Others of feminism – in much the same way that women became the Others of patriarchy.'

My understanding of past feminist writers is different. Far from a monolithic rejection of motherhood, or even a buried dislike of the process, there is a constant tension between an urge towards separation and connection. In many ways, feminism is the story of women's bid for 'freedom' *away* from motherhood and its associated repressions, in particular the stifling tie of family and community. Every single patriarchal institution, and particularly the church and state, has, historically, worked to confirm women in their dependent place: sexually, financially, morally. Feminism's answer has been to urge separation, independence and necessary risk. For those women reared in societies where the duty of the daughter, wife, mother and sister is supposed to come before the duty to self – and look around the world to the many countries and cultures where this oppressive ideology still applies – this is an entirely honourable project. Motherhood is a complex but definite bind when not freely chosen, when assumed to be one's main life task. Mary Wollstonecraft is one important starting point in the Enlightenment tradition of a new individualism which argued for recognition of women's potential rationality and therefore their equality with men. We have all benefited from her quarrel with patriarchy, even if we now, at the end of the twentieth century, recognize the interesting and sometimes fatal limits of rationality itself, as a way of either theorizing or organizing life.

At the same time there is a very different story going on, often within the same writer's life or work. Simone de Beauvoir was one of the great individualists of the twentieth century who embraced two of its most collectivist ideologies: feminism and Marxism. Shulamith Firestone, the twenty-five-year-old American who penned *The Dialectic of Sex*, wrote with the angry voice of singularity about the need for communes. For once the case for separation and independence is established – in an individual as well as a political life – the next question is inevitably circular: how to live with others, and on what terms? There is virtually no feminist writer who does not assume or stress the importance of emotional and political connection as well as autonomy.

Some of the most powerful advocates of this position demonstrated it through their life and work, women such as Sylvia Pankhurst in the early years of the twentieth century and Dora Russell from the 1920s onwards. These two, both from the comfortable middle class, represent a crucial strand of feminist thinking on motherhood that has been somewhat buried by the individualism of the 1980s and 1990s. Their work was primarily practical, their principal concern to improve the conditions of child-rearing and domestic life of working-class women. To them, the fact, and value, of motherhood was assumed; what was not acceptable was the terrible poverty associated with so much of it. We must not forget these practical women or practical policies, even if the sometimes sensible, slightly pious, tone of benign middle-class feminism is an anachronism in our age.

There is also an important personal strand we need to follow;

the secret or perhaps not so secret story behind the willed politics of a writer. (Any writer, for that matter; not just women, not just feminists.) In researching and writing the accounts which follow, I became acutely aware of whether the writer was a mother herself and at what stage in her motherhood she wrote her particular work. This is not to say that only mothers can appreciate motherhood; far from it. Simone de Beauvoir, who was never a biological mother, took a refreshing pleasure in the physicality of procreation. Dora Russell, who had three children, loathed the social acceptance, even elevation, of avoidable pain in childbirth. She adopted a more efficient tone about the whole process. Immersed in the practicalities, rather than the abstract romance, of child-bearing, she was concerned to improve the physical world into which most babies were born rather than muse on the 'flesh of my flesh'.

Looking at the political and personal context of an abstract work perhaps makes it easier to understand why someone wrote what they did and why it matters. One of the disturbing aspects of our current culture is a covert disdain for the past – for history itself – or a distortion of it to suit present purposes: it takes patience, time and not a little human sympathy to put aside current preconceptions and place ourselves in the position of those who lived ten, twenty, certainly two hundred years ago. Feminist writer Lynne Segal, analysing 'Generations of feminism', mourned this passing of time as a loss even to those who were once present and active in that history:

> Yet, what often leaves erstwhile political crusaders with little more than mournful and confusing feelings of loss and regret – whatever our capacities for irony – is the way in which new narratives emerge as collective memories fade, writing over those that once incited our most passionate actions.[2]

Old politics, like old lovers, are so easy to forget. But remembering the past is a guarantee against tyranny, including the contemporary tyrannies of 'dumbing down', in which we pretend to be more stupid than we are, or arid academicism, in which we pretend to be more clever. And as important as the act of remembrance is the importance of quarrel, the constant examinations and reinterpretations of arguments, lives, grand theses. That is why I briefly return to these writers, these women: through re-remembering we can reinvent ourselves with more competence, imagination and tenderness.

Mary Wollstonecraft: first rights

Mary Wollstonecraft is considered one of the founders of modern feminism for her *A Vindication of the Rights of Woman*. In more senses than one, we look at it as a set text: we bow before its certainty, its assumed, unchanging authority. Yet, like many pieces of significant writing, it was produced very quickly; it took her just six weeks. Wollstonecraft herself always meant to come back to it, revise it, improve upon it. It was one of half a dozen polemics written by various radicals of the late eighteenth century against Edmund Burke's *Reflections on the Revolution in France*, and, for Mary, a sequel to her own first response, the not very significant *A Vindication of the Rights of Man*.

What makes *A Vindication of the Rights of Woman* so important is partly its subject. In *The Second Sex* Simone de Beauvoir writes, 'Representation of the world, like the world itself, is the work of men: they describe it from their own point of view, which they confuse with absolute truth.' Yet over a century and a half before de Beauvoir wrote those words, Wollstonecraft had made an effort to turn the world upside down, turn object into subject. *A Vindication* presumed women to be the centre of their own worlds, however weakly and vainly they held that position. The presumption itself constitutes half the revolution of the work.

Inevitably, Wollstonecraft turned the spotlight on a particular class of women. While the whole of *A Vindication* is suffused with her passionate opposition to social injustice in general, and sexual injustice in particular, the examples that she uses are drawn from her experience as a young woman, from a comfortable but precarious background, who had had to struggle to establish herself in the world in every way. That struggle – the trials of a clever, passionate girl without hereditary advantage – is reflected in her quick-witted contempt for other more fortunate, less talented, women. As her biographer, Claire Tomalin, observes, some of Wollstonecraft's observations – about women, and mothers – date from her experience as a governess in Ireland to a large Anglo-Irish aristocratic clan, the Knaresboroughs. This family rather toyed with her: treating her first as a person of some importance and then literally dismissing her. Wollstonecraft's jealousy of her employer's fecundity and sexual allure, despite multiple pregnancies, obviously informed her later writings. Wollstonecraft felt both sexual competitiveness and class resentment towards Lady Knaresborough, but she deploys the emotions to powerful effect. As Claire Tomalin points out, Wollstonecraft in *A Vindication* 'hit the exact tone of righteous indignation that is still effective – indeed it has become the staple of much successful journalism'.[3]

Wollstonecraft's main targets are those women who are happy to make themselves men's sexual objects and use their feminine wiles to win admiration and sexual approval. 'Pleasure is the business of women's life . . . according to the present modifications of society . . . and while it continues to be so, little can be expected from such weak beings . . . they have chosen to be short lived queens [rather] than labour to obtain the sober pleasures that arise from equality.'[4] One may sense Wollstonecraft's envy of such women, as well as her more just, rational concern for their fate once beauty has faded, yet her rationality led her to the right conclusion. An education equal to men's could direct and shape women's physical and mental energies and liberate them from the tyranny of femininity and dependence on men. Women, Wollstonecraft believed, should be allowed to take up such professions as medicine (not just nursing), farming, shop-keeping and business.

How does motherhood fit into the central themes of *A Vindication*? Wollstonecraft certainly does not reject it: on the contrary she both blandly and grandly assigns most women to this, their biological task . . . 'the care of children in their infancy is one of the grand duties annexed to the female character by nature'.[5] However, crippled by their own silliness and moral and intellectual limitations they will not be good ones. Mothers, she argues, seldom exert 'enlightened maternal affection . . . To be a good mother, a woman must have sense and that independence of mind which few women possess who are taught to depend entirely on their husbands.'[6] A good widowhood, on the other hand, yields opportunity from tragedy; here, Wollstonecraft sketches a rough – if smug – portrait of the ideal woman, so absorbed in her own tasks and the proper upbringing of her children she cannot think of herself for one moment.

In the substance of her argument, Wollstonecraft's good sense cannot be disputed – from a modern perspective at least; motherhood is not bad, it is simply not enough. In her injunction to 'make your own life' as well as you make another life, Wollstonecraft lays down the basis for nearly two centuries of individualist argument on procreation and child-rearing. At the same time, the limitations of Wollstonecraft's young perceptions – of human beings, in general; of women in particular – emerge most noticeably on the subject of motherhood, perhaps because Wollstonecraft is writing as a dissatisfied daughter (who had not yet become a mother herself) rather than as a dissatisfied mother, a very different state. Her injunctions to mothers are made with the well-being of the children, not the female parent, in mind. Like so many young women without children – and it is an age question as much as anything – she invests mothers with too much power and not enough sensibility. She too simply sees the labour of motherhood as self-sacrifice or unattractive self-display rather than a complicated generosity. She too easily interprets its harshness as tyranny rather than desperation; its calm as relinquishment, rather than acceptance of self. From the inside of motherhood everything looks different.

Compare the tone of *A Vindication* to a work written just four years later when Wollstonecraft was touring Scandinavia with her tiny daughter, Fanny: *Letters Written During a Short Residence in Sweden, Norway and Denmark* (1796). The *Letters* are more descriptive than prescriptive. They are rather wistful, sad in places. By now, Wollstonecraft had been disappointed in love, borne a child, Fanny, and attempted suicide twice. The *Letters* indirectly affect these experiences, and the book seems to have a genuinely wider and more perceptive compass. Writing in Letter Number Three, Wollstonecraft observes that

> the situation of the servants in every respect, particularly that of the women, shows how far the Swedes are from having a just conception of rational equality. They are not *termed* slaves; yet a man may strike a man with impunity because he pays him wages . . .[7]

But it is her direct references to her own motherhood and her child that touch the heart. As Claire Tomalin says of the *Letters*:

> On the one hand she is a sensible and informative writer, on the other the book is personal in a way that is sometimes startling. Few travel writers and still fewer business investigators have taken a small child with them on their journey; the tenderness with which she writes of Fanny, 'my little frolicker', 'my little cherub', now 'hiding her face in my bosom', now running about on the seashore, 'the rosy down of health on her cheeks', and leaving her 'tiny footsteps on the sands', is the most touching feature of her narrative.[8]

It is more than tender; it is tragic. In the *Letters* Wollstonecraft writes of her recognition of the intense vulnerability not only of her own situation but of Fanny, illegitimate and transient through Mary's need to earn a living. She writes of a 'sort of weak melancholy that hung about my heart at parting with my daughter for the first time'. Then she goes on:

> You know that as a female I am particularly attached to her – I feel more than a mother's fondness and anxiety, when I reflect on the dependent and oppressed state of her sex. I dread that she should be forced to sacrifice her heart to her principles, or principles to her heart. With trembling hand I shall cultivate sensibility, and cherish delicacy of sentiment,

lest, while I lend fresh blushes to the role, I sharpen the thorns
that will wound the breast I would fain guard . . . I dread to
unfold her mind, lest it should render her unfit for the world
she is to inhabit – Hapless woman! what a fate is thine![9]

If motherhood renders Wollstonecraft's view of womanhood
more vulnerable and fearful than her aggressive younger self had
allowed, it also gives her writing a dimension and humanity that
A Vindication lacks.

Class acts: Sylvia Pankhurst and Dora Russell

Feminist history is as much made up of activism as of argument.
Two women who have contributed to our perspective on
motherhood, Sylvia Pankhurst and Dora Russell, have done so as
much through their campaigns and example as in the writings left
by them. Sylvia Pankhurst was the daughter of Emmeline
Pankhurst and sister of Christabel, the stars of the suffragette
movement of the late nineteenth and early twentieth century. But
Sylvia's politics, tending more towards socialism, slowly but
surely diverged from those of her increasingly élitist mother and
sister. In 1914 she set up her own branch of the Women's Social
and Political Union – the body that campaigned for women's
suffrage – in the East End of London. As she increasingly
identified with East End women and the problem of poverty,
Sylvia wanted to widen the struggle for the vote in the direction
of working-class interests. Money given to her by generous
benefactors was used to set up free nurseries to care for the
children of her East End campaigners. During the war one set up
a cost price restaurant and workshop in East London.

When, in her mid forties, she had her first and only baby, a son,
Richard, Sylvia's interests focused even more directly on the
conditions of motherhood. Sylvia refused to marry the father of
her child, stating, with some perception, that 'the tendency of the
future will see nothing remarkable in our decision to live together
and have children without marriage and without the woman
losing her own name'. As her somewhat sceptical and ungenerous

biographer, Patricia Romero, states, 'She never undertook any task without sharing it with the public at large.' In that same year, 1928, Sylvia began campaigning on maternal health, writing pamphlets that demanded welfare centres, maternity grants, legislation to help combat post-natal fever in women and a variety of measures to protect child health. In the mid 1930s Sylvia continued to agitate for a national Maternity Service; here backing up the efforts of Labour politician Eleanor Rathbone, who had campaigned for family allowances (which later became child benefit).

Later in her life Pankhurst became friendly with the young Dora Russell, who by the mid 1920s was also campaigning on what she called the issue of 'feminist mothers'. Russell was a tenacious exponent of birth control and the right to abortion and, like Pankhurst, a theoretical proponent of 'free love', as it was then rather romantically called. In her autobiography, *The Tamarisk Tree*, she describes how, as a young mother, she met opposition to her 'modest requests on birth control' and a 'fury against child-bearing displayed by the delegates to the Labour Women's Conference':

> I began to wonder if the feminists had not been running away from the central issue of women's emancipation. Would women ever be truly free and equal with men until we had liberated mothers? Demanding equality and the vote, women in the Labour movement had argued that there should now be no distinction between men's and women's questions, a view which I had more or less accepted until I came up against this issue of maternity. What rights had the working-class mother? Dependent on her man's income, she yet had no claim to a share of it: she must bear and attempt to feed and care for every child born to her . . .[10]

Over the years Russell became gradually convinced

that the trouble with traditional societies is that they completely neglect the views and needs of women. At this stage I simply felt the urge to champion the oppressed mother and disgusted though I was with false sentiment about the noble act of childbirth, I could yet visualize the bearing and rearing of children as a creative activity hitherto little understood or practised in the world.[11]

While later feminist writers have turned their minds to the question of how to reconcile motherhood and high individual purpose, few have taken up the question of the many, rather than the few, with the passion of a Dora Russell. Although known in her young days as 'The Very Intellectual Miss Black', Russell was pre-eminently practical. Her writings on motherhood have the empirical and indubitably English ring of the organized middle-class woman who knows what society needs for it to be put right, and is guided by a deep instinctive sympathy for 'others less fortunate'. Writing on 'Feminist Mothers' in 1925, Russell put her case on both ideological and material grounds. Woman, she argued, has a right not to be a mother, and a right to work and be a mother, but she has an equal right to decent conditions in which to bring up her children. 'Intelligent medicine' can guide women through the preventable misery of unwanted children, insufferable pain during labour, the potential ravages of childhood diseases. She is dismissive of the maternal instinct as anything more than 'habit almost imperceptibly learnt in tending the first, blossoming into a smooth instinctive unity with the coming of the second'.

At her essay's end, she concludes that 'feminist mothers' must demand, first of all, '. . . the recognition of their work – the most dangerous of all trades and the most neglected and despised'. Society should help women to have an education and children, at well-spaced intervals, but it 'is imperative that the woman who has children should never be shut out from public life'.[12]

Dora Russell continued to campaign, write and lecture until the mid 1980s. Her earlier work, like that of other pioneers concerned with both maternal conditions and child welfare, such as Eleanor Rathbone and Margaret McMillan, set the stage for the welfare state and the public provision of the post-war era. Russell also anticipated many of later feminism's arguments about freedom, sexual and biological. What she did not, and could not do, was anticipate the extent to which mothers would enter the workforce and there, if at all serious about their work, be required to tuck the fact of their motherhood out of sight; nor would she anticipate the lack of life chances still available to most women, either in jobs with little pay or with no job at all and dependent on the state. Russell saw child-bearing as the natural centre of women's lives; public life should be organized around it. How could she foresee that by the end of the second half of the twentieth century, society would to the same extent see child-bearing and child-rearing as subordinate to women's public or economic role, even while women themselves struggled for parity in both spheres; home and work.

Simone de Beauvoir: the vocation of the self

Simone de Beauvoir's *The Second Sex* still stands as one of the great works on women in the twentieth century. It anticipated and encouraged many of the directions taken by western women in the second half of the century. Much of de Beauvoir's influence was personal; her extraordinary life story, described in her equally impressive four-volume autobiography, set a new template for female independence: a life of sexual freedom, a life dedicated to work and politics, an unmarried life, a childless life It is both ironic and fitting that the woman who decided to have no children of her own should, instead, have spawned generations of 'daughterly' admirers and imitators. (And in later life, de Beauvoir did adopt an adult daughter, Sylvie Le Bon.) In her introduction to her book, *Daughters of de Beauvoir*, based on a film of the same name, Imogen Sutton writes:

> I always knew I wanted to have children, whereas she knew
> that she didn't want to be a mother . . . Ironically, it was
> during pre-production on the film that I became pregnant,
> and while filming in France my morning sickness was at its
> worst. So while I worked on a film about her, I was involved
> in a very different sort of experience to any she had had. And

yet I could still find a dialogue between us on the subject. Most women who appear in the film talk about her decision not to have children . . . Marge Piercy comments that it 'seemed to me a clear and sunny, rational yet felt choice'. [And] Ann Oakley says, 'Simone de Beauvoir has been a very important role model for me, as she has been for lots of other women, and in that sense she has been a mother, the mother some of us perhaps wished we had ourselves.'[13]

For de Beauvoir, in keeping with her rather severe, teacherly persona, motherhood first and foremost needs *explaining*. There is certainly no reason, intellectual or instinctual, to have children; equally, there is no condemnation of those who do. Instead, de Beauvoir judges motherhood as an action, or set of actions, that make sense within a wider context. 'Maternity,' she observes, with cool even-handedness, 'is usually a strange mixture of narcissism, altruism, idle daydreaming, sincerity, bad faith, devotion and cynicism . . .' According to her, a woman's reaction to it depends not on biology or even conscious hopes but on her 'total situation', the life she has made for herself both privately and in a public and social context. In women's attitude to childbirth, 'women give expression to their fundamental attitude towards the world in general.'[14]

While de Beauvoir is tough on motherhood and tough on the causes of bad motherhood, she is remarkably open to its many enjoyments. She takes an almost vicarious pleasure in the various stages from early pregnancy through to birth and early childhood, sharing in the joy and absorption of the women whose experience she reflects. She writes of 'the marvellous peace of late pregnancy' or of the writer Colette's perception of gestation as a 'holiday' (a view I often remember my own mother quoting to me). She is just as perceptive on the disappointment, ambivalence and anger that mother feels for child and vice versa. 'The child is the foe of the waxed floor' may not be an observation with wholly modern resonance but it captures the lack of order, in action and feeling, that young children inevitably bring to the lives of parents.

De Beauvoir recognizes that a woman's attitude to childbirth and children will depend not only on her relationship with her mother, but on her mother's own relationship to these experiences. Drawing on her knowledge of psychoanalysis, de Beauvoir sees that a woman's attitude to parenthood is, therefore, not always a conscious process:

> It must be realized that the avowed decisions and sentiments of the young mother do not always correspond with her deeper desire. A young unmarried mother may be overwhelmed by the material burdens suddenly forced on her and may be overtly in despair and yet find in the baby the realization of her secret dreams. On the other hand, a young married woman who welcomes her pregnancy with joy and pride may inwardly dislike it under the influence of obsessions, fantasies and memories of infancy that she declines to recognize openly.[15]

Even more passionately than Wollstonecraft, de Beauvoir believes that women who have purposes beyond parenthood make much better mothers; their very detachment guarantees a more authentic form of maternal absorption. They are not seeking anxiously for a reflection of themselves in the baby's gaze, but merely enjoying a sensual relationship. The writer Colette is frequently held up as an exemplary mother, principally because she keeps on writing, as opposed to those 'women who muse endlessly on their new importance'.

> The great danger which threatens the infant in our culture lies in the fact that the mother to whom it is confided in all its helplessness is *almost always* a discontented woman . . . sexually she is frigid or unsatisfied: socially she feels herself inferior to man: she has no independent grasp on the world or on the future. She will seek to compensate for all these frustrations through her child. When it is realized how difficult woman's present situation makes her full self-realization, how many desires, rebellious feelings, just claims she nurses in secret, one is frightened at the thought that defenceless infants are abandoned to her care [my emphasis].[16]

The exaggeration of that 'almost always' undermines de Beauvoir's apparent pedagogic neutrality on the motherhood question. For here she is referring back to the discontented woman in her own life, her mother Françoise, whose unhappiness and lack of satisfaction had a direct and continuing impact on her ambitious, strong-willed daughter. (Like Margaret Thatcher, de Beauvoir infinitely preferred the worldliness of her father, Georges.) This sense of past mothers as threatening, but future mothers as promising, is as much a clue to de Beauvoir's own 'personal situation' as a quasi-sociological prediction that woman's total situation is improving. Nevertheless, de Beauvoir does see the young mother of her own day − the post Second World War period − as offering something more hopeful to themselves and the next generation. The new woman

> demands to have a part in that mode of activity in which
> humanity tries continually to have justification through
> transcendence, through movement towards new goals and
> accomplishments . . . the woman who works − farmer,
> chemist or writer − is the one who undergoes pregnancy most
> easily because she is not absorbed in her own person . . . the
> woman who enjoys the richest individual life will have the
> most to give to her children.[17]

The continuity of thought from Wollstonecraft to de Beauvoir is, then, extraordinarily constant. Motherhood is tolerable as a secondary activity to the grand plan of selfhood; to the exercise of reason through education, work and action in the world. Under this rationalist scheme, lonely independence is preferable to mutual interdependence. What this view does not allow for − and here, the fact that neither the Wollstonecraft of A Vindication nor de Beauvoir was a mother is important − is the notion of a rich and continuing enjoyment, as opposed to a partial and passing pleasure, between mother and child, that does not have to justify itself so much as watch its boundaries. It is almost as if these stern women think parenthood is a pleasure to be earned, and continually justified, rather than one of nature's prizes that just happens to be granted to the lucky many.

At the same time, neither woman shows a real appreciation of what is involved in motherhood, the sheer labour of it, that might make the pursuit of other adventures or tasks difficult, if not impossible. It is interesting how often writers invoke the example of other writers – like de Beauvoir with Colette – and praise them for keeping up their interests, when writing is actually the easiest of occupations to keep up as a parent. 'All' one needs is a pen, paper, a flat surface and a sleeping (or minded) child. If it has to be, work can be done in twenty-minute stretches or after the baby has gone to sleep; it can be written – like so much of this book! – at five in the morning, before the first stirrings begin. But what of those other occupations that de Beauvoir names: the farmer and chemist, as well as the writer? A field cannot be ploughed at twelve at night, a laboratory is open only at set hours. Both professions demand co-operation with, and constant connection with, others: bosses, subordinates, co-workers, technicians, students, animals.

De Beauvoir is probably one of the last significant feminists to write about motherhood with no realistic appraisal of what women's large-scale entry into work would mean; the sheer tenacity required of women to keep 'visible', respected and, in the case of professionals, rising up a professional ladder. Like Wollstonecraft she was satisfied with the generalizing of her own personal notions. But having purpose is not the same as pursuing an ordinary career nor being a breadwinner. Having purpose is not the same as gaining or taking worldly or political power. Purpose tends to be the favoured mode of the artist: the writer, the thinker. She (or he) judges everyone else by it, and is surprised and disappointed to find most women either not marked by it in the same way or hindered by more ordinary obstacles than a lack of determination.

Betty Friedan: motherhood and the marketplace

Betty Friedan, the critic and chronicler of American suburban motherhood in *The Feminine Mystique* (1963), took the question of 'purpose' a little further on to ordinary territory. She, too, wanted to rid women's lives of emptiness. The world she describes has a distinct physical and topographical feel to it that will be familiar to anyone who has driven through an American small town, or watched a film like Douglas Sirk's *All That Heaven Allows*. Here is the land of a million neat white houses set in neat green lawns with a neat white picket fence and a well-pruned tree out front; the newspaper thrown on to the gravel drive in the misty early morning. Here is a world, too, of stifling conformity, as Marilyn French wrote in her novel *The Women's Room*:

> It is often noticed that women in suburbia, much like the women in ancient Greece, are locked into the home and see no one but children all day. The Greek women saw slaves who might have been interesting people. But suburban women have each other.[18]

In his last book, *Women and the Common Life: Love, Marriage and Feminism* (1997), published posthumously, social critic Christopher Lasch pointed out that:

> What is striking about Friedan's manifesto, when one returns to it more than thirty years later, is the degree to which it was dominated by the plight of suburban women . . . it did not seem unreasonable to interpret the 'post-war suburban explosion' as the product of a 'mistaken choice' made by a new generation of women who repudiated the active life of their predecessors and saw the family as a refuge from increasingly unmanageable conditions in the public world. 'Women with commitments outside the home,' Friedan observed, were 'less likely to move to the suburbs'.[19]

Ostensibly, Friedan was addressing that generation of women who had gone on to higher education and were proud of their achievements. Her genius was not so much in recognizing that there was a problem — others had done so — but in the detail of her *investigation* of women's failure to 'follow through' on their education, into meaningful, productive lives. Women, she saw, were sinking their lives and hopes into men, sex, family and ideal homes. 'The problem which has no name' was the consequent feeling of emptiness, of being cheated.

Friedan was concerned almost exclusively with the affluent; she had little to say about the millions of American women who had not, on the one hand, had the benefit of an education, nor, on the other, the dubious luxury of not working. Concentrating on a lost post Second World War generation of largely white, well-off women, Friedan argued the importance of work. 'For being paid is, of course, more than a reward – it implies a definite commitment.' Not any old job will do. A job must be part of a 'life plan . . . be part of the social scheme . . . to the active, ambitious woman, ambition is the thread that runs through her life from beginning to end, holding it together and enabling her to think of her life as a work of art instead of a collection of fragments.'[20]

Friedan *was* a mother when she wrote *The Feminine Mystique*. She rarely alludes to her own experience, yet it dominates the book, as it must; for she is writing at that point in a parent's life when both the magic and the difficulty of children are accepted, integrated and may perhaps even have dimmed; when the woman who has devoted her life to them starts to ask, what now? Friedan is not rejecting motherhood or family so much as taking it for granted. The book expresses restlessness rather than rebellion, a position confirmed by her later book, *The Second Stage* (1980), which, in a sort of mirror image of *The Feminine Mystique*, urges women not to jettison family life for the sake of possibly empty careers.

What is Friedan actually suggesting to women? She may urge women to take up more than jobs, but she actually elaborates little on where such paid and meaningful work might be. Christopher Lasch points out 'how little she was inclined to identify the work women ought to be doing with highly paid professional careers. She wanted women to get out of the house, but she did not necessarily want them to throw themselves into the job market.'[21]

Friedan's chief injunction was, in fact, a backward-looking

one; when she urged women to work that involves 'initiative, leadership and responsibility', she was seeking a return to the kinds of voluntary or, at least, socially committed work that women had undertaken *en masse* in the nineteenth century. Looked at in this light, Lasch argues, we should not read Friedan in the conventional way as the 'first halting step down the road since traveled by an army of more militant women . . . [but] as an attempt to mark out a road that was later abandoned. The issue, in a word, was how to revive a sense of vocation in a society destitute of any sense of common purpose.'[22]

We are back to that word 'purpose' again. Friedan, like many feminist writers before her, was, in many ways, urging all women to do as *she* did or wished to do; work with 'leadership, initiative and responsibility'. (There is no better definition of a feminist spokeswoman and campaigner than that!) It may be that even as early as this first book, Friedan shied away from more traditional ideas of career success – even while appearing to recommend it. She may have already feared, as she states in *The Second Stage,* that this path has its own emptiness, parallel to the emptiness of the domestic hearth.

An interest in social purpose rather than simple professionalism may also explain why Friedan is so vague on the practicalities of women's entry into paid work. There is very little in *The Feminine Mystique* on men's role in the social revolution she proposes. Friedan is keen to point out how getting women out of the home can benefit men; how relieved and unburdened they can feel when their wives have interests other than themselves, home and children. But it stops there. She gives no clue to the momentousness of change required if women are to be truly liberated from the cares of home and what that will mean to a male sex reared, in effect, to be serviced by women. All Friedan's directions are to women, urging them to prove and improve themselves. There is, implicitly, a great optimism about the public world's ability to take women seriously, once women themselves decide to be serious. 'Not until a great many women move out of the fringes into the mainstream will society itself provide the arrangements for their new life plan.'

Thirty years later, the 'provision of arrangements by society' has proved to be a half-way house at best. On the whole, women have adapted to the 'mainstream', not the other way round. A significant but still small number of women have interesting jobs, sufficient personal flexibility – money, actively involved partners or, more rarely these days, supportive networks – to pursue them and have children. Many, many others struggle with family and work, managing but not satisfied.

In *The Feminine Mystique* Friedan was the last of the great feminist liberal idealists. She believed capitalism could bring satisfaction to women, if they moved from being consumers to producers. But such idealism does not survive recession, social and economic inequality or the gross fact of exploitation. As a more socially conscious, politically radical generation of feminists were to discover, the solution to motherhood does not lie in an individual's adaptation to the market. The great feminist revolution lies unfinished.

~ 11 ~

Feminism II:
Everyday Rebellions and the
Small Matter of Enjoyment

None of it is as simple as we thought back then.
Sheila Rowbotham, *Guardian*, 13 May 1997

Just listen to the flamboyant, ferocious tone of the first feminists
of our own time:

> Mother is the dead heart of the family, spending father's
> earnings on consumer goods to enhance the environment in
> which he eats, sleeps and watches television . . . The home is
> her province, and she is lonely there. She wants her family to
> spend time with her, for her only significance is in relation to
> that almost fictitious group. She struggles to hold her children
> to her, imposing restrictions, waiting up for them, prying into
> their affairs. They withdraw more and more into non-
> communication and thinly veiled contempt.[1]

Or this:

> The reproduction of the species by one sex for the benefit of
> both would be replaced by . . . artificial reproduction:
> children would be born to both sexes equally, or

independently of either . . . the dependence of the child on
the mother (and vice versa) would give way to a greatly
shortened dependence on a small group of others in general,
and any remaining inferiority to adults in physical strength
would be compensated for culturally. The tyranny of the
biological family would be broken.[2]

It took me time to put together both the content and flavour of
these declarations – for they go beyond mere writing, and come
to exist within a grand political courtroom in the sky where
talented polemicists do, indeed, declare themselves – with a
certain blankness that faced me whenever I asked women about
what feminism meant to them, as mothers. They frequently
looked puzzled; rather as if I had asked them to recall a long-ago
incident or an old school friend. Sorry, said the head shake.
Another cup of tea? To some, feminism really meant little. To
others, it conjured up a picture of hostility; to men, children,
family. To yet more, feminists were like politicians in general;
larger than life characters who know nothing about 'ordinary life'.
   For a long while this puzzled me, particularly as so many kinds
of feminism have concerned themselves with what Sheila
Rowbotham recently described as the world of 'births, betrayal,
ecstasy or even the washing up'; particularly as feminism has soft-
ened in its approach to motherhood, if not family, since the mid
1980s. But my own knowledge is professional, detailed; when
rereading recently the work of Germaine Greer and Shulamith
Firestone, both quoted above, I wondered if, like a long-distance
phone call, today's women still hear the echo of that argumenta-
tive voice of nearly two decades ago as somehow representative
of today's politics? And do they perhaps mix up that relatively old
certainty with a relatively new form of feminist arrogance; those
American writers, so dominant in the late eighties and nineties,
who have had so much to say on sex, hunger, pornography,
power, self-esteem, art and great men but so very, very little to
say about motherhood? Does the 'ordinary' woman's view of
feminism's view of motherhood lie, then, between the devil of
assumed derision and the deep blue sea of acknowledged distance?

None of this is at all fair, of course, to modern feminism's varied reflections on motherhood. Nevertheless, many women's suspicion of feminist politics may still touch, tenderly, on a half truth. As I have already argued, feminism's great works of the past have always been a form of 'writing against', writing against the assumption that motherhood is all that women can do. The politics of the second wave built on that older feminist view that motherhood was an essentially restricting situation, a problem that needed solving. Greer and Firestone, both published in the early 1970s, carried this 'writing against' to new heights. The new emphasis on individual creativity and self-expression, so characteristic of the sixties, and the corresponding rejection of much more deep-rooted ideas of service and love-as-work, only fuelled their disrespect for the mother of yore and lore. Thus they can assert: mothers are the 'dead heart' of a home, unloved, unfree. From the vantage point of youthful choice, the greying mothers of their own age may well have looked like that.

But this left another story untold, an important side of women's experience unexpressed. For motherhood is not just raw biology; it is not *only* drudgery. Being a mother is calming; it is moving; it is enlightening; it is fun. These ordinary pleasures seem so obvious to most women. For them, their enjoyment or, at the very least, their acceptance of their own parenthood is not just a collapse into private life, a refusal to take up a challenge. It is a different *sort* of challenge, a place where a variety of values can be expressed and maintained. To create and rear a human being can be a fundamental expression of that most positive of human qualities; love. And yes; love-as-work. While feminism's boldest and best story – and certainly its most publicized one – has always been the tale of the one who got away, it has always had a slight difficulty with the one who stayed behind, and *liked* it. It has had worrying blind spots about this small matter of enjoyment. Even when it has been able to acknowledge the strength and pleasure, as well as the difficulties, of the mother-child bond, it has – fearing sentimentality perhaps? – not often been able successfully to create a public language to express *all* the dimensions of motherhood.

Revolt of the mothers Part 1 . . .

Earlier centuries leave us with relatively few manifestations of any individual's political thought, male or female. One characteristic of the second half of the twentieth century is the sheer numbers of people leaving a record, through articles, film, video, of what they think and feel; as a society we are deluged. Second wave feminism, which dates from the late 1960s onwards, is no exception. We have the testimony of the perceptions of many women, many mothers. As Anna Coote and Beatrix Campbell note in their account of these beginnings:

> *Contrary to popular belief, the new feminists were not footloose and fancy-free: most were married and freshly acquainted with motherhood.* 'I had been at home for about a year after the birth of my first son,' Valerie Charlton recalls. 'I found it impossible to adapt. I had the baby when I was twenty-seven, and in one year I had gone from feeling confident and in charge of myself, earning a living, to being completely collapsed and lonely [my emphasis].'[3]

These young women were society's baby boomers, reared in post-war optimism, highly educated, many of them passionately committed to left-wing politics. Yet they found themselves in a kind of political version of Betty Friedan's *The Feminine Mystique*, changing nappies while the men were out changing the world. These young women did not feel anything as simple as dislike of their children or of mothering itself. It was more that they had a sense of injustice; the individual men they knew, and the social movements they were involved in, were so much more interested in equality outside the home than within it. Sheila Rowbotham quotes a letter sent in 1971 to *Shrew*, an internal magazine of the women's liberation movement, from a woman who describes herself as an 'ardent revolutionary'. This woman could not understand her own depression, until she saw that the problem lay in the division of labour in the home. 'I challenged him on the hypocrisy of his political attitudes. Wasn't I oppressed too? He hadn't even come to terms with this fact, let alone the fact that he was my oppressor. I looked after the home and kids so that he could be free to do what he liked.'[4]

Complaint quickly became politics; women's frustration became women's liberation. Early writings of the movement are rich in a sort of 'thick description', of pleasure and guilt, the deadness of the home compared to the aliveness of political events outside. There is something distinctly modern in these young women's musings on the question of 'Who am I?' or 'Who was I meant to be?' – the question of individual identity – that is lacking from the more robust writers of even ten, fifteen years before. Sue O'Sullivan, a young mother in the late sixties, wrote like this:

> Back in Stoke Newington I sat with my big quiet wide-eyed baby and stared at him wondering who I was, who he was. I sat for hours with him on the breast, I wiped up shit, pinned nappies on . . . I was floundering badly but I think I must have looked all right. Pictures from my album show smiling or contemplative family life . . . I wasn't sure what anything meant. I'd joined the grown up world of mothers and yet I felt more unsure and lonely than ever before. I could perform all the techniques of motherhood completely. I was riveted by the baby but I had an awful feeling that being a mother didn't fit me well.[5]

Angela Coyle described her personal summer of 1968, in which the demonstrations and sit-ins reached their height, as follows:

> In August 1968 I was nineteen, but now I had this baby. I was clueless and on my own. I abandoned breastfeeding because I felt I didn't know how to do it. Life came to mean bottles, nappies and endless days of isolation. My intelligence was channelled into devising ways of passing the time, days, weeks, months. Whilst I lost the restlessness that I experienced when I first got married *things still didn't seem quite right*, my life was meant to be more . . . but what? [My emphasis][6]

This language of discontent had a literary, if not explicitly political, fore-tradition. As early as the 1950s, Doris Lessing, in her Martha Quest trilogy, had depicted the pains and tribulations of being a mother. In *A Proper Marriage* (1954), Lessing describes Quest's 'contest of wills' with her baby daughter, Caroline, over food which the child ends up smearing all over herself:

> What is it all about? asked Martha in despair. She was furious
> with herself for losing her temper. She could have wept with
> annoyance. She was saying to herself as she wiped up milk
> and grey pulp; Oh Lord, how I hate this business, I do loathe
> it so. She was saying how she hated her daughter; and she
> knew it. Soon the hot anger died; guilt unfailingly
> succeeded . . . 'My poor unfortunate brat, what had you done
> to deserve a mother like me?'

A decade later, writers like Penelope Mortimer and Margaret Drabble were writing in rich emotional detail about the conflicts and ambivalence of wifehood and motherhood. Margaret Drabble described the social context for this writing as follows:

> When we left college we had babies, fed the family, did a
> day's work, served Cordon Bleu meals by candlelight and
> were free to have intellectual conversation all evening. But
> the freedom was mockery because we were all overloaded,
> exhausted. And out of that feeling arose the women's novel of
> the sixties, it just arose spontaneously: Edna O'Brien, Doris
> Lessing, Penelope Mortimer, and a little later Fay Weldon,
> beginning to express these feelings of rage.[7]

Writers like Drabble and Mortimer were less explicit, less harsh than Lessing; Weldon was funnier. (Her 1981 short story 'Weekend' is a brilliant depiction of a wife and mother's unremitting labour and a husband's blithe blindness to it.) In her short, spare novel *The Pumpkin Eater* (1962), Mortimer told the story of a young wife whose near-obsession with pregnancy and having babies shields her from the realities of a disintegrating marriage. In her early books such as *The Garrick Year* (1964) and *The Millstone* (1965), Margaret Drabble described the pleasures, rootedness and ambiguous dissatisfactions of young wifehood and motherhood. The effect of both Drabble's and Mortimer's writing is not to criticize the family head on, but rather to build up a sense of undefined threat around the main female character that envelops the reader in the same ambiguous way that it envelops her.

But it was with the arrival of an explicitly political feminism that personal stories were 'made over' into politics. 'This novel changes lives!' shouts the bold black and silver front of my 1978 copy of *The Women's Room* by Marilyn French. It didn't change mine because I hardly had a life to change by then, but *The Women's Room* did appear to sum up a generation of older women's experience of bad and boring marriages, of longing for escape from motherhood, the risks and excitement of education, sexual love and friendships with other women and finally, the inability of even good men, new men, to truly reciprocate love and care for women and children. Here was feminism's best story line again, this time cast in social realist prose; the story that suggests women may be better off alone, unhappy, perhaps, but free. *The Women's Room*, which remains a very angry book, offered no solutions, just a lot of conflict and confusion. Its impact throughout America and Western Europe was huge. Somehow, it crystallized a mood of fury and despair that some women felt about men, and some mothers felt about the fathers of their children.

But even as French was laying down the template of one kind of feminist reaction to motherhood, another writer, the poet Adrienne Rich, was exploring the institution with more tenderness. Rich's non-fiction study *Of Woman Born: Motherhood as Experience and Institution* (1977) was a historical, anthropological and political examination of motherhood, but it was also a highly personal account of her own experience. Rich, a young mother in the fifties, was describing the Friedan generation who either gave up their work for babies or were forced, like Rich, to work not quite in secret but without domestic or public support; work was to be 'fitted in' around the babies. Rich's description of the ambivalence of mothering has a resonance even today; her use of language raises it far above even beautiful polemic. Rich is open about the physical ache, the longing she has felt sometimes just to hold a tiny baby, that can come on any of us; she is equally as open about the desperation of never having time or true mental freedom.

> . . . I remember a cycle. It began when I had picked up a
> book or began trying to write a letter or even found myself
> on the telephone with someone toward whom my voice
> betrayed eagerness, a rush of sympathetic energy. The child
> (or children) might be absorbed in the busyness, in his own
> dream world; but as soon as he felt me gliding into a world
> which did not include him, he would come to pull at my
> hand, ask for help, punch at the typewriter keys. And I would
> feel his wants at such a moment as fraudulent, as an attempt
> moreover to defraud me of living even for fifteen minutes as
> myself.[8]

Sharing and caring

What was really new about second-wave feminism was its attempt to bring men in, to involve them in the bringing up of children. Wollstonecraft, de Beauvoir, even Friedan never seriously considered this: motherhood was a problem for a woman to wrestle with alone. 'Second-wave' feminists, with their challenge to everything, including nature, began to think about the family, men and women in a quite new way. Two influential works of the period tried to think through the problem of parenting, if in quite different ways. Shulamith Firestone's unequivocal *The Dialectic of Sex* (1970), which I have already quoted from, was a full-scale assault on the biological family. Firestone believed that reproduction was the central obstacle in the way of women's true liberation. Historically, she argued, this had had to be the case but new developments in technology were now beginning to change this scenario. Her most revolutionary prediction, and suggestion, was that women should be freed from the tyranny and misery of pregnancy and childbirth, and she is quite sure that both *are* miserable experiences, by advances in technology. Hence her view that 'the end goal of feminist revolution must be, unlike that of the first feminist movement, not just the elimination of male privilege but of sex distinction itself . . .'

Firestone was, in many ways, a far seer. Thirty years on, we are indeed in possession of technology that can separate nature and reproduction: test tube babies, IVF, surrogacy. It will not be that many decades, I believe, before men may be able to gestate, and themselves feed, a human foetus. But as far back as 1970, Firestone risked naming the shape of a future that must have then seemed absurd. However, if Firestone thought babies were women's downfall, she had, at least, some solution to the problem. In its collectivist assumptions, *The Dialectic of Sex* reads very much like a product of the sixties, a product of its hope and its utopianism. In her final chapter Firestone examines the failures of some previous communalist experiments – the Russian communes set up after the revolution and the Israeli kibbutz – with an eye to improving upon them. Written at the peak of Marxist influence on the European sensibility, it assumes the development of communalist ideas which have, of course, virtually disappeared. Firestone believed that the future of the family lay in group arrangements where childcare is shared by mothers, fathers and other adults.

In *The Reproduction of Mothering* (1978), Nancy Chodorow declared, 'Women's mothering is one of the few universal and enduring elements of the sexual division of labour.' She argued that it was not just biological but social, or 'relational':

> Biological mothers have come to have more exclusive
> responsibility for childcare just as the biological components
> of mothering have lessened, as women have borne fewer
> children and bottle feeding has become available.[9]

Women do the job of mothering, she argues, because psychological tools for mothering are passed on from mother to daughter, while a son's nurturant capacities and needs have been systematically curtailed and repressed. She concluded that, 'It is politically and socially important to confront the organization of parenting.' By this, she meant, like Firestone, the creation of more collective enterprises or 'group situations'. 'Children could be dependent from the outset on people of both genders and establish an individuated sense of self in relation to both.'[10]

Things were changing at street level, too. The bleakness of so much writing by young mothers, the traditional pessimism of the young, was matched by the practical optimism of young energy. There were many attempts to set up alternative ways of living, from group houses, to community nurseries, like the Dartmouth Park Hill nursery which opened in north London in 1972, to bunches of women just living together. In the year before she died, the journalist Jill Tweedie wrote, in a letter to me, that the brief period she had lived in such a house, just with other women, was one of the happiest times of her life.

It is odd, now, to look back at these 'experiments in living'. They seem both a little absurd and utterly sensible. Perhaps this is because their innovators' very willingness to risk absurdity, and challenge the natural, was what made their ideas and practice more commonplace for the generations that followed. Even if most people do not practise what they preach, most of us in 1998 believe that men should be actively involved with children; the idea of 'new men' is no longer new. Some of the other ideas of the seventies have fallen by the wayside; for example the notion that non-parents should be involved intimately and actively in bringing up children. Writing about this particular aspect of the experiments in loving, Marsha Rowe concluded that, 'The women who are non-biological parents feel like the governesses of old – no-one knows quite how to treat them.'[11] What's striking now is how many of these political and emotional projects required the very element lacking in modern lives: time. Time to make social relationships anew; time to 'work out new ways of relating to the children', time to involve little boys in cooking, and little girls in carpentry, as they tried to do at the Dartmouth Park Hill nursery; time to deal with all those new men who were 'unsure' of their child-relating capacities. The neo-conservatism of so many men and women today arises from this simple lack of hours, as much as a dearth of hope.

From women's liberation to many feminisms . . .

It is one of the most commonplace observations about feminism that at some undefinable point, like a river that spawns many tributaries, feminism became feminisms. Like many commonplace observations, it is true; a movement that held conferences and marches, however full of debate and disagreement, became something else; a gentle or not so gentle clamour of voices. Some branches of the new spawning feminism took up a more militant relationship to men and sex; some retreated into a gentler world of women alone; some turned their attention to the politics of the nation. But what is of particular interest here is how almost every significant change, and multiplication of, feminisms led to a more tender approach to motherhood.

One of the dominant currents in the new multiplicity of viewpoints was what has been called 'difference' feminism or, in some other quarters, cultural feminism. Crudely, this looked to what was good in women's actions and behaviour, and particularly their caring qualities. Rather than rejecting women's mothering capacities, some writers, notably Carol Gilligan *In A Different Voice* (1982), saw in these capacities a different ethical system which demanded equal respect to men's ethical system. Building on the work of psychologist Jean Baker Miller, Gilligan argued that traditional developmental models emphasized the masculine path as one of individuation and separation into adulthood: full maturity was therefore premised on a lack of connection, rather than an ability to connect and separate, separate and connect, over and over again. Furthermore, men's aggression, Gilligan believed, stemmed from their inability to make satisfying human relationships. Gilligan argued:

> As we have listened for centuries to the voices of men and the theories of development that their experience informs, so we have come more recently to notice not only the silence of

women but the difficulty in hearing what they say when they speak. Yet in the different voice of women lies the truth of an ethic of care, the tie between relationship and responsibility, and the origins of aggression in the failure of connection.[12]

Here, then, was a politics that recognized and valued, if in a rather abstract way, what women actually did, their 'caring'. In this vision, mother was no longer the 'dead heart' of the family, but an autonomous individual with a different, perhaps better, set of values than the all-powerful, worldly father. It is no coincidence that this slightly later generation of feminists, those of the early eighties, were more able to 'see' women and their power, of whatever kind, than the women who came to young adulthood in the sixties and early seventies, the Greers and the Firestones, who seem much more in thrall to the absent, powerful, bullying father. As women became more visible, more powerful in society, they both turned their attention to other women and slowly withdrew power from the nightmare patriarch of the past. (So that, today, our image of malehood is often a deflated, weak one.) There were limits to difference feminism, however. A more caring view of womanhood does not explain Myra Hindley or women's participation in fascism or girl gangs; more importantly, it can be seen to hold women back from the inevitably dirty world of public debate where many increasingly thought feminist voices should be present. Socialist feminist Lynne Segal expressed this view:

> Women's sensibilities are seen as disqualifying them from the 'nasty' world of economic and political power, but equipping them for the socially ill-rewarded work of childcare and, of course, the general servicing of men.[13]

In the real world things were not quite so simple. Feminists of all political hues were influenced to varying degrees by aspects of difference feminism but were not that restrained in their involvement in the 'dirty' world of economics and politics. The 'womanist' iconography of campaigners against the American

siting of missiles at Greenham Common is a good example of
how a pro-woman stand could, for a short while at least, sit
comfortably with a radical politics.

Black feminism also knocked the idea of mother as the 'dead
heart'. For a start, the experience of most young black women,
particularly if they were Afro-Caribbean, was of mothers who
had always worked outside the house. Black and Asian women
wrote of their mothers often with more respect than many of
their white peers; respect for their mothers' lack of privilege,
rather than miserable reliance on it; respect for their fortitude in
the face of racism. Black feminism posed feminism with a
different set of questions, a different political agenda from old and
one that was very much to do with the 'nasty' world of politics
and economics. As Beverley Bryan, Stella Dadzie and Suzanne
Scafe record in their sober and moving 1985 account of black
women's lives in Britain, many black mothers had been unable to
find decent childcare when they had had to work. There are
heartbreaking stories of having to send babies to childminders and
finding them 'soaking wet. The nappy had been left on all day',
or of even having to foster out a baby so that a mother could
work: 'He was a fat baby when I took him there, but when I went
to visit him he was so skinny.'[14] But respect for a mother's work
was not the same as romanticism: American writer June Jordan
put her conflicting feelings about her own mother, who died
worn out, like this:

> And I thought about the idea of my mother as a good woman
> and I rejected that, because I don't see why it's a good thing
> when you give up, or when you co-operate with those who
> hate you or when you polish and iron and mend and endlessly
> mollify for the sake of the people who love the way that you
> kill yourself day by day silently . . . I cherish the mercy and
> the grace of women's work. But I know there is new work
> that we must undertake as well: that new work will make
> defeat detestable to us. That new women's work will mean
> we will not die trying to stand up: we will live that way:
> standing up.[15]

Mothers in the mainstream

By the late eighties, yet another strand of feminism had well and truly entered the mainstream. By now, several campaigners of the seventies had moved into professional policy positions: one or two had even got to Parliament. From them issued a stream of papers, pamphlets, books and ideas which by the early nineties had coalesced into quite a powerful agenda for a 'family friendly' feminism.[16] Journalists who had previously laboured, under-rewarded, on 'movement' magazines or alternative papers were increasingly placing articles and their faces in the newspapers that reached millions. Journalists and writers, such as Angela Neustatter, Angela Phillips, Yasmin Alibhai Brown, Yvonne Roberts, were writing about the various problems they encountered with childcare, work, employers, men and the state, and the public policy implications of these issues. Some magazines, like *Cosmopolitan* and later *She*, and a few features pages, chiefly the *Guardian* Women's Page, offered space and some encouragement to feminists who wanted to talk to the whole, sceptical world.

The triumphs and glamour of Bourgeois Feminist Triumphalism (BFT) had made their mark here, too. The arrival of Madonna and Margaret Thatcher made an older feminism look just that, old, worthy. But while the women's magazines, ironically, were able to incorporate BFT's glammier aspects without undue disrespect to feminism's more collective aims, newspapers, largely run by men, were anxious to rid themselves of the whole 'worthy' package. It was the last straw for many of the liberal contingent when the *Guardian* Women's Page was satirized by Dennis Potter in *The Singing Detective*. Being in the business of selling newspapers, they wanted to reflect the new young brash politics; feminism as entertainment rather than feminism as politics. Sex, shopping, cinema, soap opera, self-esteem, the dilemmas of royalty: these subjects convey the feel of the new post-BFT feminism just as surely as the 'issues' of family, wages, racism, the dilemmas of trade unions convey the feel of an earlier period. New-generation feminists reflected the change more in their language than their content; while still taking up many political subjects, the tone of post-BFT feminism is more ironic, less sympathetic, more confident and less anguished than the earlier writing of 'women's liberation'.

What did this mean for motherhood? If I shut my eyes and summon up a picture of who or what this popular newspaper-led feminism was concerned to represent – and sell to – she is not the classic BFT: the pinstripe mobile-phone-sporting caricature of the share dealer's floor. She is a young-ish, pleasant-ish, professional woman. If she is not a mother she wonders a lot whether, and how, she will ever become one. If she is a mother she is just as likely to be a single mother, who may even have chosen to have a baby from sperm donation, rather than the full-time stay-at-home model of middle England. She may be a publisher or a lawyer or even a lecturer but she is more likely to belong to one of the new media-related professions than one of the caring professions such as social work or teaching. She goes to the gym, likes sex (probably more than the men or man she's having it with), and gossips a lot with her girlfriends. She is interested in designer clothes, lipstick, the whole 'looks' package and scorns a slightly mythical older feminism which tells her she shouldn't be. If she is a working mother, she will probably be part-time but ambivalent about it. Certainly, she is tough, work-minded; there is no obviously 'caring' aspect to her. She is increasingly dissatisfied at what workplaces are doing to her/not doing for her. Hers are a set of reasonable demands for pre-school care, after-school clubs and respect on the job.

The toughness of post-BFT feminism was a reflection of the dead hand of politics. During the eighties and early nineties both the British and American governments were doing and saying little about working mothers. The backlash was truly entrenched and there was a general air of pleasured defeatism about women trying to 'have it all'. With the end of both history and the socialist states in the East, radical politics appeared dead. Two books of the period reflect this defeatism and mild despair; the individual's attempt to cope with the new individualism.

Revolt of the mothers Part 2 . . .

The first was Betty Friedan's much maligned *The Second Stage*, published in 1981. Here, Friedan was trying to answer her own earlier argument, to put her finger on a sense of unease she felt about her political daughters, the women who had learned the lesson of *The Feminine Mystique* only too well:

> A young woman in her third year of Harvard Medical School tells me 'I'm going to be a surgeon. I'll never be a trapped housewife like my mother. But I would like to get married and have children, I think. They say we can have it all. But how? I work thirty-six hours in the hospital, twelve off. How am I going to have a relationship, much less kids, with hours like that? I'm not sure I can be a superwoman. I'm frightened that I may be kidding myself. Maybe I can't have it all. Either I won't be able to have the kind of marriage I dream of, the kind of medical career I want.'[17]

Friedan touched on many of the subjects that were to obsess women (and newspapers) for the next decade: the ticking of the biological clock, the clash between work and family, the fear that women would choose not to have children, the impact of recession and job insecurity on the male psyche. The book is shrouded in fear and suppressed rage at the right-wing forces of reaction, from Christian revivalism to Islamic fundamentalism, which were trying to push women back into the home.

The Second Stage received a rather unfriendly reception from some feminist quarters, mainly because of Friedan's hostility to separatist feminism (then at its height), lesbianism, and her corresponding embrace of the family. Yet in her formulation of a family-friendly feminism, Friedan merely anticipates many of the demands of a mainstream feminism that was to develop over the next decade: in particular, that men and women together find solutions to caring for children and working. As a political animal who had gained her voice in a less miserable era than the eighties, Friedan had the confidence to actually state that we ignore human needs for love, sexual, parental or familial, at our peril. Once again Friedan assumed that men and employers had changed far more than they had, yet her emphasis on the limits of a career way of life and the importance of 'passionate volunteerism', only this time without female self-abnegation, for civic society was terribly important. Friedan understood that there are all sorts of human effort, that the effort of career is not the only effort worth making nor the only success by which we should judge ourselves. 'Life lived only for oneself does not truly satisfy men and women. There is a hunger in Americans today for larger purposes beyond the self. That is the reason for the religious revival and the new resonance of family.' Communal concerns engage the better parts of people's nature, because they transcend the 'culture of narcissism' that so characterizes contemporary society. She was also able to use that word 'capitalism', which so many feminists shy from deploying.

Just over ten years later, British feminist Rosalind Coward tried to tackle the root of modern women's dis-ease from a more personal perspective. In many ways, the catchy market-oriented title *Our Treacherous Hearts, Why Women Let Men Get Their Way* (1992) did not accurately reflect the scope of the book, which ranged much wider than men's intransigence or women's self-betrayal. Coward was attempting to analyse a trend she spotted among women to return to the home, giving up the struggle to balance work, home and relationships. According to her, this was mainly a flight from conflict; from the difficulties that feelings of envy and competitiveness caused women at work, from the unarticulated conflict with men about the sharing, or not sharing, of domestic tasks at home:

> Even when women achieve at high levels, work is often less vital to a sense of self than it is for men. It can it seems be cast off in favour of something 'more real'. The notion that family and children represent a more important, more 'real' priority is repeated by women from all walks of life.[18]

Women, Coward claimed, often redirected their own buried

competitiveness and aggression to the project of full-time mothering, or on to their husband/partner. It was easier for a woman to urge her man on in his workplace or projects, to help *him* to success, than it was to help herself to a success she did not feel entitled to herself. One consequence of this more traditional division of labour in the workplace was a reinforcement of the woman's role at home.

Coward's book paints a gloomy picture of human and work relations. Rather like the feminism of the sixties, but this time with a modern psychoanalytic touch, Coward problematizes women's pleasure with motherhood. Why, she asks, do women submerge themselves in children so? She applies the same questioning approach to women's inability to handle competitiveness and envy in office politics, in itself a measure of how far the new feminist individualism had broken from the political perspectives of the previous decade.

Coward's book is clearly a reflection of the time in which it was conceived and written, a fact she has acknowledged herself since. Bourgeois Feminist Triumphalism was at its height, and any woman who felt conflicts about 'making it' searched her soul for signs of personal weakness. I was not a mother then, but I remember the feel of that time, the way that professional women, the kind of women Coward interviewed in her book, talked; the edge of anxiety, resentment, jealousy, particularly of other women. Women were terrified of appearing a failure, yet this fear was written into everything about them, from their body language to their frenzied overwork. The single child-free woman was a particular threat. Young, mobile, free, more available for male attention, she was inevitably going to prosper in certain working environments, especially as old-fashioned ideas about what a woman could do were fading in the face of the icon's achievement. In many ways, a single woman's femininity now added to her working power and allure, as long as she could be present, give time.

In contrast, mothers found themselves at a huge disadvantage. They had delayed parenthood until either it could be delayed no longer, or they believed that their work position was relatively stable. Yet they remained near enough to their younger selves to remember what *they* once thought of those whey-faced women who were always whispering into phones to nannies and rushing off at five on the dot. And then they became one of the whey-faced; perpetually distracted, perpetually passing from one world to the other, never feeling fully present in either. Their femininity was not expressed in womanly allure but by the actual weight of dependence; a child on them: them on a child. Even the pleasure of mothering became a kind of revenge against women who 'did not have them' or would not have them: both justification and compensation for what they saw themselves losing.

And yet all this discontent found no formal means of protest: it was like a lot of individual conversations that never quite joined up, a lot of personal scraps of unhappiness that further divided the women experiencing it rather than bringing them together. This, then, was the second revolt of the mothers; a passive protest against private conditions and public assumptions which was mainly experienced as unpleasant feelings of personal failure. Once femininity as a form of personal stylishness was accepted, it became clear that the femininity which counted against women was the femininity of 'caring' – of the work assigned to women as women: motherhood and other caring responsibilities. While an earlier feminism could discuss and respect these qualities, and various forms of difference feminism could elevate them to something special, mainstream feminism was in a bind. It wanted women to be taken seriously, but it wanted the weight and difference of their experience to be taken seriously too. And while so many of the new generation of feminists wrote in clear, certain tones, this mainstream popular feminism was often much less confident about politics than the older movement of the seventies. It was as if mainstream feminism dared not beat the system over the head, or not a system it was still trying to join.

Tales from the periphery

At this point in feminism's story of motherhood, I decide to take an hour to listen to the story of Tracy, twenty when I talked to her, a young white mother living on a grim estate on the rim of Basildon: a very smart young lady who regretted that she hasn't the brains to be Prime Minister. Like everyone's, Tracy's life story is long and complicated. Her mother beat her up so badly she left home at thirteen and went into care; then she went into her first flat, my first 'survival home', she called it. Her baby son was born in the flat, a tiny place. By the time he was ten months old, she was on anti-depressants because she couldn't get the buggy down the steps. 'I couldn't get out.' With amazing persistence, she telephoned the council 'every other day until they gave me a house. They just had to give me it.'

I visited her there. I have never been in such an empty space. There was a couch and a television and a phone in the living-room. That was about it. She had sold most of the furniture to buy clothes for her son. She had one remaining item to sell, her son's playpen. 'I won't go below fifty for it. But I don't seem to be getting anywhere with selling it,' she said, in a puzzled voice. Tracy had been in a steady relationship with her son's father for four years; he was an unemployed manual worker. Willing to work almost anywhere, he had not yet been able to get a job. 'It's just doing his head in. He *cries*.' Tracy had tried to get a job with British Telecom, but she failed the exam: 'You had to remember all these numbers, I couldn't do it.' But she was planning to take the exam again.

'The single thing that would make a difference to our life would be ... money. M.O.N.E.Y.' She spells it out for me. 'We're on rations, really. Burgers, pies. Sometimes when I'm lucky we can get minced meat to make a spaghetti bolognese or shepherd's pie ...'

When I remind myself of her story, her clear-headed but, at present, hopeless materialism – 'I need £250 a week, at least' – I see all the places where she snags against feminism's easier presumptions. For Tracy, her baby is not a problem, her man is not a problem, her independence is not at issue, her work is not a problem. She just has no money and no-one she can trust to leave the baby with if she ever did get a job. I suppose you could say Tracy is surviving, and when you're surviving you need things to have dilemmas. That's the one thing lacking from Tracy's life, from her naked living-room: objects, property.

It would be too easy to say feminism does not speak about mothers like Tracy. The varied work of writers like Ann Oakley, Sheila Rowbotham, Beatrix Campbell, Yvonne Roberts, Sue Innes give the lie to that. The work of an organization like the Maternity Alliance, which campaigns for maternity rights for women on low incomes, indicates that there is a politics, still, that acknowledges poverty. But such politics will always have an uphill struggle in a culture run by those with plenty of 'things' themselves and too little political imagination. And that imagination, that ability or desire to think about lives other than those similar to our own, has declined over the years, as economic pessimism and personal selfishness has been further sanctioned. Modern feminism, too, has moved away from its material roots, towards a greater and greater interest in representation, in ideas about women, in women's ideas about themselves, rather than a direct concern for minimum standards of life.

And yet poor mothers did worst of all under the years of conservative government. Nearly a third of babies born in the early to mid 1990s are born to parents who live on means-tested benefits. The gap between incomes widened during the 1980s as a result of both rising unemployment and the lowering of taxation on those with higher incomes. These raw figures have direct impact on everything from birthweight – 9.5 per cent of babies born to mothers alone were of low birthweight in 1994 compared to 4 per cent of babies born to families with fathers in a professional occupation – to infant mortality. While the death of young children has declined over the twentieth century as a whole, investigations into Sudden Infant Death Syndrome (cot death) suggests some correlation between social class and propensity to this early tragedy.[19]

If every indicator shows that women and children who were poor got poorer, it is doubly wrong that they also became the forgotten political subjects of an era. The language of aspiration was deemed wide enough to include us all. But what happens when your aspirations are for something so basic, it never occurs to somebody else that you don't have it or can't get it? A banana for your baby to eat and mash about in his or her hands, a bus fare to a green place for your children to play or a safe place to work?

In 1992 I visited a factory in a small back street of Birmingham. Its address, incredibly, was 10 Downing Street, which coincidence helped me in placing an article in a national newspaper on the strike that had been going on there. A group of Asian men and women were in a long, weary battle with their management over union recognition and health and safety in the workplace. I talked to some of the women: one of them had miscarried while handling some chemicals; she was sure, as you would be, that the two were connected. The sadness of that story was compounded, for me, by the political isolation of these women. It may be too easy a parallel but when a similar strike occurred in 1976 at a photo-processing plant in north-west London, the Grunwick dispute, thousands of supporters from Scargill's 'flying picket' miners to sceptical metropolitan feminists thronged there. Grunwick was part of a collective story. Burnsall was a lonely struggle.

It was not just mothers on income support or in factories whom feminism appeared to forget for a while. It was all those women who make up the burgeoning parts of the new economy, particularly the ever-expanding service sector: women in low paid, casualized or shift work, the woman who got the job at British Telecom that Tracy tried for. Women with as severe a time crisis, as worrying fatigue as professional women, but probably with less time to reflect upon it.

Many contemporary feminist writers, particularly journalists, make this same point, in private. Whenever they want to write about something or someone other than Princess Diana or adultery or serial killing or sexual harassment – I exaggerate, but the point is fair – they come up against the entertainment problem. Poverty, mundanity, ill and undernourished kids, especially those committing no joy-riding crime, mothers pushed to the limit of their endurance but still standing – in other words, not committing some appalling act against their children; all this and so much more simply does not qualify as entertainment. If marketing feminism as alarming, amusing, relevant, witty,

controversial, and all those other adjectives that describe and
proscribe entertainment, has been one of popular feminism's
greatest victories, then the absence of stories that don't attract
such easy adjectives has been the inevitable underbelly of failure.

New mothers, new feminism

Modern feminism – shaped by diversity, difference and even the
Daily Mail – has, then, made its uneasy peace with motherhood.
Its most public concern is no longer the private world of caring
but the public question of how to reconcile work, and particularly
successful work, with parenting. In May 1997 the *Guardian* ran a
three-part serial on Britain's top fifty women, the powerful new
female faces of our time. In one of the commentaries
accompanying the series, third-wave mainstream feminist
Natasha Walter wrote of her hope and belief that young,
confident, professional women will no longer have to pay
extreme penalties, in terms of their career, just because they have
children. Concrete support from men and private or public
childcare will allow them to continue with their work, albeit at a
slower pace; 'If the acceptance of career breaks and flexible
working leads men and women to slow down for a bit in their
thirties and forties, that isn't going to bring the whole
establishment shuddering to a halt.'[20] Walter quoted Ruth Kelly,
one of the new young women MPs to enter Parliament in the
landslide of 1997 and who gave birth to a son just under a month
after the election, who, in her turn, cites the example of Harriet
Harman, one of the few feminist examples of public motherhood
during the eighties:

> Harriet Harman is one of the most respected women in
> politics. She was seven months pregnant when she was elected
> and went on to have two more children. I'm going to be really
> committed to my family, but I'm also committed to my work.

This sentence heartens and disheartens me simultaneously. The
optimism of Ruth Kelly's (relatively) young energy, her

certainty that it can be done, means, I am sure, that it will be done: that she, too, will have her family and her work. Certainly she will be better off than most if, as Natasha Walter asserts, 'Her husband will, she is sure, take an equal role in family life.' However, the House of Commons will not help her much as there is little precedent, yet, among MPs or political professions generally for 'career breaks' or a slower pace of work during crucial periods of 'private' life. Perhaps the 'feminist mothers' of the new Parliament will have changed that by the end of the first term.

But I also want to insert words of warning, to remind us of the importance of the language of feeling. How can we use this language without it sounding like a 'return to the home' movement or simple pessimism? How can we find ways to talk of the extraordinary pull, joyful and burdensome, of motherhood without always trying to put it in its place? How can we talk about the toll it takes on a body, literally, in the very cells and flesh of oneself, the fact that creation of another individual takes blood, milk, sleep, calm and time – always time, inevitably time – from the person who creates it? How can we find a way to honour this effort without excluding women from the public sphere? I mean only that there is something in Ruth Kelly's understandable certainty about her future as a mother that risks obscuring what the experience is really about, obscuring the experience that other women are having, all in the attempt to be taken seriously.

In Ruth Kelly's brisk, worldly assertiveness we see one way, at least, in which feminism's terms of reference have both widened and contracted. There is much more confidence about 'out there', the public world; much less honesty about 'in here', the home and the heart. The best of those young mothers of the late sixties and early seventies were able to talk, without undue self-pity, about blood, bodies, sleep, time, moods, ambivalence: the very stuff of this primal connection. They possibly did not have much idea of what they wanted, beyond a recognition that what they did in the privacy of their home was a form of politics, a social act that needed social recognition. And they wanted their freedom, within reasonable boundaries. This was not a freedom from responsibility. This was not a freedom as envisioned in its most extreme form by Marilyn French in *The Women's Room*, a walking away. It was the freedom that might come from sharing the children they had created with another. It was the freedom that comes from knowing that the person or people who share your most intimate life 'see' you for who you really are. That society, too, 'sees' what you do: finds a place for it, a respect for it.

Nowadays the most open writing on motherhood is likely to come from the genre of autobiography, such as Fiona Shaw's searing *Out of Me* (1996), a story of a post-natal breakdown, or psychoanalysis, such as Roszika Parker's *Torn in Two* (1995), her impressive and moving study of maternal ambivalence. Compare this to the go, go, go for it girls approach that mainstream feminism, perhaps unwittingly, promotes now.

Motherhood is at risk of becoming a little too neat in this vision. It is like a package that we each carry around: *my* parenthood, *my* children. Ruth Kelly is right to admire women who have held their own in the public arena. It takes a certain toughness to have a public life and rear one, two, three or more children. But I think we probably do not know what it has cost those individual women who have done it and, schooled in toughness as they are, they almost certainly will not show us now. Nor should the full-time model be our only guide. As an almost continuous full-time worker, someone like Harriet Harman offers us a completely conventional example. She, not society, has made all the adjustments.

There is a risk, too, that the work ethic has seeped too far, too deep into all our thinking. Feminism must not, along with government, forget that bringing up children is a form of work; neither motherhood nor fatherhood should need so much justification beyond itself. Even in its new acceptance of motherhood, feminism is, once again, urging women to be so much more. Perhaps this is inevitable. As long as society both foists most of the jobs associated with parenthood on women and yet gives them no credit for it, that may always be feminism's job. It seems a pity. It seems a pity that it is still not able to be the political voice that reflects the experience of motherhood, material and emotional, of someone like Tracy or of all the other women I talked to; the pleasures of the park, laughter in the bath; motherhood as both the affirmation of, one crucial metaphor for, all that really matters in life.

~ 12 ~

The Best of Both Worlds: Towards a New Politics of Motherhood

> . . . I want all this marked on my body. We are the real countries, not the boundaries drawn on maps with names of powerful men . . .
>
> Katherine, speaking at the end of *The English Patient*,
> screenplay by Anthony Minghella, 1997

Yesterday, finally, I saw her. Young, tall, black and elegant, she was pushing an elaborately pretty pram and talking business on a mobile phone. High heels, of course. She was a feature editor's dream, a modern female icon; the apparently democratic embodiment of the aspirational ideal. (If Thatcherism could not, in the end, give everyone a home, at least they got the booby prize, a mobile phone of their own.) Here, surely, was a perfect example of the new motherhood, one young woman who was not going to let a baby or two get in her way, a woman who could bottle-feed and write a job application at the same time.

Why, then, did I want so much to follow her home to see how her story panned out? I nearly did, I was that curious. Curious to see where she lived, to see who, if anyone, greeted her at the door. Curious to see who took the baby from her and what they did then and for exactly how long. I was curious, in short, for all the myriad details that make up a real life, the only kind of life worth talking about. All these thoughts were going through my mind as I passed that young woman on the hill. If this was a detective story, that young black woman would be the key witness.

Yet I hold the key to the story myself, of course. An interview is a form of benign stalking. Talking to so many people in depth is the equivalent of following them home. You don't learn the 'truth', exactly, but you get a chance to check descriptions of a life against observable domestic details, for instance. You absorb all sorts of emotions, veiled and overt. 'I do not ask the wounded person how he feels . . . I myself become the wounded person.'[1] When I replay some of my interview tapes, which I do from time to time, what strikes me, above all, is the incredible wealth of detail. If political talk is partly the ability to speak in generalities about the things that should concern us, personal talk is a never-ending reaching into, and reflecting upon, the million moments of our lives that really concern us. Women tend to do this personal talk better than the abstract kind. They feel more comfortable in the concrete. But how do we make generalities from all those moments? How do we speak a political truth?

Listening to those tapes once again reassures me that perhaps I know more of my young mother with her mobile phone than at first I thought. It reassures me that I might be able to close my eyes and convincingly conjure up the place where she lives and with whom and how. I have talked, after all, to quite a few young women, black and white, like her. There was the young mother who worked as a receptionist at a health centre. Her manner was very animated but, close up, I could see how tired she was. All she wanted was to be at home with her baby son. Then there was the woman who was bringing up her child on her own and had arranged a place in college to do a foundation year, with the ultimate aim of studying film. Plans were in place; she talked about the future with excitement. But, like so many tough, bright mothers, or those, at least, below a certain income, it had been a long time since she went out. She said she could not care less. She had to be dragged out by friends who, affectionately, told her she had got boring since she had the baby, but how much any or all of this was bravado, I couldn't tell. That's what I mean about never quite knowing the truth about people. I could tell she

didn't like questions about the father of her child, and I could tell
she didn't like them partly because she doesn't like *him* and partly
because she feels sad and bad for her son that he will not grow up
with a father in place, as she did. I was told as firmly as the world
is always told, 'He knows his father's name and where he lives and
who knows, maybe in the future, they will get something going
between them.'

Perhaps now I can follow that young woman walking down
the hill, talking on the phone while she pushes her baby back
from the childminder. She finishes her call as she turns into her
road, folds the phone away, fiddles for her keys. She lives in a
second-floor flat on a reasonably well-ordered estate, now
managed through a Housing Action Trust. There is damp on the
kitchen and living-room walls but the walkways are clean and
quiet, and intruders are kept to a minimum by a new gate system
which you operate with a smart card. It is a Thursday afternoon.
Once she has settled the baby, she will spend the rest of the
evening chatting on the phone, watching television, eating, but
alone. She will not be going out at the weekend either. After rent,
bills, and food, most of her money goes on childminding fees. On
Sunday afternoon she'll go up to see her mother and father,
talking on her mobile again from the bus stop to the house,
intriguing some other passer-by with her style and chutzpah. But
as the afternoon wears on, she will become bad-tempered because
it's work next day and her current job, as a 'junior administrative
officer' – truer title: filing clerk and office run-around – bores her
rigid. She has greater dreams for herself; she would like to design
her own clothes. Everyone says how elegant she looks, and on so
little! Her two best friends always want to borrow from her and
then complain that they never look as good as her, even though
they're wearing the same things. 'It's how you wear stuff,' she
says. 'It's how you stand, walk, sit.' Her designer dreams for
herself are there, but beyond the rock of today's reality. For the
moment, they are out of sight.

It is not quite the story summoned up by the image, is it? It is
not quite the story we want to hear.

The two faces of competence

Keep that young woman in mind as I ask my final questions, suggest some preliminary answers.

I said, at the beginning of this book, that I wanted to investigate what has got better or worse in mothers' lives; I suggested then some obvious answers. One of the most important advances, without doubt, is that women's competence is no longer at issue. Culture spreads the word of possibility to us all, young, old, thin, fat, black, white. My young mother may never become a dress designer, but she does not have to stumble upon some rare book in a library that tells of one extraordinary woman of her times who has already done it; she does not have to experience the epiphanous moment of old to believe that she can do it too. We are deluged with images confirming women's ability to do and to dazzle, to earn and endure; for that, at least, we have Bourgeois Feminist Triumphalism to thank. (And I mean that most sincerely.) With proven competence come wider horizons and greater mobility: the intrepid woman traveller of old has been replaced by legions of women at ease in airport check-ins; masses of us are now at home, at least for a time, in a foreign land.

The problem for modern mothers lies in a different interpretation of the same word: competence. Society both assumes and relies upon women's competence to be mothers without helping them sufficiently to maintain their already proven public and work skills, the other kind of competence. A committed parent carries a heavy, delightful weight. Yet the exact nature of this weight is one of society's best-kept secrets. One often reads the standard, throwaway line, in feminist and non-feminist work alike: 'Women do the double shift,' or 'Women retain responsibility for the home.' The very fact that it appears as a mere line of text in an article or manifesto or even a book mimics the lack of importance attached to it in the world; *yet it remains one of the most important statements made about women today, on the cusp of the twenty-first century, around the world.* We have to linger on that throwaway line and understand what it really means, for until we understand what it really means, we cannot tackle so many of the other problems associated with it.

It is this fact, for instance, which gives the lie to equal rights feminism, the idea that women need only enter the public world, prove their competence, over and over again, for women and men to be equal. Equal rights feminism is not so much a theory nowadays as an underlying attitude, a particular tone of voice. When Mary Wollstonecraft says to women, keep yourself busy and you will be a better mother for it, the beginning of this tone of voice is apparent. When de Beauvoir barks at us to farm, to write, to enter the chemist's lab, it is present once again. It is the tough approach of battle-hardened characters that says, in effect, get on with it. Don't let your motherhood be a bar to freedom and opportunity and risk and reward. Don't let your motherhood be a bar to hard work of the other, better, kind. And many women have, throughout history, done just that: got on with it. For many in low-paid or low-skill jobs on which their survival depended, there was no choice. Throughout history, mothers have worked in dangerous and debilitating occupations, to support a family. The female slaves who built American capitalism bore, often, their master's child and returned to the field that same day. For the first women professionals, their motherhood could not be a hindrance in another way. Like someone hiding the fact of pregnancy, it was crucial that they did not let their motherhood 'show'. Children were often looked after by nannies or sent to boarding school. Yet, as Rebecca Abrams notes in her book of interviews with some of the pioneer professionals, there was a price to be paid for that concealment:

> Determination to succeed is frequently offset by this kind of
> shoulder-shrugging acceptance, and it is noticeable
> throughout these interviews that these independently-minded
> and undeterrable women often seemed *surprisingly prepared to
> accept the status quo*. When they challenged so much, it is
> striking what they seemed not to think of challenging [my
> emphasis].[2]

Not any longer. As more and more women, and more and

more mothers, have developed ambition, hopes and plans, this approach will no longer do. Today's mothers veer between two emotional and practical stances, often on the same day. On the one hand, they show a slightly martyred acceptance of their responsibility for the home and children, that fatalism which Gramsci described as 'nothing other than the clothing worn by real and active will when in a weak position'. There are, after all, many compensations to giving up the outside struggle in whatever form it takes. If it is stopping work altogether, one can concentrate on home and children with a relatively clear head and light heart. If it is accepting a low-key, low-paid work life – 'just jogging along' as one woman called it – there is a sort of simplicity to that too. If it is shouldering all the work of the home, this, at least, eliminates tensions between partners.

Other women go a different way. They decide to stretch themselves to full capacity, usually by working full-time, because they need the money or want to keep visible or want to keep future avenues open. Choosing this option can have definite effects on a woman's mental and physical well-being. Every study of working mothers shows they are stretched to their limits of endurance; exhaustion is one of the most common words to come out of my own, and many others', accounts. But these women want to remain in control of their own meanings, their own money and, to a certain extent, their own destinies. Conservatives of all hues may talk about valuing women in the home but they don't say anything about valuing them anywhere else; difference feminism may say women have a superior ethical system, but if no-one else recognizes it, what's the point of having it at all? So modern mothers operate two different ethical systems at the same time; they exercise both kinds of competence, the caring kind and the calculating kind.

And then they collapse.

In her book *Hystories* (1997), writer Elaine Showalter argues that Chronic Fatigue Syndrome, also known as ME, is a form of modern hysteria, one of the major psychosomatic disorders of the late twentieth century. Whatever the organic elements that trigger and maintain CFS/ME, most sufferers admit that an

element of depression is involved in the condition. I have become
intrigued, recently, by how much this condition of debilitating
tiredness and suppressed anger – one working definition of
depression – reflects contemporary women's troubles. Many of
those struck by it tend to be women in their early to mid life;
high-achieving 'Type A' characters are particularly susceptible.
The twenties, thirties and, increasingly, the forties are, of course,
the child-bearing years. They are also the decades when work
lives are past promising beginnings; they are becoming confirmed
and consolidated. Or not. It is only speculation on my part but
could the condition be a particularly dramatic form of rebellion
by women who simply cannot see the road ahead for themselves,
who do not see a way through the many responsibilities they
hope and are expected to take on in life? Is CFS/ME a sensitive
individual's expression of the impossibility of meeting a set of
social expectations, made worse by the fact that society presents
us with more and more examples of women who do; the so-
called icons who appear to achieve professional and personal
success, or at least have good jobs and children? CFS/ME stories
often centre on women with heavy family responsibility and
draining jobs that offer little reward, in terms of status or money;
another crucial difference from the icons. Here, culture may not
offer new possibilities, but may pile on impossible pressure.

From nature to skills: the importance of domestic democracy

What then, of men? I have already argued that we should not read
as much into the new fatherhood as we might wish. While there
has been a dramatic revolution in images of fatherhood, and in
men's ability to express their feelings *about* fatherhood, women
still do more of the work of parenting. It is really that simple.

Yet it is possible to see some optimistic signs, and not only in
metropolitan households influenced by feminism, libertarianism
or common sense. I see it in my own household – influenced,
incidentally, by all three. I have partly been able to work and
enjoy my children because I share my home and my life with

someone who is prepared to work less than the 'average man' and enjoy his children more than the 'average man'. Nature still reigns in some respects – I was the only one who could get pregnant, give birth, breastfeed – but in more subtle, difficult ways that are not subject to easy description. This part of nature begs questions rather than answers: how much does a young child need its mother more than its father? How much deeper does the once-fibrous connection of mother and child go, and how long does it last? I know I often find it harder to leave my 'girls' than their father does, but how much is that my trained sensitivity to my own sensitivities? Personally, I do not believe in fighting my own nature that much; if I find I can't leave my ten-month-old daughter for much longer than a day then I will not do it. Many a woman has had this kind of realization; it bothers me a lot less than some.

But I do believe in fighting culture or convention all the way. There is no biological law that says looking after a baby means only women can press the commands on the washing machine or wash up a pile of dishes. There is no natural law that says only women can pack the children's clothes for a holiday or go out and buy a three-year-old five new pairs of socks. The most important feminist lesson of the last thirty years has been that the so-called natural division of labour is really about *a range of skills that can be shaken up and redistributed by those who have a will to do it*. As a young woman, I taught myself, in no particular order, to handle money, drive a car, change a fuse (or just about), address a meeting, chair a meeting, learn a trade and practise it with reasonable competence, and how to realize greater dreams, also to do with my profession, that required iron discipline. I was lucky in my late twenties to meet a man whom I not only loved but who had, in his time, learned how to cook, clean, shop, listen as well as talk, and iron fifteen shirts for as long as it took to listen to one side of a favourite cassette.

Children are often the crunch point for apparently egalitarian couples. Before children, there is so much less to do and both partners are more willing to experiment. Just after a baby is born, everyone is tired, grumpy, elated: overwhelming love for a tiny helpless creature can make women start acting like their own mother in more ways than one. Then, the real challenge begins. The hardest of the new skills to acquire, for men and women, are not how to prepare baby rice, manoeuvre a pushchair or change a nappy but how to spend an afternoon with two fractious under-threes without pulling out your own hair or falling asleep in lassitude. The writer and Reith lecturer Marina Warner said somewhere that she was never any good at getting down on the floor and playing about with bricks and things; many women aren't. It is particularly hard when, as I said in my personal beginning to the book, you have already spent half a lifetime learning how not to be a conventional woman. And the boredom, chaos, invisibility and sheer lack of value associated with being with young children over long periods of time is too hard for most men to overcome, unless they are unusually committed or they have to.

We may not have anything approaching an equal sharing of skills between men and women but what we do have is a new negotiation over those skills. I recently listened to a couple discussing who does what in their house. It just happened that he climbed up ladders and changed light-bulbs and she put the dirty washing in the machine. It just happened that she liked cooking up plates of lasagne for gangs of visitors and he was good at chilling and opening the alcohol. On the surface, then, everything was as it 'should' be. Except for two things. He was saying that he wanted to cook and might try it soon; she had recently been under the bonnet of a car and fixed some small technical thing, and it felt like a great victory. So there was change. But it was the *conversation* itself that was new. Our parents' generation simply did not discuss the division of tasks in this way, and it took second wave feminism to make this personal conversation political.

However, the phrase 'the personal is political', which now carries so much baggage from the past, will no longer do. We must, instead, talk about *domestic democracy*; the importance of all adults in a household contributing their equitable share to the maintenance of the place where they live. If we truly achieved that, we would be half-way to a social revolution.

New labour, new families

The failure to address this question of domestic democracy is one reason why the current debate about the family is so sterile; it has no understanding of the new and necessary challenge to 'essential natures'. Journalists like Melanie Phillips and the communitarian thinker Amitai Etzioni have written a great deal about the need to underwrite the family: among other things, they have proposed that marriage be made more attractive and divorce made more difficult. They have both condemned the selfishness of the new individualism and the lack of time modern parents spend with their children. These thinkers are too preoccupied with form over content. They are more concerned to resurrect a mythical family of old than pay attention to the detail of new family formations. Cohabitation, which has risen sharply over the last two decades, does not merely represent a *lack* of something; moral fibre, commitment to children. Like many people, my own ethical system involves concepts of high fidelity and long-term loyalty. However, as I believe that these qualities are more likely to come from genuine reciprocity between partners and parents, friends, and eventually parents and children, I look to an ethically informed love to do the job rather than rules and contracts. This is why, despite twelve years of happy union (with the same person!), I am not, have not been, and never will be, a married woman.

The lived reality of many arrangements such as mine, and this includes many married people, is radically different from an older generation. 'Mother' goes out the door to work as often as 'father'. He puts the children in the bath as often as she does. This is not subversive of family life, but a sensible new egalitarianism that needs consolidating, not dismantling. The organization of the family of old can no longer describe our future. For instance, a potent mix of economic power and personal disappointment has created a situation where many mothers now live with their children on their own. We may not like it — although, quite frankly, I am more interested in whether the women themselves like it — but we need to address the strengths as well as the

weaknesses of that fact. To suggest that the state withdraw basic
financial support from single mothers, and their children, is
punitive and wrong. Instead, we should understand why so many
women prefer to be, or find themselves left, on their own. There
are some answers in this book, of which the most important is that
many men still need to learn how to 'take care' of themselves and
others. That, to answer Freud and the Spice Girls, is what women
really, really want.

Most important of all, the new motherhood will only take that
jump from image to reality if a real new fatherhood comes to
exist. What do I mean by that? Let me discard my usual
impossibilist instincts and be, for the moment, a gradualist, a mild
and patient social reformer. For my young mother with her
mobile phone, it might mean the father of her child
acknowledging his paternity in a real not a romantic way, and
beginning to take that responsibility; giving money and time to
that baby in the pram. For the rabidly ambitious corporate lawyer
who calls leaving for the office at eight in the morning 'a really
late start', it might mean thinking through what he is going to
feel, fifty, knackered and really rich, with a daughter who has
grown up to be a seductive stranger. For the distracted father who
has every other weekend with the progeny of his acrimonious
divorce, it might mean trying actually to *be* with that little girl and
boy rather than endlessly making calls on his mobile phone to try
and fix up things to do, or burying himself behind his newspaper.

In my ideal world, the new fatherhood means something much
much more radical. It means a man in sufficient charge of his own
working time, and his own feelings, to contribute a meaningful
half to his children's life and the maintenance of his own
household. And I *mean* a meaningful half.

Like all radical changes, it would be painful. Those men who
have, through divorce, widowhood or other circumstances,
become sole carers of young children are irrevocably changed by
the experience. They do not become token women, but
something much more complicated. They are exiled equally from
the world of 'showy' fatherhood and the business-as-usual world
of motherhood, the world of the playgroup and park culture. I

recently watched an older father spend an entire afternoon at a local drop-in centre without a word passing between him and the dozen women there; it was as if his presence was a kind of embarrassment or affront. These men have 'given up' a great deal of the privilege of traditional masculinity but they would not like the exact words 'given up' because they have gained so much in the process. Yet they *have* lost, as women do – opportunities to train or to travel or to throw themselves into the great life-altering project or to go to the pub and drink with the right, or wrong, people. These losses give men an insight into the complexity of a life that not only asserts the bland fact that children and the self and work all matter, but which acts upon these truths, by *giving all these things equal weight.* They may not be welcome down among the women, but they understand this much about mothers.

But how will men who are not forced through bereavement or relationship breakdown to take their fair share in the care of children begin to do more? We can talk about changing work patterns and women needing to relinquish their 'power' in the home, although my skin does prickle with irritation when that line is trotted out too frequently, but too much emphasis on these questions sidesteps the important question of conscious intention, even courage. As Suzanne Moore says, 'The issue does not seem to me to be one of men's inability to shake off social conditioning, but of men's refusal to give up a good deal. This is about power.'[3] It is interesting that a generation of men influenced by feminism or the sixties are the most likely now, in young middle-age, to be domestic democrats. They are less conservative than the Thatcherite generation that followed them, the generation that allowed post-feminism to tell them there wasn't a problem with domestic life or that it had been solved. Among them, too many collapse back into the old ways, or updated versions of their parents' ways. Nature and tradition are invoked once again. It was politics that changed one generation of men: it is only politics that will change future generations.

It's beyond me

But what of society's wider role, its famed collective
responsibilities to its children? For too long, having and bringing
up children has been left to 'individual choice', which usually
means left to women. Now we have a government that believes,
in principle at least, that state and community should contribute
to the care of young children. It is not my job to provide
blueprints for government, especially one that will not spend
money I think it should spend, but certain general principles seem
obvious to me. The first is that, if we accept caring is a job, then
we should go about making more jobs out of caring. As a society
we accept this to a certain extent. Social workers, nurses, home
helps, nursery teachers all do a job that women were once
supposed to do for free. The beauty of society, that concept
Margaret Thatcher refused to believe in, is that it can take
political and financial responsibility for private problems. A
decent society should pay towards the care of its most vulnerable
citizens: children, the elderly and the ill. The problems of an older
welfarism – bureaucracy, even corruption – show us that
provision should be as flexible and as direct as possible. Child
benefit, once called family allowance, has proved to be one of the
most successful, if minimal, forms of channelling money from the
state directly to the individual who most needs it; usually, the
mother. There is an unanswerable case for substantially increasing
this benefit, which should remain universal, and clawing back the
excess, in tax, from the relatively and very wealthy.

There is also a case for providing a decent carer's income to
anyone who decides to stay at home and raise a child, care for an
elderly relative, nurse a sick friend or partner. Unlike unemployment benefit, which is, after all, a payment for *not* doing something, a carer's income would reflect the active, engaged nature
of bringing up a child. Both employed and unemployed men
should be encouraged to claim it as much as women. It should be
granted on the basis that it does not preclude its recipient from
taking some work, nor from at any time going back into work for
however long they want. In other words, taken with other

measures that sanction and encourage paid work that women want, the risk of 'returning women to the home', the expected political charge against it, would be minimal.

The failure of the old welfarism also shows us that provision for children should follow the lead of parents. As I described in Chapter 7, thousands of parents, especially women, have set up their own childcare and community initiatives; some of these services already charge a small fee and are thus on the cusp of the private and public sectors. All they will need is a little local flexibility and a reasonable grant to keep costs and further fees down to a feasible minimum. Investment in these projects will not only provide decent places for children to go; it will also provide new jobs which will, in turn, have a marvellous effect on that extraordinarily important measurement, Gross Domestic Product. Modern investment in caring should take its ideological cue from the experiments of early second-wave feminism, by actively involving fathers, non-parents and encouraging young men, like Jackie's son in Cardiff, to train as crèche, playgroup or nursery workers.

Time to go home

But the creation of a new respect and financial reward for caring must go hand-in-hand with a significant redistribution of paid work. The second job of a society serious about giving children a good start is to free up everybody's time, not just women's. Six months' maternity leave plus half a lifetime's part-time work, the most familiar female option, leaves the question of father time untouched. Paternity and parental leave, one a question of weeks, the other a question of three years at most, will make only a small dent in existing practice. By creating more jobs overall, everyone can work less hours; in short, we should establish a creative part-time culture in which the very word 'part-time' would cease to exist. Two questions inevitably arise. One, how could most people afford it? And what about ambition, the fevered desire of a few to work as long and hard as they like in return for the golden reward of personal success? There are no easy answers, but this occurs to me immediately; if one breadwinning man is bringing in a full-time wage and his wife is staying at home, then they could, theoretically, bring in the same amount to the household with both of them out at work half the week. Add to that a generous or at least realistic child benefit, and maybe a graduated carer's income, and there is enough. (I will return to that important word 'enough' in a moment.)

And what of ambition? To return to my gradualist/realist self for a moment employers could change our 'long hours culture' overnight if they sent out serious signals that working long hours is a sign not of success but of inefficiency. It is either their failure for not designing jobs that can be done in the hours allotted, or an employee's inability to buckle down and get his or her work finished in time. Seriously successful women with young children provide an excellent model here; many of them are renowned for their punctual time-keeping and fearsome efficiency. If the editor of a newspaper or a chief executive in local government, or a partner in a law firm, indicated that any male employee, parent or not, who was working over his or her hours was being seen as inefficient, buildings would empty at five o'clock sharp. People with sad or non-existent home lives would just have to find something else to do in the early evening. And the very ambitious and childless, that supposed ideal model against which all other workers cannot hope to measure up to? They could go home and write a film script, climb a mountain at the weekends, or even have a child, without the expected penalties.

Will any of this happen, in the real world of motivated corporate Britain? I have my eye, in this respect, on certain of my male contemporaries, those who have already made their mark on the world and are of an age to become parents. To paraphrase Germaine Greer's question at the end of *The Female Eunuch*, 'What will *they* do?' Will the more powerful among them set new standards of necessary minimalism, or will it, for the next generation, all be business as usual?

And what would the best scenario mean for the many mothers who have been forced to renounce their ambition, gracefully or not? It would mean new work and, just as important, play possibilities.

It would mean they too could run companies and marathons. They could swim, see the latest film, send e-mails, not just once every blue moon, but regularly, over and over again. They could get a life, at last; secure in the knowledge that their children were not, always, in the care of a loving stranger but with one of the most important people in their lives: their father. What mothers need to enjoy the best of both worlds is, above all else, more time.

Having less of it all: towards a new moral ecology

Some of the most interesting thinking of the latter half of the twentieth century has been in the ecological sphere, our recognition that the earth does not have infinite resources, that we must respect and conserve the resources we already possess. We need to develop a parallel *moral ecology*, one that recognizes a limit to infinite expansion; of income, power, ambition and consumption. The new mother depends on it because in order for her to have more – time or money – someone else has to have less. One of the negative effects of Bourgeois Feminist Triumphalism was the inherent implication that equality meant a few women having a lot more of what a few men had; power, fame, money, even access to weapons. But this morality created Margaret Thatcher, a feminine mother without respect for many of the living values of her own sex and with a blindness to those without access to any of these things.

In the years since the height of Thatcherism and BFT, we have seen the growth in influence of that mysterious force 'middle England', which directly reflects the 'more is better' values. This middle England is not to be found only in green-belt land. It dwells in the cities as well as the country; middle England, or middle Britain, shops in Glasgow's Buchanan Street as well as in Worcester's shopping malls. Middle England is shorthand for a habit of the heart. J. K. Galbraith cogently described it as 'the culture of contentment', in which the majority of the population in the western economies can now live a fairly affluent lifestyle, while a significant minority are consigned to economic desperation. This minority are called the underclass: an impolite synonym for the poor. Yet the 'contented' majority are anything but. When one's life is guided only by the need to have things, or rather when the possession of property defines so much who you are, rather than providing a mere material basis for a decent life, you never can have enough. The rise and rise of the credit card is proof enough of that. Middle England, which is riven with its own form of debt as pernicious as the more discernible debt of the poor, thrives on material acquisition. And parenthood becomes yet another reason for consumption as proof of true existence. I shop at Baby Gap therefore I am.

New Labour drew this group to its proverbial bosom and promised it would never take away what it had so honourably earned. But how do we mark the point where honourable aspiration becomes naked greed? When do we start to invoke the interests of the famed community? New Labour's landslide of May 1997 showed what more it could have risked if it had dared; the party could have proposed taxing the very rich to give to the poor. It could have risked a greater form of economic egalitarianism in the name of that abstract notion, the community, of which it likes to talk so much. Instead, it confirmed everyone's feeling that 'what is mine, is mine'.

What this means, quite simply, is that the poorest mothers will not get the help they need. And that might include my young mother with her mobile phone, keeping up such a good show on her hundred and something pounds a week take-home pay. It will certainly mean that for the Glasgow young woman community-worker Bob Holman encountered in spring 1997:

> While writing this piece, a young woman called in to our
> Easterhouse project. Hungry, isolated, in debt and tired of pro-
> tecting her kids from the needles lying around the stairs, she
> wept, 'I can't go on.' One of her kids asked for, and devoured, a
> banana. This is not fiction. Her poverty is as real as the £100,000
> a year being paid to Labour ministers. I gave her food.[4]

Far better, he added, if our project 'could offer a crèche, a food co-op, a warm community café'.

Rare are the representatives of middle England, among them the most caring mothers possible, who show much understanding that there are children living just ten minutes' walk from where they live without enough to eat, children sitting in rooms as bare as Tracy's, with one TV, a couch and a threadbare carpet. No politics of motherhood is going to mean very much unless we include those children, those mothers. If charity is about taking on the problem as a 'caring' individual, politics is about taking it on as a responsible society.

A moral ecology recognizes that basic wants must be supplied before surplus requirements are satisfied, and it genuinely recognizes 'the needs of strangers'. In his book of the same name, Michael Ignatieff laid out the dimensions of this necessary civic modesty when he returned to the utopian dream of the Greek polis:

> Its human dimensions beckon us still: small enough so that
> each person would know his neighbour and could play his
> part in the governance of the city, large enough so that the
> city could feed itself and defend itself; a place of intimate
> bonding in which the private sphere of the home and family
> and the public sphere of civic democracy would be but one
> easy step apart; a community of equals in which each would
> have enough and no one would want more than enough; a
> co-operative venture in which work would be a form of
> collaboration among equals. Small, co-operative, egalitarian,
> self-governing and autarkic: these are the conditions of
> belonging that the dream of the polis has bequeathed us.[5]

We are so far from that vision, it is easy to lose sight of it; easy to lose the sense of locality, modesty, equality that inevitably fashions the good society. Instead, we bob about hopelessly in the sea of globalization and greed. Even the once most untouchable aspect of motherhood, procreation, has become a question of calculation, multiplication and 'moreness', as the sad saga of Mandy Allwood, the woman who became pregnant with eight babies through fertility treatment and who subsequently miscarried every foetus, so tragically showed. There really was no more room in the womb.

All through this book, I have tried to separate image from reality; not just in the obvious sense that five gorgeous successful mothers in *Hello!* magazine do not a revolution make. Nor even in the less obvious sense, that for all our media reflection of ourselves we consistently leave out the most vulnerable, because they are least likely to be consumers and because we do not want to remind ourselves of what we all fear; poverty. I mean something more profound; that by living so much through culture, which is where the body of society's sense of itself is now created, we have forgotten the sometimes more mundane power of politics. At the same time, politics is losing its power to genuinely offer change to the people, which accounts, in the words of French writer Cornelius Castoriadis, for 'the frightening emptiness of contemporary political discourses'. Worse, we even live politics *as* culture, judging our Prime Ministers and Presidents by how they present themselves as much as by what they do.

As a result of this passivity, we all slowly accept the end of history or the end of socialism or even the end of the possibility of real change itself. So we acquiesce in the worst of our contemporary realities; the material, miserable realities.

This brings me back to my young mother with her mobile phone; for she, too, lives out so much of herself through personal style; she, too, uses style as the legitimate weapon of the have-not-enoughs, style as an act of compensation, even revenge. But it is not enough for the rest of us to admire and forget. If we go that step further and enter her life, sit with her in that damp kitchen with its peeling, moist walls, we will learn something important. We will see that she needs not only a personal dream and an actively involved father, she needs not only a good job and a safe crèche. She needs a kitchen and living-room free of damp, a play space for herself and her son, and somewhere to go for rest and recuperation. She needs unpolluted water and enough money for fresh food. The beauty of the best of feminism is that it gives her the best possible idea of who she might be, today or in the future. It gives her the confidence to ask for what she needs and wants, and hopefully the self-knowledge to be angry when it is refused her. It offers her, too, the chance of the best of both worlds; the fulfilling private life and the connections of the wider public world.

Even still, she needs something more. She needs a society that remains curious about, and compassionate towards, her. She needs a society that does not leave her neither to fight, nor indeed to flourish alone. She needs a society that believes that the moral and material requirements of this young mother, of low income but high expectations, are as crucial to its own well-being as they inevitably are to hers. In that young woman's necessary future, then, lies the resolution of a question that has always engaged the kindest and finest minds of the past; the question of social as well as gender justice, the imperative necessity of a greater economic as well as moral parity between all our citizens, regardless of the cloak of class education or even confidence, the face we too often defensively turn to the world.

What, then *must* we do?

Notes

Chapter 2. Asking the Right Questions: A Sort of Introduction

1. For just one example, see feature on Maeve Haran in 'Having it Both Ways', *Sunday Times*, 23 June 1991.
2. *The Times*, 25 July 1990.
3. *The Times*, 23 September 1994.
4. 'Femail', 29 February 1996.
5. *Guardian*, 11 April 1995.
6. *Vogue*, September 1995.
7. *Daily Mail*, 5 February 1997. See also: 'Fathers are Vital, Too', *The Times*, 11 June 1996; 'Honey, I'll look after the kids', *Daily Telegraph*, 22 January 1997; 'Dad's the Word', *Guardian*, 4 February 1997.
8. See, for example; Kate Saunders, *Sunday Times*, 6 November 1994; Suzanne Moore, *Guardian*, 3 November 1994; Janet Daley, *The Times*, 27 April 1995.
9. 'Babies on Benefit', *Panorama*, BBC, 20 September 1993.
10. Andrew Stephen, 'Mum vs Dad', *Telegraph* magazine, 26 November 1994.
11. 'Missing Mum', *Panorama*, BBC, 3 February 1997, and *Observer*, 9 February 1997.
12. *Independent on Sunday*, 19 January 1997; *Sunday Express*, 19 January 1997.
13. *Guardian*, 6 January 1997.
14. Slavenka Drakulic, *How We Survived Communism and Even Laughed*, Hutchinson, 1997, p.27.
15. *Best of Young British Novelists*, Granta, 1993.

16. Adrienne Rich, *Of Woman Born: Motherhood as Experience and Institution*, Virago, 1977, p.21.
17. *New Statesman*, 10 January 1997.
18. See, for example, 'I would rather live now', A. S. Byatt in the *Daily Telegraph*, 30 October 1995. Introduction to pamphlet on 'Tomorrow's Women', *Demos*, 1997.

Chapter 3. Great Expectations: New Ethics, New Icons

1. Olwen Hufton, *The Prospect Before Her: A History of Women in Western Europe, Volume One 1500–1800*, HarperCollins, 1995.
2. Henley Centre, Planning for Social Change, *Shaping Factors*, 1996–7.
3. Christopher Lasch, *Women and the Common Life: Love, Marriage and Feminism*, ed. Elisabeth Lasch-Quinn, Norton, 1997, p.99.
4. Rebecca Abrams, *Woman in a Man's World: Pioneering Career Women of the Twentieth Century*, Methuen, 1993, p.xxviii.
5. Margaret Stansgate, *My Exit Visa: An Autobiography*, Random House, 1992, p.74.
6. Ibid., p.70.
7. See, for example, Melissa Benn, 'Brace Yourself for the Backlash', *Cosmopolitan*, February 1992.
8. *Hello!*, 5 April 1997.
9. Mary Wollstonecraft, *A Vindication of the Rights of Woman*, Penguin, 1992, p.243.
10. *Elle*, November 1995.
11. Julie Burchill, *Sex and Sensibility*, Grafton, 1992, pp.199–204.
12. *Daily Express*, 17 August 1987.
13. *Daily Express*, 10 May 1989.
14. Hugo Young, *One of Us*, Macmillan, 1989, p.514.
15. For just one example of such an interpretation of Thatcher, see Beatrix Campbell, *The Iron Ladies: Why Do Women Vote Tory?*, Virago, 1987, pp.238–44.
16. For two examples of a very different approach by famous women to their mothers, see Simone de Beauvoir, *A Very Easy Death*, Penguin, 1966; interview with Brenda Dean, in the *Guardian*, 17 June 1992.
17. Hugo Young, *One of Us*, p.4.
18. *Guardian*, 13 May 1997.
19. Julie Burchill, *Sex and Sensibility*, Grafton, pp.245–63.
20. *Daily Mail*, 15 February 1997.

21. See, for example, Suzanne Moore, 'She Who Must Not Be Obeyed', in *Head over Heels*, Viking, 1996.
22. *Daily Mail*, 13 April 1990; *Independent*, 10 January 1992.
23. See, for example, 'Taking the Rearing View', *The Times*, 12 February 1992.
24. Style and Travel, *Sunday Times*, 23 June 1991.
25. *Mail on Sunday*, 1 October 1995.

Chapter 4. Work: The Politics of Time

1. Kate Figes, *Because of Her Sex: The Myth of Equality for Women in Britain*, Macmillan, 1994, p.75.
2. Christine Gowdridge, A. Susan Williams and Margaret Wynn (eds.), *Mother Courage, Letters from Mothers in Poverty at the End of the Century*, Penguin 1997, p.192.
3. Patricia Hewitt, *About Time. The Revolution in Work and Family Life*, Rivers Oram Press, 1993, p.24.
4. Ibid., p.9.
5. Ibid., see pages 8–15 in particular.
6. Ibid., p.14.
7. Ibid., p.15.
8. *Guardian*, 20 May 1992.
9. Juliet Mitchell, *Woman's Estate*, Pelican, 1971, p.38.
10. Source: Liz Speed, Equal Opportunities Commission.
11. Cynthia Cockburn, *In the Way of Women: Men's Resistance to Sex Equality in Organisations*, Macmillan, 1991, p.76.
12. Personal conversation with me, early 1996.

Chapter 5. Work: The Puzzle of Ambition

1. Antonia Kirwan-Taylor, 'When the juggling stops', *Vogue*, September 1995.
2. For by far the most powerful of these, see Polly Toynbee's 'Scaring mothers? It's *Panorama*'s bit of fun', *Independent*, 4 February 1997.
3. 'Paper tigresses', *Vogue*, April 1996.
4. *Guardian*, 23 October 1996.
5. Henley Centre, *Planning for Social Change. Shaping Factors*, 1996–7, p.148.
6. Scarlett MccGwire, *Best Companies for Women. Britain's Top Employers*, Pandora, 1992, p.117.

7. *Independent*, July 2 1997.

Chapter 6. Home Truths: Androgyny, the New Father and the Housewife

1. Adrienne Burgess, *Guardian*, 4 February 1997.
2. 'Parenting in the 1990s', findings, Social Policy Research 106, October 1996.
3. *Social focus on women*, Central Statistical Office, 1995, p.14.
4. Dr Kalwant Bhopal, 'Domestic Labour in South Asian Households in London. Paper presented at conference 'The New Family?', University of Leeds, 24 May 1996.
5. *Guardian*, 5 March 1997.
6. Adrienne Burgess, *Father Reclaimed*, Vermillion, 1997.
7. Liberal Democrat Election Manifesto, 1997.
8. *Independent*, 5 October 1995.
9. *Daily Telegraph*, 22 April 1996.

Chapter 7. Down among the Children: From Self-reliance to Snobbery

1. Helen Wilkinson and Ivan Briscoe, *Parental Leave: The price of family values?*, Demos Project Report, 1996, p.4.
2. The Daycare Trust, 'The Childcare Gap', 1997.
3. Patricia Morgan, *Who Needs Parents? The Effects of Childcare and Early Education on Children in Britain and the USA*, Institute of Economic Affairs, 1996.
4. Angela Phillips, 'The Tied Cottage Effect', in *Storia: A Woman's Eye View of Britain Today*, Pandora, 1990, pp.118–19.
5. Figures issued by Working for Childcare, 1996.
6. The Daycare Trust, 'The Childcare Gap', 1997.
7. Ibid.
8. Perhaps one of the NCT's biggest policy successes was its involvement in the shaping of the 1994 Changing Childbirth legislation, one of the few genuinely radical, and woman-friendly, measures introduced by the Conservative government of the early 1990s. Changing Childbirth, the implementation of which the NCT continues to monitor, offers women more choice in their antenatal care and birth; much of the substance of the legislation drew on changes already being advocated and practised by groups like the NCT and the Active Birth Movement. As Barbara Kott

says, 'It was so different in the early 1970s, when you think about it. You went in, had an internal examination, a full pubic shave and enema. You were left on your own. The midwives were probably too busy to come and see you much. You always gave birth on your back and everyone had an episiotomy [a cut]. All that has changed.'

9. The Daycare Trust, 'The Childcare Gap', 1997.
10. *The Times*, 22 January 1993.

Chapter 8. Babies on Benefit: Alternative Cardiff Conversations

1. Clarence Thomas, the black judge accused of sexually harassing his young employee Anita Hill, constructed his self-defence on the basis of character partly by contrasting himself with his sister, Emma Mae Martin, a poor woman on welfare. As one commentator on the Thomas debacle described it: 'In a speech to Republicans (who practically invented the role of welfare queen) he had made Martin into a stock character in the Republican scenario of racial economics. His point was to contrast her laziness with his hard work and high achievement to prove, I suppose, that any black American with gumption and a willingness to work could succeed. Thus, a woman whom he had presumably known and loved for a lifetime emerged as a one-dimensional welfare cheat. For Thomas, it seemed, all the information that needed to be known of his sister compared her to him: she was a failure on welfare and he was a high-ranking official . . . [but] it turns out that she was only on welfare temporarily and that she was usually a two-job-holding, minimum-wage-earning mother of four. Unable to afford professional help, she had gone on welfare while she nursed the aunt who had suffered a stroke but who normally kept her children when Martin was at work . . . Martin belonged to a mass of American women who were caregivers to the young, the old and the infirm.' From Nell Irvin Painter, 'Hill, Thomas and the Use of Racial Stereotype', *Race-ing Justice, Engendering Power: Essays on Anita Hill, Clarence Thomas and the Construction of Social Reality*, ed. and with an introduction by Toni Morrison, Chatto & Windus, 1993.
2. For example, during the passage of the Human Fertilization and Embryology Act, 1989, there were at least two attempts by

members of the House of Lords to ban lesbians access to artificial insemination.

3. Angela Y. Davis, 'Outcast Mothers and Surrogates', *American Feminist Thoughts*, ed. L. Kauffman, Blackwell, USA, 1993 p.362.

4. For the most recent expression of this view, see 'Reclaiming the moral high ground for children's sake', interview with Melanie Phillips, in *Family Policy Bulletin*, Family Policy Studies Centre, Summer 1997.

Chapter 9. Party Impressions

1. *Guardian*, 12 May 1997.
2. See, for example, *Daily Express*, 8 May 1997; and a report on 'Blair's Babes' in *She*, July 1997.
3. *Daily Express*, 8 May 1997.
4. Jane Taylor, 'Don't Call Me Babe', *New Statesman*, 16 May 1997.
5. Joanna Coles, *Guardian*, 21 April 1997.
6. Charlotte Adcock, *What Women Want on Politics*, Women's Communication Centre, March 1997, p.vii.
7. *Guardian*, 17 April 1997.
8. *Prima*, October 1996.
9. Steve Richards, *New Statesman*, May 1997.
10. Patrick Wintour, *Observer*, 11 May 1997.
11. *New York Times*, 1 August 1996.
12. Barbara Ransby, 'US; the Black poor and the politics of expendability', *Race and Class*, Volume 38, October–December 1996.
13. Labour Party Manifesto, 1983.
14. Labour Party 'Strategy for Women', 1996.
15. Beatrix Campbell, *The Iron Ladies: Why Do Women Vote Tory?*, Virago, 1987, p.155.
16. *The Times*, 6 November 1996.
17. Patricia Morgan, *Who Needs Parents?: The Effects of Childcare and Early Education on Children in Britain and the USA*, Institute of Economic Affairs, p.10.
18. Blake Morrison, *Independent on Sunday*, 6 April 1997.
19. *Daily Mail Weekend*, 26 October 1996.
20. *Prima*, October 1996.
21. *Guardian*, 24 March 1995.
22. Michael Young and A. H. Halsey, 'Family and Community Socialism', Institute of Public Policy Research, 1995.

23. *Independent*, 16 March 1995.
24. See, for example, Helen Wilkinson, *Time Out: the costs and benefits of paid parental leave*, Demos, 1997.
25. For the full story of Lucy Hovells' campaign, see Beatrix Campbell's article on Sedgefield in the *New Statesman*, 8 May 1997.
26. Statement from Harriet Harman, Minister for Social Security, 15 July 1997.
27. Personal communication with Lucy Lloyd, Daycare Trust.
28. *She*, July 1997.
29. See, for instance, interview with Tessa Jowell, *Independent on Sunday*, 20 July 1997.

Chapter 10. Feminism I: The Not So Secret History

1. Maureen Freely, *What about Us? An Open Letter to the Mothers Feminism Forgot*, Bloomsbury, 1995, p.13.
2. Lynne Segal, 'Generations of feminism' in *Radical Philosophy*, no. 83, May/June 1997.
3. Claire Tomalin, *The Life and Death of Mary Wollstonecraft*, Penguin, 1992 (revised edition), pp.135–6.
4. Mary Wollstonecraft, *A Vindication of the Rights of Woman*, Penguin, 1992, p.146.
5. Ibid., p.271.
6. Ibid., p.272.
7. Mary Wollstonecraft, *Letters Written During a Short Residence in Sweden, Norway and Denmark*, Centaur Press, 1970, p.27.
8. Claire Tomalin, *The Life and Death of Mary Wollstonecraft*, p.228.
9. Mary Wollstonecraft, *Letters*, p.66.
10. Dora Russell, *The Tamarisk Tree, My Quest for Liberty and Love*, Virago, 1978, p.175.
11. Ibid., p.176.
12. 'Hecuba, Feminist Mothers', *The Dora Russell Reader: Fifty Seven Years of Writing and Journalism, 1925-1982*, Pandora Press, 1983, pp.23–36.
13. Penny Forster and Imogen Sutton, *Daughters of de Beauvoir*, Women's Press, 1989, pp.2–3.
14. Simone de Beauvoir, *The Second Sex*, Penguin, 1976, p.521.
15. Ibid., p.510.
16. Ibid., p.528.
17. Ibid., p.539.

18. Marilyn French, *The Women's Room*, Sphere, 1979, p.98.
19. Christopher Lasch, 'The Sexual Division of Labour', in *Women and the Common Life: Love, Marriage and Feminism*, ed. Elisabeth Lasch-Quinn, Norton, 1997, pp.105–6.
20. Betty Friedan, 'A New Life Plan for Women', *The Feminine Mystique*, Penguin, 1963, p.310.
21. Lasch, 'The Sexual Division of Labour', p.113.
22. Ibid., p.114.

Chapter 11. Feminism II: Everyday Rebellions and the Small Matter of Enjoyment

1. Germaine Greer, *The Female Eunuch*, Paladin, 1971, pp.251-3.
2. Shulamith Firestone, *The Dialectic of Sex*, Paladin, 1972, p.19.
3. Anna Coote and Beatrix Campbell, *Sweet Freedom: The Struggle for Women's Liberation*, Picador, 1982, p.15.
4. Quoted in Sheila Rowbotham, *The Past is Before Us*, Pandora, 1989, p.106.
5. Sue O'Sullivan, *I used to be nice: sexual affairs*, Cassell, 1996, p.4.
6. Angela Coyle, 'Where Were You in '68 sunshine? A Time in the Life of . . .', *Red Rag, A Magazine of Women's Liberation*. Undated.
7. Olga Kenyon, *Interviews with ten women writers*, Lennard Publishing, 1989, pp.27–8.
8. Adrienne Rich, *Of Woman Born: Motherhood as Experience and Institution*, Virago, 1977, p.23.
9. Nancy Chodorow, *The Reproduction of Mothering, Psychoanalysis and the Sociology of Gender*, University of California Press, 1978, p.5.
10. Ibid., pp.214–17.
11. Marsha Rowe, 'Changing Childcare', *The Spare Rib Reader*, 1982, p.11.
12. Carol Gilligan, *In a Different Voice*, Harvard University Press, 1982 p.173.
13. Lynne Segal, *Is the Future Female? Troubled Thoughts on Contemporary Feminism*, Virago, 1987 p.147.
14. Beverley Bryan, Stella Dadzie, and Suzanne Scafe, *The Heart of the Race, Black Women's Lives in Britain*, Virago, 1985, p.30. See also Hazel Carby, 'White Woman Listen! Black Feminism and the Boundaries of Sisterhood', *The Empire Strikes Back: Race and Racism in 70s Britain*, Centre for Contemporary Studies, London, 1982.

15. June Jordan, 'Many Rivers to Cross', *Moving Towards Home, Political Essays*, Virago, 1989, p.125.
16. For example, Anna Coote, Harriet Harman, Patricia Hewitt, *The Family Way, A New Approach to Policy-making*, IPPR, 1990; Harriet Harman, *The Century Gap*, Vermillion, 1993.
17. Betty Friedan, *The Second Stage*, Michael Joseph, 1981, p.22.
18. Rosalind Coward, *Our Treacherous Hearts, Why Women Let Men Get Their Way*, Faber, 1992, pp.24–5.
19, All the figures in this paragraph are taken from Alison McFarlane 'Figures Bearing on Maternity Poverty', in *Mother Courage, Letters from Mothers in Poverty at the End of the Century*, Penguin, 1997, pp.195–208.
20. *Guardian*, 28 May 1997.

Chapter 12. The Best of Both Worlds: Towards a New Politics of Motherhood

1. Walt Whitman, *Song of Myself*, Penguin, 1995, p.54.
2. Rebecca Abrams, *Woman in a Man's World: Pioneering Career Women of the Twentieth Century*, Methuen, 1993, p.xxx.
3. Suzanne Moore, 'Sloth about the house', *Head Over Heels*, Viking, 1996, p.114.
4. *Guardian*, 11 June 1997.
5. Michael Ignatieff, *The Needs of Strangers*, Chatto & Windus, 1984, p.107.

Index